POLICING THE CITY

Policing the City

ROB MAWBY

*Social Work Research Unit,
University of Bradford*

SAXON HOUSE

British Library Cataloguing in Publication Data

Mawby, Rob
  Policing the city.
  1. Police – England – Sheffield
  I. Title
  363.2'09428'21   HV8196.S/

ISBN 0-566-00277-9

Published by SAXON HOUSE
Teakfield Limited,
Westmead, Farnborough, Hants., England.

Printed in Great Britain by David Green (Printers) Ltd, Kettering, Northamptonshire

Contents

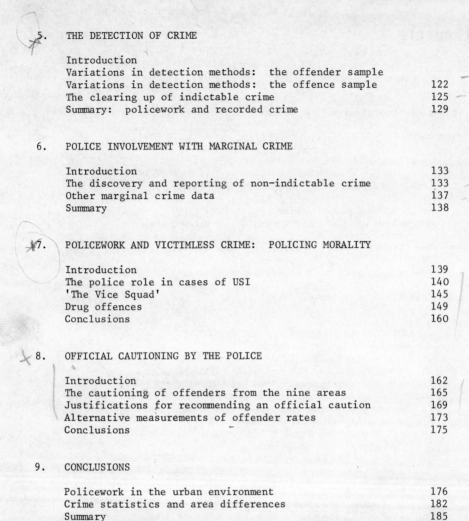

Foreword

The Sheffield Study on Urban Social Structure and Crime is a research project which has been undertaken by the University of Sheffield over the last decade. Those accustomed to American style social science research budgets might immediately think that a decade long project must have employed scores of research assistants and consumed hundreds of thousands of pounds; so let me disabuse them of such ideas. Only three people – John Baldwin, Rob Mawby, and Polii Xanthos – have ever been employed on the project full-time, and the total amount received in research grants from sources outside the University has been less than £15,000. The style of the project, in short, has not been that of the large corporation, but that of the corner grocery shop.

Working on this scale has its disadvantages, but also its advantages. One of the principal gains is that those who work on the project can be given a fair amount of freedom to develop ideas and research strategies in their own way, whilst not destroying the overall unity of purpose of the Study as a whole. In a large project, such a procedure could only be anarchic, but in a small enterprise – given goodwill on all sides – it works.

It is out of this context that this book has emerged. In the first stage of the Sheffield project, reported in The Urban Criminal (Baldwin and Bottoms 1976), we had done some preliminary theoretical work on urban crime, and also carried out an intensive analysis of recorded crime for the whole of the city of Sheffield. Given the known limitations of recorded crime data, this was explicitly intended only as an exploratory, hypothesis generating stage of the research (see the published volume for details). But there were a number of different directions in which subsequent research could have gone from this stage.

Rob Mawby joined the team when the analysis of the data on the first stage had been completed, and John Baldwin had left Sheffield. As the only full-time worker on the project at that stage, he was given primary responsibility for deciding which direction of research to pursue. His orientation toward labelling theory, his scepticism (despite our caveats) about some aspects of the approach used in The Urban Criminal, and his strong prior research interest in policing and law enforcement – all these led inexorably in one direction, to a much closer examination of the way in which official offence and offender rates were created in areas with contrasting recorded rates. For example, there were two pre-war council housing estates, demographically very similar, and separated only by a single main road, but with official offence and offender rates different by as much as a factor of three or four. The question of whether these different rates were the result of differential law-enforcement processes on the two estates cried out to be investigated.

So questions of this kind became the second stage of the project, which is reported in this book. I shall not weary the reader by reciting here the methods of investigation used or the details of the results, for these can of course be found in the body of the text. Suffice it to say that as a result of a very detailed analysis, there was very little to suggest that differential policing contributed to the different official crime

or offender rates as between different residential areas. Even results
which at first sight might seem to support a 'differential labelling'
interpretation of criminal statistics on closer examination failed to do
so. For example, it is shown in chapter five that residents of the high
crime rate areas had a significantly higher proportion of their known
offences cleared up by 'indirect detection': that is, by offences admitted during routine police questioning of those who were caught for
other offences. This seems to be exactly the sort of escalatory, self-
fulfilling prophecy that one might expect - and indeed it does seem to
indicate that detectives might devote more energy to 'clearing the books'
when faced with offenders from known 'criminal' areas. On the other
hand, the analysis of offences in the residential areas shows that there
was no greater tendency for known offences committed in the high-rate
areas to be first discovered and recorded due to an indirect detection;
and the same was true when considering the source of the police's first
knowledge of offences (as opposed to their detection of the offender)
even within the sample of offenders from the residential areas. In
other words, the apparently greater enthusiasm for questioning offenders
from high-rate areas about their alleged other crimes resulted in more
admissions from high-rate area residents about crimes already reported
to the police by other methods, but this did not affect either the official
offence rate for the area (since the reporting was being done already by
others) or the official offender rate for the area (since each offender
only counts once in this rate, however many crimes he admits).

The remarks in the previous paragraph will already have introduced to
the reader the complexity of some of the distinctions which necessarily
have to be made if one is to deal adequately with the problem of interpreting the recorded criminal statistics for different geographical
areas. The discovery or reporting stage, the recording stage, the
process of detection, and the differential handling of known offenders
all have to be considered, for each has its own set of processes; and
all the time one has to be aware of the difference between the offence
rate of an area and the offender rate (as well as other secondary
distinctions of a like kind). It has become fashionable in recent years
either to write off the criminal statistics as 'useless', or to point
out (correctly) that they are the end result of a bureaucratic process
but not to enquire with any precision what that process is. It is a
great merit of Dr Mawby's study that he has shown the weakness of these
positions. In their place, he has provided a set of concepts and
distinctions which make much clearer exactly what it is that criminal
statistics are comprised of, and has then applied these distinctions in
a thoroughgoing way to his own data.

Dr Mawby's study is, however, not just about criminal statistics. As
the title of the book implies, it contains also some fresh insights on
the policing of crime in the city, perhaps most notably in the chapter
based on interviews with the uniformed police themselves (chapter 3) and
in the chapters on marginal and victimless crimes (chapters 6 and 7).
These and other sections of the book will repay careful study by those
interested in the sociology of policework in an urban context.

Where does Mawby's study leave the Sheffield Urban Project? He has
demonstrated here that differences in official crime rates between
selected areas are not the result of differential law-enforcement
processes, and we have other evidence suggesting that they are only to a
limited extent the result of differential public reporting. Hence, so

far as we can judge with the available research instruments, there are 'real' differences between the high crime rate and the low crime rate areas in the extent of criminal behaviour actually occurring in the districts, and being committed by residents of the districts. What has deliberately not been attempted in this book is any explanation of those differences. But in a final volume of the research project that crucial explanatory problem will be addressed - and that will take us away from the role of the police towards that of the housing authorities.

A. E. BOTTOMS
(Professor of Criminology, University of Sheffield and Director of the Sheffield Study on Urban Social Structure and Crime).

Preface

This book arose from my period as a research assistant in the Centre for Criminological Studies at the University of Sheffield. Without the help of the project director, Tony Bottoms, it would not have been possible to develop the research to this stage, and I am extremely grateful to him for his constructive advice and encouragement throughout. In addition Monica Walker has been a source of help both with statistical advice and proof reading, and Christine Fisher has been a conscientious adviser at the drafting stage.

Most of all, I would like to express my thanks to the South Yorkshire Police whose cooperation made the research possible. It is not uncommon for academics to take it for granted that organisations should cooperate willingly with them. On the contrary, as has been noted recently (King and Elliott, 1978) many of the subjects of criminological research have little to gain and much to lose by allowing access to outsiders. I am therefore especially grateful to those members of the police force who contributed their time and expertise on this occasion.

R. I. MAWBY,
November, 1978.

Introduction

The book has developed out of the second stage of a long term project in Sheffield, concerned with crime in the city. The first stage of the research, where official statistics were used to consider offence and offender characteristics, has been written up elsewhere (Baldwin and Bottoms, 1976). The second stage has been described already in my PhD thesis, submitted in 1978 (Mawby, 1978 (i)), and is based on research carried out during my time in Sheffield from 1972 to 1975. During that period I was concerned to see how far area differences in recorded crime rates were an artefact of the police discovery and recording processes for offences, and with this aim considered a variety of sources on crime in different parts of the city, including police statistics, records kept by other official agencies, like the GPO (on telephone kiosk vandalism and television licence evasion) (Mawby, 1977 (i); 1979 (i)), and information gained directly from residents on their past offences and victim experiences (Mawby, 1979 (ii); Bottoms et al, forthcoming).

Here I have concentrated more directly on the material available from official police statistics. I have considered a variety of recorded sources kept by the police, pertaining to situations regarded as 'real' crimes, minor crimes and related incidents of a non criminal nature. The only police data related to offences not used are records of motoring offences. Although other aspects of policework like public order maintenance during demonstrations, pickets, and football matches would be included where the police decided to make an arrest, this study is essentially concerned with police action in relation to criminal and 'quasi-criminal' behaviour. Whilst a study of policework in other situations might produce a rather different picture, I can make no appologies for this. The day to day life of the average policeman is oriented towards the control of crime, and Policing the City is an attempt to describe the policing of criminal incidents, by police and members of the public alike.

What I have attempted is an investigation of the records, using both a comparison of different types of incidents which were defined and categorised and an analysis of the information contained within the records themselves (for example on how a crime was discovered, how an offender was identified, etc.). In these ways I have tried to assess the influence of different agents on the creation of official statistics, and consequently, the extent to which official data are unreliable or invalid measurements of crime details.

In this context, the emphasis has changed notably over the years. Whilst Cressey was able to assert in 1964 that 'Despite all their limitations, the criminal statistics give information which is important to our understanding of crime and delinquency and to hypotheses and theories about them' (Cressey, 1964; 50), the prevailing academic opinion today is that official records are so suspect that they may be disregarded.

The main theoretical forces behind this charge have been diverse. On the one hand, labelling theorists have rightly pointed to the truth that

1

criminal or deviant behaviour is dependant upon legal and cultural definitions and the recognition of individuals as deviants depends on the operations of law enforcement agencies (Becker, 1963). At the same time conflict theorists, including Marxist sociologists, have focused on the role of the state and its agents in determining the nature of 'social order' and the means of maintaining it (Taylor et al., 1973; Turk, 1969). On a rather different level, phenomenologists and ethno-methodologists have been concerned to detail the transactions that take place between police and public, the extent to which police intervention is dependant upon their reading of particular situations and the negotiations which may preceed police decisions to arrest (Sacks, 1972).

It seemed to me, at the outset, that these critiques of the role of the police in relation to crime statistics were weighty and that any research which failed to take them into account was founded on insecure ground. In this sense I was considerably sceptical of the first stage of the Sheffield research since, despite the careful disclaimers of the research team, it was ultimately dependant upon definitions of crime expressed in official statistics. The research exercise, then which had sought to compare areas of the city according to the offences committed there and offenders residing there, seemed to me to be suspect. I felt that it was crucial to a continuation of the research that a subsequent stage should incorporate a critique of the role of the police in the production of statistics. I anticipated that such an exercise would reveal that area differences in offence and offender rates were to a large extent due to different police styles, and the differential involvement of the police, in contrasting areas of the city.

In fact I found no such thing. An area analysis of policing patterns revealed that there was little or no evidence that differential policing affected the relative offender rates of contrasting residential areas. Similarly, although there was some suggestion that offence rates may have been affected by the extent of police presence, the distinctions found were between residential and other areas, rather than between different types of residential area.

On the other hand, there were other differences within the data. In particular, the nature of the victim and the visibility of the offence seemed to exert considerable influence on the role of the police. On another level, there was a wealth of information on the role of the police at the detection stage, one part of the law enforcement process which has received limited attention in the past.

In rewriting the research findings in book form, therefore, I have shifted the focus somewhat. While the original aim of the research was to consider the effect of differential policing on area crime rates, here I have focused on the role of the police (and other agents) vis a vis crime committed in certain residential areas of the city, or by residents of those areas. Within this framework I have analysed differences - at the discovery, detection and cautioning stages - according to a number of variables, of which area characteristics form only a part.

In chapter one I have reviewed literature on the role of the police in the production of crime statistics. Following this, chapters two and three are focused on the areas covered in the research, first in terms of the picture presented by the statistics, second through the eyes of the police who work in the areas. Then the bulk of the work (chapters four to eight) is devoted to the role of the police and other agents in these areas.

As I have already noted, the results were surprising. Consequently in chapter nine I end by reconsidering the role of the police and the extent to which their influence is constrained, and the implications of the research for the study of criminology.

1 Crime Statistics and the Role of the Police

Official crime statistics, both directly and through their presentation by the media, provide us with what is perhaps the clearest and most commonly accepted image of the national crime situation. Details of offenders who have been caught, or prosecuted, have served as sources used by politicians and academics alike in attempts to describe the nature of the 'criminal population', the extent of the 'problem', and the measures which need to be taken to solve it.

But how much do official statistics actually tell us about crime? While official data of any sort have been treated with considerable caution by social scientists, this is especially the case when we consider criminal statistics. As one classic text has noted, for example, 'The general statistics of crime are probably the most unreliable and the most difficult of all statistics.' (Sutherland and Cressey, 1960; 25).

The reasons behind this type of statement are all too clear. On the one hand, not all crimes are reported to, or discovered by, the police, and even those which are may not be recorded as such by the police. On the other hand, at least half of those crimes which are recorded remain unsolved, with the result that details of the offending population are even less adequate.

Once we accept this, however, the way in which we proceed can vary considerably. On the one hand, we may consider these inadequacies to be so serious as to undermine any attempt to utilise existing statistics, (the view taken by many contemporary theorists); at the other extreme, we may see them only as 'minor irritants', a position generally adopted by traditional criminologists.

With few exceptions, the positivist empirical tradition within criminology, of which Sutherland and Cressey were important representatives, took this latter position. For example, they began with a strong cautionary section on the inadequacies of official data: 'It is impossible to determine with accuracy the amount of crime in any given jurisdiction at any particular time. Obviously a large proportion of the crimes committed go undetected, others are detected but not reported, others are reported but not officially recorded. Consequently any record of crimes, such as crimes known to the police, arrests, convictions, or commitments to prison, can be considered only as an 'index' of the crimes committed. But these 'indexes' of crime do not maintain a constant ratio with the true rate, whatever it may be .... Both the true rate and the relationship between the true rate and any 'index' of this rate are capricious 'dark figures' which vary with changes in police policies, court policies, and public opinion. In the United States the variations in this 'dark figure' in crime statistics make it almost foolhardy to attempt a comparison of crime rates of various cities, and it is even hazardous to compare national rates or the rates of a given city or state in a given year with the rates of the same jurisdiction in a different

year. International comparisons are even more difficult' (Sutherland and
Cressey, 1960; 25).

However, having accepted that the statistics were highly suspect,
traditional criminologists almost invariably went on to base their
theories on precisely those statistics. Almost inevitably this led to
the assertion that, particularly as far as offenders were concerned,
official statistics differed more in quantity than in quality from the
total crime pattern (Cohen, 1955; see also Matza, 1969; 98, for a criticism of this approach). A good example is provided by Cressey: 'Despite all their limitations, the criminal statistics give information which
is important to our understanding of crime and delinquency and to hypotheses and theories about them. Similarities and differences in crime
rates for certain categories of person are so consistent that it can be
reasonably concluded that a gross relationship between the category and
crime exists in fact .... The statistics on ordinary crime so consistently show an over representation of lower class persons that it is
reasonable to assume that there is a real difference between the
behaviour of social classes, so far as criminality is concerned.'
(Cressey, 1964; 50).

This was not, of course, a view which was held unanimously. A number
of criminologists doubted the extent to which 'known' crime (or 'known'
offenders) were representative of the totality. In consequence, a
further aim of many critics was to be able to produce estimates, or
alternative measurements, which could be used to portray a 'real crime
rate'.

At an extremely crude level, it was therefore not uncommon for criminologists to hazard guesses as to the proportion of crimes which were
excluded from official statistics. However, a more subtle extention of
such attempts came about through the use of self report and victim
studies. Here members of the public (or specific groups) were asked
directly either about crimes they had committed or about their experiences as victims. These approaches served two ends. On the one hand they
provided, for a given sample, what was considered a reasonably accurate
picture of crime. On the other hand, by comparing the results with
official statistics, they allowed criminologists to make general estimates of the amount of unrecorded crime.

This empirical tradition of 'going behind' the official statistics
clearly depends on the twin assumptions that a true crime rate is attain-
able and that victim and self report studies are valid and reliable means
to that end. But each of these assumptions may be questioned.

In fact, criticism of the empirical tradition has been made forcibly
over the last fifteen or so years, especially by those interested in the
theoretical background to the statistics creation processes.

In particular, social scientists have become more interested in the
social processes behind the creation of official statistics, as research
objects in their own right, and less interested in the 'dark figure' of
crime as a methodological obstacle. At the same time, the possibility of
being able in any way to discover a 'true crime rate' has been widely
discarded.

According to Bottomley, this new theoretical perspective developed with the work of Wilkins: '(I)t was with his introduction of the 'decision stages' concept that he began to break rather newer ground. He discussed the various kinds of statistics, <u>not</u> in relation to whether they were 'reliable' measures of different aspects of criminal behaviour, but in relation to the kind of decisions which they reflected, which could have an independent influence upon the future progress of individuals through the criminal justice system.' (Bottomley, 1973; 3)

These points of decision, which Wilkins calls 'gates', became the focus for a multitude of articles from a wide variety of sociologists and criminologists. In one early, and frequently quoted article, Kitsuse and Cicourel illustrated this new perspective where the focus of interest shifted from a concern with the 'incidence' of crime towards an analysis of the 'processes' behind the crime statistics: 'Thus, the questions to be asked are not about the appropriateness of the statistics, but about the definitions incorporated in the categories applied by the personnel of the rate-producing social system to identify, classify and record behaviour as deviant .... Rates can be viewed as indices of organisational processes rather than as indices of the incidence of certain forms of behaviour.' (Kitsuse and Cicourel, 1963; 131).

Criminal statistics, according to this view, measure the willingness of the police to go out and discover crime and the ways in which they record their findings (if at all), and the extent to which the public define situations as requiring police intervention. However this does not necessarily imply that, with care, official data may not be used to consider crime related issues (as opposed to police related issues), unless one accepts a position of extreme relativism. Perhaps the best example of such a stance is given by Douglas in his analysis of records on suicide. 'It is a fundamental part of the argument through this work that there does not exist such a thing as a 'real suicide rate'. Suicides are not something of a set nature waiting to be correctly or incorrectly categorised by officials. The very nature of the 'thing' is itself problematic so that 'suicides' cannot correctly be said to exist (i.e. to be things) until a categorisation has been made' (Douglas, 1967; 196).

Of course, Douglas' research was concerned with suicide, rather than crime as such. However, if we consider the argument vis-à-vis crime statistics, the critique becomes clear. According to this perspective, there is no such thing as a real crime rate, because for this to be so there has to be an agreed universe of meaning and of moral values. Clearly there is no such thing, with the result that we have a number of alternative definitions of 'reality', (i.e. crime) which are realities in their own right and are not reducible to one total reality. Consequently, even if we ignore problems related to the incompleteness of various accounts, a review of police records, victim statements, or self reported 'offender' accounts will give us different answers based on the different moral evaluations of crime with which each of these groups, and each individual within each group, is making.

The principal difficulty with the Douglas approach, which has been pinpointed by Hindess, is that if relativism is accepted at this extreme level, the social scientists' observations become no more than one alternative account of an account (Hindess, 1973; 26). It is, therefore, notable that Cicourel, who alongside Douglas was the main object of Hindess' attack, has responded by implicitly accepting Hindess' argument in this respect (though certainly not in all respects). That is, whilst Cicourel asserts that in principle no 'real' crime rate can be discovered, he argues that 'research on juvenile justice can be used to improve crime statistics and to estimate and to control possible sources of error' (Cicourel, 1976; xix).

But clearly, once one accepts that official statistics can be improved, it is illogical to deny that a 'real' crime rate exists (if not, the concept of 'improvement' is meaningless). It therefore appears that Cicourel is saying that, as a philosophical ideal, an objective omniscient observer could know what the real crime rate is, but that the social scientist's research instruments can never place him in this position because of the differential moral evaluations of research subjects. Despite this, though, we can edge closer to this reality by better research methods, even though the reality itself is unattainable.

Similarly, the position taken here is that it is possible to talk in the abstract about 'a real crime rate' although in all practicable senses it is impossible to approach any measurement of this reality. That is, what we can do is to attempt to get behind some layers of the mask, accepting that while a complete demasking operation is impossible it is feasible to construct measurements of crime which are less invalid than others. Moreover, the whole tenor of the present research process is towards the view that a careful use of alternative research sources and methods may allow us to go some little way towards presenting some representation of that reality.

Where the aim of the exercise is comparative, this point is particularly salient. Taking the official crime rates for different areas of Sheffield, this research aimed at assessing how far the various processes behind the official statistics were instrumental in influencing contrasting rates. On one level then, the exercise follows in the tradition set by Cicourel and Douglas, where the object is to consider in more detail the processes involved. On another level though, following Cicourel's acceptance of Hindess' critique of relativism, the processes involved are considered in terms of how far they differentially influence crime rates in different areas. That is, a variety of research instruments, but principally certain features of officially recorded crimes are used to assess the extent to which we may remain confident that areal crime rate differences reflect differences between 'real' crime rates rather than being merely artefacts of the recording processes. Thus, while in no sense are we able to approach a measurement of 'real' crime rates for the various areas of the study, an attempt has been made to assess the degree of confidence we may have that differences in the 'real' crime rate are reflected in those measurements, however imperfect, which we do have.

Of course, one element which conflicts with Cicourel's stance - crucially - is the use of official statistics as a source, a possibility which Cicourel appears to discredit, and this issue will be raised in a subsequent section of chapter two.

However, at this juncture it is clearly appropriate to continue this introductory overview by discussing some contributions to the debate which have been made in research on the police. The most important element of these contributions is that which focuses on an acceptance that the role which the police define for themselves is not as an agency involved in the mechanical recording of all crime. Essential to the

7

police role is an element of discretion, which is evident at the level of determining what the nature of the job is, how it can be carried out most appropriately, and what sorts of criteria may be relevant in helping to determine appropriate action in particular incidents.

THE POLICE AS A DISCRETIONARY LAW ENFORCEMENT AGENCY: AN INTRODUCTION

A crucial step towards an understanding of the discretionary power of the police was made in early research on the police in Britain and America, by Banton (1964). He distinguished two functions of the police - the keeping of public order and the enforcement of the law through prosecuting lawbreakers - which he encapsulated in the terms 'peace officer' and 'law officer' respectively. Quite clearly these two roles are not necessarily mutually compatible - the decision to arrest may in certain circumstances provoke rioting, for example - and yet they have been assigned similar importance since the creation of the Metropolitan Police in the nineteenth century.

One study which developed these differences was that of Wilson in his comparison of alternative policing styles which he saw as dominating police practices in different American cities. In his early work, Wilson described two styles - the 'professional' style (where action is based on a fixed code of regulations leaving little room for discretion) and the 'fraternal' style (where discretion plays a key role) (Wilson, 1968 (i); 9-30). In his later and more extensive study, Wilson enlarged the model into one which incorporated three policing styles - the legalistic style (based on the professional style), the watchman style (based on the fraternal style) and the service style:

(i) The legalistic style. Here, according to Wilson, the police model approached the rigorous application of legal principles. That is, those who broke the law were almost always prosecuted. Discretion, in terms of the proportion of offenders handled informally, was kept to a minimum.

(ii) The watchman style. In contrast the watchman style centred on the maintenance of good order. Where illegal action was visible to the police, arrest did not necessarily follow. How the police acted, or what sanctions they applied, depended on how best order could be maintained or restored.

(iii) The service style. This alternative appeared according to Wilson, to be the least common of the three, being confined to middle class communities where police and public showed a common definition of order. Thus discretion was widely used, not as a means of maintaining order, but, within a wider definition of the police role as a helping one, as a means of acting in the best interests of the community (Wilson, 1968 (ii)).

Wilson's model seems to allow different crime data to be accredited with different degrees of validity, depending upon the policing style operating in that context. However, an additional advantage is that his typology can be applied at various levels of analysis. That is, different styles may be appropriate according to:

(i) The bureaucratic organisation of the police force. Wilson implies that the attitudes of the police chief may be crucial in determining which style is adopted within a force. He also suggests that, subject to public opinion, the style may change. Thus, in a period of concern over police corruption, or the prevalence of vice, a legalistic style may be adopted to demonstrate that the police are incorruptible/in control.

(ii) The type of offence. Clearly some offences are less easily dealt with according to the legalistic model. In particular offences committed by a large proportion of the population, like motoring offences, cannot all be handled formally. In these circumstances, either the watchman style (give an informal warning, but if the offender creates trouble by arguing, book him), or the service style (advise motorists) may be adopted.

(iii) The area being policed. Wilson specifically relates his typology to the type of area being policed. In particular, he suggests that the service style is seen as appropriate in middle class communities. Here the policeman may see himself as a 'servant' of the community, where his clients are usually met in the role of victims or complainants rather than offenders. Moreover, even where the client is an offender - especially a juvenile offender - common sense interpretations of the cause of delinquency are likely to encourage the officer to adopt a position where he co-operates with and is sympathetic to the best interests of the parents, rather than one where the matter is dealt with formally.

Wilson's typology is useful to the extent that it sets the discretionary processes which may be employed by the police within a wider framework. Notable within this framework is the role of the public, both in terms of its willingness to sanction general police practices and in terms of the relationship between police and public. In a later section of his book, Wilson returns to a discussion of the role of the public on another level, namely, by concentrating on the amount of control the police have over 'input'. In focusing on the role of the complainant in controlling police discretion, Wilson introduced an area of debate which was later developed by Reiss (1971), and it is a point which will be reviewed in the next section. The extent to which the police, in developing distinctive styles, are dependant upon their relationships with the Public has, however, been discussed in the British context by Cain (1973).

Cain's research was originally situated within the role theory model of Banton and appears to have altered course both during the practical research period and the writing up stage. Partly because of this, her comparison of two police forces, one rural and one urban, is not as specifically paralleled to the Wilson typology as the reader might expect.

Nevertheless, the two policing styles described by Cain seem to be fairly similar to the service and legalistic styles distinguished by Wilson. In the rural force, the reliance of the policeman on the local community for co-operation and off duty social contacts, pressures him into a type of service relationship. In contrast, in the urban force the relationship between police and public is more formal and the possibility of basing social life around colleagues rather than members of the general public make the service style less necessary and less appropriate. It therefore seems that operations are more often conducted according to the legalistic style. Cain's research was not, of course, directly concerned with an analysis of crime statistics, although it provides some details of how the use of discretion influences recording. However,

9

following Cain's distinction between police operations in the two forces, it is possible to argue that her analyses undermines any reliance on police statistics from the rural area to a greater extent than is the case for the urban area.

This however, is to keep the discussion of policework on the level of formal role models. One great advantage of Cain's research, and more recently the personal account of Holdaway (1976) is to focus attention on the ways in which the police create for themselves an environment in which they are able to maximise job satisfaction. The working mandate of the police is monopolised by routine patrol work and boring and repetitive tasks, the bulk of which may be seen as entirely unrelated to 'real policework' (Lambert, 1970; Punch and Naylor, 1973). The police consequently might be expected to modify formal work patterns so as to create a more satisfactory working environment. According to Cain they do this through the use of what she calls 'easing mechanisms', for example the creation of 'safe areas' where they can relax while on duty, or the search for potentially exciting aspects of the job (for example public order incidents which may provide the opportunity for a 'free for all'). In essence then, the ways in which the police act in certain situations may often be understood not merely in terms of how they are interpreting their official role, but also in terms of how they can maintain a degree of interesting yet unproblematic work.

One further important element in police decision making as it affects crime statistics, however, relates to how the police react when confronted with a possible arrest situation. Quite clearly the police do not make decisions within a moral vacuum. Their interpretation of behaviour, and appropriate ways of dealing with it, will be determined by the stock of knowledge which they have built up over their time in the job, their training and their individual background perspectives. Take for example the case of juvenile delinquency. Given that the police are confronted with a juvenile who has committed a criminal act, they are afforded (or allow themselves) sufficient discretion to deal with the case in a variety of ways - by administering an unoffical caution (otherwise known as a cuff round the ear), by recommending an official caution, by calling in other agencies, or by recommending prosecution.

Piliavin and Briar, in analysing this situation in the American context, suggested that the police distinguish between cases by building up a complex picture of the offender so as to be able to 'measure' his degree of guilt. That is, the incidents although important, become only part of a comprehensive analysis of the 'true character' of the offender, wherein such factors as hairstyle, clothes, demeanor, sex, and social class may be incorporated. '(B)oth the decision made in the field - whether or not to bring the boy in - and the decision made at the station - which disposition to invoke - were based largely on cues which emerged from the interaction between the officer and the youth, cues from which the officer inferred the youth's character. These cues included the youth's group affiliations, age, race, grooming, dress and demeanor. Older juveniles, members of known delinquent groups, Negroes, youths with well oiled hair, black jackets, and soiled denims or jeans (the presumed uniform of 'tough' boys), and boys who in their interactions with officers did not manifest what were considered to be appropriate signs of respect, tended to receive the more severe disposition.' (Piliavin and Briar, 1964).

Piliavin and Briar undermine the validity of data in the official records - on race, social class and sex - which social scientists take into account in formulating their theories. However, Circourel goes further than this by asserting that agencies may make these judgements according to common sense equivalents of precisely those theories which the social scientist uses. For example, the police may use information on the home circumstances of juveniles in coming to a decision on whether or not to prosecute, such that a relationship between maternal deprivation (as a psychological theoretical construct) and delinquency (as officially processed) is created.

Cicourel illustrates this by comparing juvenile court data from two cities. He found that in one city official delinquents (i.e. those prosecuted) commonly came from broken homes, whilst in the other city this proved not to be the case. On investigating further, he found that the difference lay not in the incidence of deprivation among delinquents, but in the importance placed on deprivation as an explanatory variable by the decision-makers in one city. That is, since in this one city deprivation was seen as symptomatic of delinquency, known delinquents who came from broken homes were proportionately more likely to be prosecuted. Since the majority of sociological studies of deprivation and delinquency have relied on prosecution records (or even probation files), it would appear that the results of such studies are questionable. (Cicourel, 1976).

The important message to be derived from these examples is not however a pessimistic one. It is not that official statistics are of no use, but that they must always be handled with care. The first task of the researcher, then, should be to consider the constraints which have been placed on the production process. One way of so doing, which has been carried out with considerable rigour by Bottomley (1973; chapter 1) is to analyse the various different constraints on police decision making which may operate at different times, and indeed many of these will be covered more fully in subsequent chapters. However, as an alternative approach one may consider the influence of police (and other agents') decisions on the resulting statistics by looking in detail at their roles at different stages of the law enforcement process. Quite clearly there are at least four theoretically distinct parts of the process:

(i) The discovery of crime by the police or the reporting of crime to the police by other agents.

(ii) The detection process, i.e. the way in which crimes which are known are cleared up. In many cases this stage may not be distinct, in that crime discovery and offender detection may be simultaneous. Nevertheless, it is necessary, as will be argued in chapter one, 'The discovery and reporting of crime', to keep a clear distinction at least until the facts are known.

(iii) Police recording processes, i.e. the ways in which the police record (or fail to record) information which is in their possession.

(iv) The handling of identified offenders, which at the pre-court stage involves decisions over whether or not to caution an offender, formally or informally.

The rest of this chapter is devoted to a detailed review of earlier

11

research as it applies to these four stages. The objective is that these sections will provide an introduction to the rest of the book, where the distinctions, especially between the discovery and detection of crime, will be considered in depth with relation to policework in Sheffield.

THE DISCOVERY AND REPORTING OF CRIME

Until relatively recently, the role of the police in the discovery of criminal incidents has been accepted, almost unchallenged, as of fundamental importance in the law enforcement process. That is, the recorded crime rate is considered to be basically indicative of police organisation. Even now, for example, it is common to find references to assumptions such as that a larger police force leads to the discovery of more crime (McDonald, 1976), or that the distribution of the police throughout the city affects the recorded crime rate in different areas. (Wiles, 1975).

Of course, in addition many authors have at the same time recognised that there are limitations to the number of crime discoveries made by the police. Wilson, for example, stressed the role of the public, whilst Duster (1970) introduced the dimensions of publicness of offence and presence of victim as variables which controlled police influence.

The public/private dimension is perhaps most clearly distinguished by Stinchcombe (1963). He noted that the ability of the police to intervene in different situations depended on whether they were sheltered by the institution of private space. That is, not only does privacy mean that many illegal acts remain invisible, but the legal situation also curbs police invasion of private areas. Since, according to Stinchcombe, more lower class activity took place on the streets, more lower class behaviour was open to scrutiny. Consequently it is arguable that the lower class appear more frequently in police statistics because their activities are more open to surveillance. Take the extreme example of the tramp:

'Few of us ever see a policeman in those places where we spend most of our time; a 'tramp' sees one wherever he goes, and the policeman has the discretionary power to 'run him in'.' (Stinchcombe, 1963).

In the discovery of crime, then, quite clearly the discretionary power of the police varies considerably. It is not something which can be assumed to operate in all situations or in respect of all types of crime. Nevertheless, because there has been an interest among sociologists of deviance in marginal crimes, (with considerably more research undertaken in these areas than with regard to minor thefts or even to serious professional crimes) public order and victimless offences, the result is that it is precisely in those areas where the influence of the public might be expected to be least that the role of the police has been described in most detail. So for example, Skolnick's (1966) research concentrated on prostitution and motoring offences, Foote (1956) and Bittner (1967) detailed police reactions to vagrants, whilst Young (1972) considered drug offences.

However, a consideration of police involvement with the more general field of crime reveals a somewhat different pattern. Lambert's (1970) study of the Birmingham police, for example, portrays the police as an

agency which operates largely in response to requests from the public.
Similarly, in America, the most notable study of the discovery and reporting processes, by Reiss (1971) revealed a pattern dominated by what the
author calls 'reactive' policing, with incidents initiated by the police
themselves (i.e. 'proactive' law enforcement) in a minority.

Reiss found that of 5,360 mobilisations of the police, (for whatever
reason), 81% were citizen invoked by phone, 5% by personal contact made
by a citizen, and only 14% by police initiative. Given that the police
operate largely as a reactive agency, Reiss goes on to suggest that the
discretionary power involved is largely in the hands of the public, not
the police:

'Thus is becomes apparent that citizens exercise considerable control
over police patrol work through their discretionary decisions to call the
police'. (Reiss, 1971; 11).

'Given the absence of a sense of civic responsibility to mobilize the
police, and the essentially reactive character of much policing of
everyday life, the citizenry has enormous power to subvert the system by
its decision to call the police or not'. (Reiss, 1971; 69).

These points form an important corrective to studies which have stressed the amount of discretionary power the police have, and they are
supported by ongoing British research by Bottomley and Coleman (1976)
and Chatterton (1976). They do not deny the existence of police discretion. On the contrary it would appear that three levels of discretion
have been distinguished. At the first level, the discovery and reporting
of incidents, the role of the police may be limited; at the second and
third levels, the recording of such incidents and the handling of suspects, the role of the police is more prominent. However, at this
initial stage at least it appears that more consideration must be given
to the role of the public — why do they frequently not report offences,
and what consequences does this have for the types of offences common in
the police statistics?

As has been shown, research in both America and Britain suggests that
the police act as a receptive agancy, to whom crimes are reported by
members of the public. Unfortunately, despite the overwhelming proportion of offences reported to the police by the public, none of the
published studies include any meaningful breakdown of different types of
complainant. Information of this type is most commonly available from a
rather different source — studies which concentrate on the victim as a
unit of analysis. At this stage, it is perhaps best to distinguish
between two victim categories — where the victim is an institution or an
organisation (called herein a corporate victim), and where the victim is
an individual, whether or not the object of the offence is himself or his
property (called herein an individual victim).

Perhaps the classic early study of the decision making of corporate
victims was Cameron's research into shoplifting in Chicago. Cameron was
particularly interested in the processes involved in the detection of
shoplifters and the decisions taken whereby known shoplifters were either
cautioned or prosecuted. In particular, she noted that:

(i) Only a very small proportion of shoplifters were caught, even in
stores employing detectives.

(ii) Of those who were caught, only a few were prosecuted. Indeed, widespread discretion was necessary; if all known shoplifters had been prosecuted, store detectives would have spent all their time in court.

(iii) Fundamental to the decision on whether or not to prosecute was an attempt to categorise shoplifters according to their degree of professionalisation, remorse, likelihood of further offences, etc. (namely, a distinction between the 'booster' and the 'snitch'). As this process operated, the result was that prosecuted shoplifters differed in a number of important respects from known shoplifters - for example, they were more likely to be lower class, black, male, and come from certain areas of Chicago (Cameron, 1964).

Cameron's findings were paralleled by Robin's research into the ways in which three department stores dealt with offences by their employees. The companies had three courses of action open to them - prosecution and dismissal, dismissal only and retention of the offending employee. In fact, over three years, only 17% of known offenders in three companies were prosecuted. However, within this overall total, there were a number of differences - for example, the percentage prosecuted varied between companies, and different grades of employee were relatively more or less immune (for example, 60.9% of cleaners were prosecuted, compared with 26.3% of sales staff). (Robin, 1970). Although an earlier British study, by Martin, did not deal with the question of the differential handling of different offenders, like Robin, Martin found firms reluctant to involve the police. (Martin, 1962).

The validity of those findings, particularly regarding the extent to which different types of offender escape prosecution, have been questioned recently, particularly in larger, more statistical studies of shoplifting (Hindelang, 1974; Cohen and Start, 1974). Nevertheless, the extent to which the corporate victim holds discretion over whether or not to invoke the legal process is not disputed. Moreover, one further distinction has been added. Hindelang in a study of shoplifting, found that shops which employed professional specialist detectives were more likely to prosecute offenders than were shops which relied on ordinary staff to discover and handle offenders. (Hindelang, 1974). If this may be generalised one must assume that the proportion of offences which is not passed on to the official law enforcement agencies is higher than even Cameron and Robin suggest.

A rather different approach to measuring the victim's involvement in reporting crime is the questionnaire victim study which was first used extensively in America by the President's Committee on Law Enforcement. Although the most quoted studies carried out for the President's Committee were household surveys, in fact the programme also included a survey of corporate victims.

The results of this survey are reported in Field Surveys 111 volume 1, (Reiss, 1967). Unfortunately the report is written in such a way that many questions relevant to the present discussion remain unanswered, but nevertheless some of the findings are pertinent.

A sample of businesses and organisations in police precincts in Boston, Chicago and Washington DC, was taken, and questions about victimisation during the past year were posed, notably in respect of four types of crime - burglary, robbery, shoplifting, and 'bad check problems'.

Overall, it appeared that 'bad check problems' and shoplifting were
particulary common - with 55.0% and 46.8% of firms mentioning them,
respectively; on the other hand rather fewer organisations experienced
burglaries (19.8%) and robberies (9.9%).

Reiss stresses that area rates were not in line with what police data
would have suggested, and that some areas with low reported rates had
high survey rates. However, little information is given about the extent
of reporting burglaries and robberies to the police. This is particularly unfortunate, since information on 'bad check problems' and shoplifting
indicated that in each case the majority of victims did not routinely
call the police - only 32.9% of shoplifting victims and 19.0% of 'bad
check problem' victims in fact did so and in each case the most common
reason for not reporting incidents was a concern to extract compensation
from the offender, i.e. if the offender was willing to pay up, further
action was unlikely.

This victim survey is so far the main one to consider the actions taken
by corporate victims. On the other hand, household victim surveys are
fast becoming a common research technique, (Hindelang, 1976; Skogan,
1976; Sparks, 1977) and were indeed incorporated into the Sheffield
study.

The President's Commission on Law Enforcement commissioned two major
household victim studies, one a pilot survey in the District of Columbia
(Bideman, 1967), the other a national survey (Ennis, 1967). In each
case, households were asked specific questions about crimes committed
against them or their individual members during the past twelve months,
and details of actions taken by the victims. The information thus allows
two types of comparison to be made:

(a.i) Comparison of the amount of crime as recorded by or known to
different agencies - in particular crimes committed against individual
victims, crimes reported to the police, and crimes processed in police
statistics.

(a.ii) Comparison between different units - in the national survey
different parts of the country, in the Columbia survey, different precincts - and different crimes.

The results illustrated the important roles played by both victim and
police in the process:

(b.i) In the Columbia survey, an estimated 31,400 offences were
committed, of which 1,700 were reported to the police (54.1%); however,
of these only an estimated 7,991 (47.0% of those reported, 25.4% of all)
were classified as crimes by the police. In other words only a quarter
of crimes against individual victims were recorded as crimes by the
police, and the selectivity factors were divided equally between victim
and police - the victim, according to what he decided to report, the
police, according to how they recorded the complaint.

(b.ii) Certain types of offence seemed to be reported more readily
than others. For example, the National Survey found that more serious
offences were more likely to be reported than less serious offences
(60% of grand larcenies, but only 37% of petty larcenies were reported)
and that marginal offences were particularly under reported (only 10% of

consumer fraud cases were reported).

On the other hand, the Columbia survey found rather fewer differences between precincts. Comparing three precincts, one (the 14th) with a very low offence rate and good police-community relations, one (the 10th) with a high offence rate, and one (the 6th) a high status low offence rate area, it appeared that differences between the total offences against individual victims and offences reported, were similar. However, considering police action, it appeared that the police in the 14th precinct were least likely to record complaints as crimes (38.2%), whilst the police in the 10th precinct were most likely to (56.4%). The conclusions here then, are that whilst the extent of police discretion is similar to that of the victim, police discretion in recording varies between areas to a greater extent than does victim discretion in reporting.

The more recent victim studies in America and Britain provide additional evidence on the characteristics of reported and nonreported incidents and victims. For example, Hindelang (1976) in describing a victimisation study in eight American cities which was funded by the National Criminal Justice Information and Statistics Service, shows a high degree of non-reporting by victims. Comparing the extent of nonreporting on a number of variables, he shows that crimes against corporate victims were more frequently reported than those against individual victims, that 'serious' incidents were more likely to be reported and that younger and male victims were among those least likely to involve the police. However, race, income and offender/victim relationship were inconsistently related to nonreporting (Hindelang, 1976; chapter 14).

Sparks' findings for London are in agreement with the American data in at least two respects - with 'seriousness' of offence related to reporting but social class of victim unrelated (Sparks, 1977; 122). In addition though, Sparks' data, because it is based on areal comparisons (in the same way as the early American Research) does allow differences to be considered on this dimension, even though, once again, the areas are rather large. Sparks concentrated his research in three areas of London - Kensington (with the highest recorded crime rate of the three), Brixton and Hackney. Comparing the three areas, (Sparks, 1977; 157), he found that according to the respondents' accounts 34% of crimes were reported in Brixton, 35% in Hackney and 40% in Kensington - that is the area with the most crime had the highest reporting rate. However when the estimated police recording rate was considered a rather greater difference emerged - with some 22% of reported incidents recorded in Hackney, 31% in Brixton and 43% in Kensington. The result of these two processes appeared to be that about twice as many incidents were recorded in Kensington as in Hackney, with the implication that much of the difference in official crime rates may be due to victim reporting practices and (especially) police recording policies.

An area comparison seems to indicate then that police recording differences between areas may be crucial. On the other hand, victim reporting differences seem to be slight, at least as far as present research findings are concerned. This finding, which is perhaps somewhat unexpected, supports earlier research carried out by Maccoby et al. (1958). They compared two areas, one with a high delinquency rate, the other with a low rate, and found no difference in the proportion of victims reporting offences. Thus, at least in terms of victims' descriptions of their actions, there appear to be only minimal indications of area differences.

One other way of considering the reporting process from the victim's perspective, however, is to ask victims what their reasons were for non-reporting. Clearly much criminological research concerned with sub-cultural or anomic explanations of criminality is pertinent here, since these theories assume areal differences in attitudes towards the police, which might be.expected to be related to nonreporting.

However, there is little evidence to support this link with reporting patterns. Sparks, for example, in comparing attitudes to the police with reporting policy, concluded that 'in our sample, the relationships bet-ween expressed general attitudes to the police and the nonreporting of incidents are not at all strong' (Sparks, 1977; 119).

Similarly, evidence from all the published studies indicates that the main reasons for nonreporting centre on victims' perceptions of the seriousness of the incident and the likelihood of action being in any way effective. Indeed, in the light of other findings - on police recording and detection, it appears that victims' presumptions are not unrealistic!

What then, do victim studies tell us about victims' motivations to report crime? As Hindelang concludes:

'(I)t is primarily what happens to the victim rather than who is victimized that determines whether the victimization is reported to the police. It is interesting to note, however, that those who are the most fearful of crime - older respondents and women - were more likely than their less fearful counterparts to report victimizations to the police. However the nature of the victimization is a more powerful determinant of nonreporting than is either the age or the sex of the victim'. (Hindelang, 1976; 401).

Given the lack of any consistent differences according to both social class and area of residence of the victim, and the lack of any signifi-cant amount of anti-police feelings amongst those not reporting crime, the findings would appear in no way to support any assumptions which link subcultural factors to victims' decisions to involve the police.

However, thus far the emphasis has been on the victim - the extent to which he reports offences to the police. In addition, though, it is pertinent to ask what factors are involved in reports by complainants who are not the victims - how many offences are reported by witnesses; what are the reasons for their involving themselves?

It is interesting that practically no criminological research has been carried out on the role of other members of the public in the reporting of crime. This is especially surprising considering the emphasis which has been placed recently on 'correcting' those perspectives which have put too much emphasis on the role of the police.

In fact, this may well be the reason for the lack of information. Originally, a great deal of research focussed on the role of the police. In response, studies like those by Reiss and Bottomley and Coleman have been more concerned with redressing the balance than with analysing precisely who the complainant is.

Turning to the American victim studies, the same trend is apparent. In neither Field Surveys 1 or 11, in which the household victim surveys are

reported, is any information on nonvictim reporting included. Only in
Field Surveys lll, volume ll, on public perceptions of crime and law
enforcement, is any interest shown in nonvictim reporting, and here the
results are not given in any great detail:

'Residents were (also) asked whether they had ever seen or witnessed an
event that looked like it might be a crime that they did not report to
the police. Only one per cent of all residents said they had seen such
an event and not reported it.'_ (Reiss, 1967; 67-68).

Since no information is given of the number who had reported such
incidents, this information is of little value!

All residents were then asked why they thought a lot of people did not
call the police when they saw a crime committed - the answers correspond-
ed to those from the victim surveys:

'The two major reasons given by residents why they think people don't
call the police in such cases are that people don't want to be bothered
by taking the time or by getting involved, given by 44 per cent of all
residents, and that people have some other reason for not reporting it,
such as protecting the offender, fear of reprisal, or that it is none of
their business, given also by 44 per cent of all residents.' (Reiss,
1967 (ii); 68).

Unfortunately, the report gives no indication of variations in reasons
or reporting practices between areas. This is a notable omission,
because Maccoby's study (quoted above) had already found areal differences in actions taken by witnesses.

Maccoby did not, in fact, distinguish between types of action taken,
and calling the police is of course only one alternative. Nevertheless,
she did find areal differences in the extent to which witnesses actually
did something whereas, it must be remembered, she found no such differences in the actions of victims. Where the respondent was not the victim,
60% of witnesses in the low delinquency area but only 40% in the high
delinquency area involved themselves in the incident. In addition,
Maccoby notes:

'It is interesting that while we found no area differences in respondents' own opinions about whether it was all right to interfere with other
people's children, we did find some differences when we asked whether
other people in the neighbourhood felt it was all right. In the high
delinquency area, people more often said that their neighbours believed
one ought to mind one's own business (22% said this, as contrasted with
9% in the low delinquency area).' (Maccoby, et al, 1958; 48).

In conclusion, then, this section has highlighted the extent to which
the initial decision on whether to instigate the law enforcement process
is taken by a member of the public. Whilst there has been scant attention paid to seeing who exactly the complainant is, the role of the
public in general would appear, at least at this initial level, to be
crucial.

This is not to say that the police have no discretion. It must be
stressed that victim studies in particular have found a considerable
discrepancy between the number of offences recorded by the police and the

number which respondents say they reported to the police. The extent to which the police redefine incidents so as to treat them as noncriminal incidents or as less serious crimes, is therefore, not inconsiderable, and focusses attention on the whole range of police recording practices, rather than on merely the indictable files. In addition, it must be re-emphasised that as yet none of the critiques has touched the role of the police in the detection process.

DETECTION: THE HIDDEN DIMENSION

Given the number of studies which have concentrated on policework, it is no less than incredible that the role of the police in detecting offenders has been so inadequately considered.

This is not to say that the issue has not been appreciated. McClintock and Avison, in their detailed survey of crime in England and Wales, for example, noted:

'Studies on crime detection rates indicate the need for a knowledge of the extent to which the police are faced with genuine problems of detecting unidentified offenders at the time when the offence is reported to them. Such cases have to be contrasted with those crimes which are automatically 'solved' when reported to the police or when the offenders are caught by the police in the course of committing the crime, so that no problem of detection arises.' (McClintock, Avison, 1968; 109).

This point was echoed in other studies by the Cambridge Institute of Criminology, where high detection rates for sex and violence offences were attributed to the fact that in most cases the offender was known to the victim (McClintock, 1963); as can be seen from the official crime statistics, (see Table 1.1) the clear up rate for such offence types is far higher than in the case of say robbery and burglary, where the detection process usually starts from a 'cold trail'. Thus, although Bottomley and Coleman had little new information to report from their pilot survey in Hull it was at least admitted that the use of forensic evidence, notably fingerprints, was most uncommon!

Table 1.1
Percentage of offences 'cleared up' according to main offence groupings
1972 (Bottomley and Coleman, 1976; 49)

	Bottomley sample	England and Wales
Violence	79	81
Sex offences	69	77
Burglary/robbery	22	37
Theft/unauthorised taking	43	29
Handling	100	100
Fraud	97	83
Other	49	59
Total	41	41

The other major feature of the detection process which has been documented by British studies is the so called 'indirect detection'. This is the case where, as outlined by Baldwin (1972) in the first stage of the Sheffield research, an offender who has been caught for one offence admits to having committed other offences. Clearly there is an incentive for the police to increase the detection rate, i.e. 'clear the books', in this manner, and they may do so at the expense of accuracy. Thus offenders may be persuaded, or 'bribed' into admitting to having committed a whole range of offences which they in actual fact did not commit.

At this stage, it appears that the British research has been largely empirical, meticulous, but inconclusive. The problems surrounding the detection process have been appreciated, but no real information has been provided on the various ways in which cases are cleared up, except in the case of indirect detections.

The American research provides a contrast to this. Rather less concern with the methodological problems has been voiced, but a more comprehensive, if unsubstantiated, analysis of the theoretical implications has been made.

To a certain extent this is, once again, due to the concentration of much research on victimless crimes, where police discovery of the offence is almost inevitably bound to detection of the offender - yet even here there is practically no information on some aspects of detection, for example, police sources in arresting drug offenders.

More theoretically, other studies have concentrated on the extent to which the labelling process provides the police with a ready source of 'suspects' from whom an offender can be discovered; as Matza puts it, the police employ a 'method of suspicion' to clear up offences:

'The main bias of police operation has little to do with how policemen act when persons fall under incidental suspicion. Instead, it follows from how and when police look when no one has fallen under incidental suspicion. The main bias flows from the method of suspicion - a form of regular police practice that utilises essential thieves and those resembling them as suspects.' (Matza, 1969; 183).

What is crucial about this method of detection, according to Matza is the extent to which it is divorced from the actual case in hand - instead it is a method used by the police to clear up 'cold' crimes:

'The method of suspicion employs police knowledge of known criminals to expedite their apprehension and the subsequent clearing of complaints. It displays the police strength towards a corps of suspects and uses a variety of means of associating offences with a person who is methodically suspect. No incident excites police attention. The suspicion derives from police knowledge regarding identity and resemblance. Thus, the actual implementation of the method of suspicion is outgoing, it seeks a regular suspect in the hope that any one of a whole series of uncleared offences can be settled.' (Matza, 1969; 192-93).

But how common is detection by this method? Matza, despite a notable lack of any evidence, leaves the reader in little doubt. He lists three detection techniques, direct witness, which he dismisses as uncommon except for highly specific offences like traffic violations, the 'classic

20

method' (à la Sherlock Holmes) as used in homicide cases, and the method
for many 'ordinary' offences:

'Using the most dubious justifications imaginable - debatable regular-
ities produced partly by the very methods they use - police search in
different ways for offenders depending on the nature of the offense.
Putting aside direct witness, which is important only in the traffic
offenses, the methods range from the classic mode, still apparent and
important in homicide, to the bureaucratic mode, the main method for the
staple offenses of larceny, burglary, and even sexual deviation.'
(Matza, 1969; 184-85).

As a theoretical exercise, this categorisation is clearly worthwhile.
However, one looks in vain, in this or any other research, for critical
evidence that the method of suspicion is common, much less the most usual
means by which suspects are apprehended.

It is easy to create an image of police in patrol cars scouting dubious
areas on the lookout for suspects, or knocking up ex-cons in the middle
of the night to check alibis. For example, Piliavin and Werthman's vivid
description is often quoted:

'From the front seat of a moving patrol car, street life in a typical
Negro ghetto is perceived as an uninterrupted sequence of suspicious
scenes. Every well dressed man or woman standing aimlessly on the street
during hours when most people are at work is carefully scrutinized for
signs of an illegal source of income: every boy wearing boots, black
pants, long hair, and a club jacket is viewed as potentially responsible
for some item of the list of muggings, broken windows, and petty thefts
that still remain to be cleared; and every hostile glance directed at the
passing patrolman is read as a sign of possible guilt.' (Werthman and
Piliavin, 1967; 56).

However, nowhere does one find the question: 'Does it work? Do the
police really clear up many offences this way, or is it rather a fruitless exercise, no matter how often attempted?' Since, as has already
been noted, the detection rate for 'cold' offences such as burglary is
relatively low, there is, even without further evidence, some reason to
question Matza's statements.

Of course, the method of suspicion is based on a common police practice
- the use of a co-ordinator to compare the M.O. (modus operandi) of an
offence with the M.Os employed by known offenders (Conlin, 1967; 224).
However, it differs in that in Matza's account the stress is placed
rather less on the technical details of the offence and more on the moral
status of the suspects. Thus, it is implied, the police react to an
offence by positing that:

(i) A person, or pool of people, are the sort who could have committed
the offence.

(ii) A particular area is particularly likely to contain offenders,
in specific cases.

These hypotheses, for this is all they in fact are, appear to be based on
a number of assumptions which certainly should be examined in some detail
and where possible tested. For example:

(i) How often do the police in charge of an inquiry have a clear enough picture to be able to act? Is it not likely that in many cases the picture will be so vague that few 'suspects' come to mind, or, alternatively, any number of 'suspects' could be considered?

(ii) How far is a police definition of suspects dependent upon the assumption that the offender lives near the scene of the crime - if it does, how correct is this view?

(iii) Even if it is correct that the police do concentrate on particular individuals and suspects, how frequently does this method result in an arrest?

This last point is particularly important empirically. It often appears to be the assumption of labelling theorists that the theoretical grid used by the police as an aid to detection creates (or at least magnifies) differences in offender rates. However, nowhere is there any concrete evidence in the American research that 'the method of suspicion' is a common feature of detection techniques.

The present research was not originally designed with a view to testing detection variables, largely because, following earlier research it was assumed that such information would be either vague or just unobtainable. However, this was not the case, and a substantial part of the project has been devoted to an analysis of detection patterns. In this respect it is extremely interesting to note that another piece of research at the same time by Chatterton in Manchester focussed on many similar issues, albeit not on an areal level. It is therefore especially relevant to consider his findings on detection. (Chatterton, 1976).

Chatterton found that 24% of arrests were the result of the police discovering the offence taking place and 2% were based on fingerprint evidence. Other modes of detection by the police which could fit the 'method of suspicion' - search (7%), enquiries (11%) and 'other units' (7%), accounted for a relatively small proportion of arrests, whilst other 'instantaneous' arrests accounted for 49% of arrests. This stresses the extent to which arrest is dependent upon factors known at the time the incident is originally reported or discovered, especially upon whether the police catch the offender in the act or the offender is named at the time of reporting by a member of the public. Chatterton stresses the extent to which the public are involved in the detection process:

'Combining the totals of these arrests by the members of both departments (uniformed and CID) which were clearly cases in which members of the public played an active part in the process leading to the arrest, e.g. the cases in the 'normal', 'implicated', 'radio call' and 'detained' categories, we are provided with a grand total of 669 arrests (49%) of all arrests for crime. Almost half of all arrests for crime were cases in which the public had provided the police with a prisoner. Inasmuch as this excludes the cases in the 'search' and 'other unit arrest' categories where members of the public may have played a critical role in the apprehension of the accused, this figure may in fact underestimate the extent of public participation in the arrest process. Examining the total of arrests for both departments combined where the mode of detection was unequivocally police initiated, i.e. the arrest cases in the 'enquiries', 'fingerprints' and 'police initiated' categories, we are provided with a total of 497 cases, representing 37% of all crime arrests on the Research Division. Even in these cases, however, the role of the public may have been more significant than at first seems to be the case.' (Chatterton, 1976; 110).

If this study is at all representative, it appears that even in the sphere of detection the role of the public may be considerable. But if this has not until recently been appreciated by academics, the same cannot be said of the police themselves. Books by ex-officers and texts in police training stress the point. For example, a Home Office Committee reported in 1938:

'Efficient detection still depends and must always depend mainly upon the capacity of the police to obtain, sift and draw deductions from information coming from all sorts of sources and all sorts and conditions of people in all walks of life.' (Home Office, 1938; 40).

At roughly the same time an ex-policeman wrote:

'In the tracing of the criminal the police are to a great extent dependent on help from the general public; and it is largely by means of interviews that the required information is obtained.' (Morrish, 1940; 54).

Similarly, Conlin, in a more recent text book stresses the overwhelming importance of the public in the detection process:

'(I)nformants are an essential part of a detective's stock in trade and are necessary to detect crime. The term informant, however odious it may sound, also covers every citizen who, having an interest in seeing that offenders are punished, is able to provide information for the police which may lead to the detection of crime .... Basically, then, the police force would be inadequate, inefficient and unable to cope with crime if it were not for the informants, paid or unpaid, mercenary or dutiful, who oil the machinery of the police organization with their vital pieces of information.' (Conlin, 1967; 220-21).

Thus, whilst the emphasis laid by Matza on the method of suspicion has been accepted uncritically by many academics there are indications, in other research and in the writings of the police themselves, that the role of the public in the detection process may be rather larger than has been assumed. Summing up current thinking, Bottomley and Coleman terminate their discussion of detection, not with a conclusion but with a thoughtful invitation to future research:

'Hopefully, future research will provide more evidence in the light of which such claims and counterclaims can be reviewed; the truth of the matter, as so often, may lie somewhere uneasily between the extremes, but a growing familiarity with the social reality of reported crimes in an urban community inclines us towards a truth of a rather different kind, namely that the real problematics surrounding undetected crime and undetected criminals lie not so much in the initiative discretion and detection methods of the police but in the role of other members of the public who crucially influence both the definition of crime and ultimately the social construction of official crime data.' (Bottomley and Coleman, 1976; 56).

The relative importance of the police and other agencies in the detection process, which is considered in more detail in chapter five, thus covers ground which has been left untouched by much past research.

POLICE RESPONSES TO REPORTS MADE BY THE PUBLIC

Evidence from victim studies indicates that whilst a high proportion of offences are not reported to the police, of those which are reported a significant proportion are not recorded as such. Therefore even where police control over the discovery of crime is constrained, the police may have sufficient power to accept, reject or reclassify those incidents which are reported to them by the public.

A recent monograph on the role of the police as recorders of information (McCabe and Sutcliffe, 1978) brings this point into sharp focus. The authors spent a considerable amount of time in the stations of the Salford and Oxford police in an attempt to describe and analyse the ways in which the police responded to citizens calls. The research method used basically 'soft' data, and no attempt was made to consider the extent to which police recording decisions may be influenced by features of the complainant or the incident itself, although the nonrecording of domestic disputes is specifically mentioned. Despite these obvious limitations however, the authors succeed in impressing on their readers the considerable amount of discretion the police may have over whether or not to record incidents, and in the former case how to record them. As the authors conclude:

'The decision to accept or reject a report that a crime has been committed is an essential part of the discretion exercised by all police officers but particularly by those of the lowest rank who are in closer contact with the community.' (McCabe and Sutcliffe, 1978; 85).

An acceptance of police discretions at this level, of course, tells us little about the reasons behind the use of this discretion. Why do the police choose to record some complaints as crimes whilst others are either not recorded at all or recorded in files relating to noncriminal matters?

A simple answer would be that the police redefine complaints made to them by the public into the appropriate legal category, excluding those which the public feel are crimes but the police 'know' are not. However, as was stressed in the introductory section to this chapter, it is frequently misleading to consider these negotiations in terms of a 'right' or 'wrong' decision - rather the police, like the public, have their own definitions of the criminal - qualities of different types of behaviour, and in some circumstances these definitions may be at variance with the legal definition. For example, as has been pointed out on numerous occasions, police reluctance to define domestic violence as an indictable crime, even where physical injury is evident, is a case in point (Pizzey, 1974; House of Commons, 1975). In cases such as this, the police may well make use of legal ambiguities. In other cases also, it is frequently unclear as to whether or not a crime has been committed - as McCabe and Sutcliffe show, for example, the police usually avoided recording the offence of stealing by finding and instead made use of the lost property book where they were not totally worried that a loss was due to theft.

The motivation behind police decisions may be based on the relative seriousness of the incident with which they are dealing – thus, as Bittner (1967) and Wilson (1968(ii)) have shown, in high crime situations the police may ignore minor incidents; in a low crime area such incidents may be considered in an entirely different light. In addition though, it is also true that the police may avoid recording incidents in order to enhance their working environment. On the one hand, it is quite clear that record keeping and report writing are ascribed low priority by beat policemen, and will be avoided where possible. Thus a lost property record may be preferred to a crime report since the amount of paperwork is less. On the other hand, by avoiding recording certain types of complaint, the police officer may thereby avoid actually investigating incidents which he considers boring or potentially problematic, for example, domestic disputes or vague complaints of vandalism. In this context also, incidents where there is little chance of an arrest may go unrecorded, as one means of influencing the detection rate.

These points are commonly accepted. They do however, create some problems in relation to the present study, where the main sources of data are police records, and where information which is not recorded is, by definition, lost to the study. In the particular context of this research, this point needs to be considered in more detail, and will be returned to in chapter two. At this juncture, however, it is perhaps appropriate to stress that to accept that there are pressures towards nonrecording is not to accept that nonrecording is always likely – rather, in certain circumstances it may be highly unlikely. In particular as McCabe and Sutcliffe (1978; 80-81) acknowledge, where recording is given high priority by senior management, i.e. where information storage is a management goal, discretion may for some types of incident be curbed, and indeed this is compatible with Wilson's model of different police styles. A more professional police, with a greater appreciation of the use of record keeping, may thus be expected to discourage nonrecording.

Research does indicate, however, that the role of the police at the recording stage may be such as to allow a certain amount of discretion. One aspect of this may be that some offenders, as well as offences, go unrecorded. Moreover where an offender is identified and recorded the police in most cases have the power to decide whether or not to proceed – it is therefore important to consider police discretion at this level.

DEALING WITH OFFENDERS

In sections 'The discovery and reporting of crime' and 'Detection: the hidden dimension', a wide range of research projects have been discussed which cast considerable doubt on the primary role of the police. At the discovery and reporting stage it is evident that the role of the public is considerable; at the detection stage there is little evidence that the role of the police is crucial and some suggestion that the public play a not inconsiderable part in the process.

In contrast, whilst the view of the complainant may still be important, there is a lot of evidence that in deciding how to deal with known offenders the role of the police is that of a primary gatekeeper, whose decision is crucial. Correspondingly, a number of studies have concentrated on police discretion at this level.

Here there are some notable differences between British and American research. While in reviewing the American literature it is practicable to distinguish between those processes which take place in the field and those which involve the formal and recorded use of discretion (Bottomley, 1973; 43-73), in Britain research has largely been restricted to the latter area. If we consider formal and on-the-street dispositions together, however, it is clear that the bases for the decisions cover similar ground. Essentially there are five areas which may be important in distinguishing those who are further subjected to the law enforcement process and those who are diverted out of the system. These are:

   (i)   The framework within which the decision is made
  (ii)   The nature of the crime
 (iii)   The wishes of the victim
  (iv)   'Objective' characteristics of the offender
   (v)   The attitudes, manner and overall moral stature of the offender.

Taking first the influence of the wider framework, it is evident that local or national expectations on policy will considerably influence the extent to which offenders are cautioned. In a study of the Madison police, for example, Shannon (1963) found considerable differences between departments and over time; similarly Wilson (1968) and Miller et al (1968) have revealed area differences which they attribute to organisational factors including the professionalisation of the police.

In Britain, reviews of statistics of formal cautions by McClintock and Avison (1968), Steer (1970) and Ditchfield (1976) reveal considerable differences between forces and differences moreover which cannot be explained according to the nature of the local crime situation. In addition, the Children and Young Persons Act of 1969 marks a change in police practices, with a notable increase in the proportion of juveniles cautioned since that date (Ditchfield, 1976).

Considering police decision making in specific cases, the influence of the victim has been noted in a number of studies. In America for example, La Fave (1965) stressed the importance of the victim, both in terms of the victim's willingness to co-operate (which may be vital to a successful prosecution) and in terms of police evaluations of the victim's moral worth and in particular his right to victim status. In these respects, of course, police handling of complaints of rape, and in particular domestic violence (Parnas, 1967), are notable examples. Similarly in Britain Steer found that taking the reasons given for cautioning males aged seventeen or more, some quarter of cases included the complainant's wish that the offender should not be prosecuted, and a similarly high proportion of cautions appeared to be based on the conception of the victim as at least partly to blame. These two justifications are, according to Steer, typified in the examples of domestic violence and unlawful sexual intercourse with a girl aged 13-15 (Steer, 1970, 27-40).

The role of the victim cannot then be ignored, even at this later stage of the law enforcement process. However, it is not clear how far the police are controlled by the wishes of the victim, or use features of the victim/offender relationship or the expressed attitudes of the victim to justify decisions which they themselves would have made anyway. In this respect, the nature of the victim may be seen as one factor which the police take into account in making their decisions, where this helps them to build up a picture of the offender and his motives. Similarly the seriousness of the offence and the objective characteristics of the offender may help the police to form a picture on which to base their decisions.

The nature of the offence is an obvious cue, since it is an indication of the extent to which the offender is committed to a criminal career. On the one hand, certain types of offences are more likely than others to end in the offender being cautioned. On the other hand, it is equally clear that more detailed features, such as the value of goods stolen, the amount recovered etc. may be vital components and indeed it has been argued by some that the amount stolen is a considerably more important indication of cautioning policy than is the nature of the offender. (Hindelang, 1974; Cohen, 1974).

Turning to those factors related to the offender himself, numerous studies have revealed a greater likelihood for some offenders to be cautioned than others. Here a number of common factors have been distinguished, with race (in America), age, sex, previous record and social class frequently found to be related to cautioning policies, although it is sometimes difficult to judge how far the interrelationship between these variables may produce certain spurious correlations.

However, if we are to understand the reasons for these relationships, it is necessary to 'appreciate' (using Matza's terminology) the decision making process from the point of view of the officer-in-charge. Here two sorts of consideration may be crucial. First, the police are concerned to distinguish between 'real offenders' and those who 'just happen' to have committed an offence, and will attempt to build up a picture of the motives behind the offences, pressures on the offender, motive of the offence etc., ultimately to decide whether the offender 'needs' or 'deserves' punishment, or alternatively, whether he is likely to offend in the future. In arriving at their decisions the police may indeed make use of similar sets of 'facts' to those discussed by academics:

'Police develop indicators of suspicion by a method of pragmatic indication. Past experience leads them to conclude that more crimes are committed in the poorer sections of town than in the wealthier areas, that Negroes are more likely to cause public disturbances than whites ...' (Werthman and Piliavin, 1967; 75).

There may however, be a bitter irony in this process:

'It may be true that the police regard Negroes more often as potential recidivists, and there are statistics to show a higher Negro crime rate - but by enforcing the law in this way they are, of course, simply ensuring a self-fulfilling prophecy.' (Hood and Sparks, 1970; 77).

The decisions taken by the police, both in the field and in the station, may thus be analogous to the decisions arrived at within the courtroom. One other element, which may well be common to both stages, is the demeanor of the offender. Whilst this may, along with other more 'objective' factors, be a cue by which the police distinguish the 'deviant' from the 'misguided', it is perhaps more likely to relate to a second area of police concern, the necessity that they should receive appropriate respect. This is important in the relative privacy of the police station; in the street, where the presence of an audience could provide the script by which the reputation of an officer is either made or broken, it is vital that the officer does not loose face. Consequently:

'A juvenile who publicly causes damage to the dignity of the police, or who is defiant, refusing the help offered by the police, will be considered as needing court supervision, no matter how trivial the offence ...' (Goldman, 1963).

The capacity for police discretion over the disposition of known offenders, whatever the bases for its use, is thus unchallenged, and in Britain, despite the clear intention of the Children and Young Persons Act (1969) it is evident that the influence of other agencies in influencing police cautioning practices is minimal (Priestley, 1977; 25). It appears, therefore, that whilst in the discovery of crime, and to some extent its detection, the role of the public is considerable, the importance of police discretion at the recording stage and in the disposition of known offenders is more crucial, although not exclusively so. At this point though, before going on to discuss the results of the present research in any detail, it may be useful to summarise earlier findings in so far as they are related to area crime differences.

POLICE RESPONSES IN DIFFERENT AREAS

As with most modern sociology, area of residence is not a factor commonly studied in research on law enforcement. For example, studies of the use of discretion by police and other law enforcement agencies have concentrated on a few 'personal' items, like sex, race, age and social class.

One exception to this pattern is Cameron's study of shoplifting. Within the study, she compared the areal distribution of prosecutions from court data with that from the stores' files on all known shoplifters. Her conclusions that there were considerable differences in the distribution of the two types of data led her to cast doubts on the reliability of official records in general:

'Explanations of the so called 'delinquency areas' (the site of delinquent subcultures) have usually been based on the premise that the rate of arrest or conviction adequately of even approximately reflects the real rates of crime of those residing in different urban areas. The study of shoplifting presented an unusual opportunity to study, for this type of crime, a rate of arrest much closer to the actual crime than the official arrest rate and to compare the rate derived from the store data with the official arrest rate ....

'The court cases show the characteristic concentration at the center of the city of the rate of arrested women per 1,000 female population. The rate declines as one approaches the middle and peripheral areas .... Altogether this ratemap of shoplifters resembles closely the residential maps of persons arrested for other types of crimes, or, indeed, indices of almost all other sociopathic phenomena. The rate at the first quartile of census areas is approximately 7.5 times the rate of the third quartile of census areas.

'The rates by census areas of persons arrested for shoplifting at Lakeside County however show no such concentration at the center of the

city. The dispersal is slightly greater ($Q_1 = 6Q_3$) and the areas with
the highest rates are not concentrated at the centre of the city only but
extend along the entire shore of Lake Michegan ....' (Cameron, 1964).

Cameron's study provided quantitative evidence of the <u>effects</u> of discretion on areal variables. This is particularly striking when it is
compared with the extent to which the area dimension is introduced in
other studies without any direct evidence of its relevance.

Cicourel, for example, has posited:

'My observations suggest police and probation perspectives/follow
community typifications in organising the city into areas where they
expect to receive the most difficulty from deviant or 'difficult' elements to areas where little trouble is expected/and where more care should
be taken in dealing with the populace because of socio-economic and
political influence. /The partition of the city into areas of more or
less anticipated crime provides both police and probation officers with
additional typifications about what to expect when patrolling or making
calls in the areas./ Thus the officer's preconstituted typifications and
stock of knowledge at hand leads him to prejudge much of what he encounters,/ which an independent observer does not always 'see'. Thus particu-
lar/ecological settings, populated by persons with 'known' styles of
dress and physical appearance, provide the officer with quick inferences
about 'what is going on/ although not based upon factual type material he
must describe sooner or later in oral or written form.' (Cicourel, 1976;
67).   \ neq.

This stance at least merits some credibility, even if it is the somewhat subjective assessment of an observer. Even the most charitable
critic could not say the same about a similar observation from Wiles:

'Enforcement agencies cannot hope to exercise active control in all
situations at all times, and decisions have to be made as to how scarce
resources are to be employed. Historically the beginning of policing in
England are linked to a fear of the danger presented by the new urban
proletariat, and the solution to the practical problem of control was a
greater use of police patrols in those areas of the city where the danger
was concentrated. The unintended consequence of this, however, was that
the extra presence of the police produced extra knowledge of crime in
those areas. The result was an over-representation in the statistics of
crime in those areas most heavily policed, which in turn provided the
necessary evidence to support a policy of differential patrolling. The
pattern today is no longer a simple one of urban areas, but rather a
differential police presence between different social situations, according to their perceived differences as criminogenically inducing – a
judgement which in parts draws upon the frequency with which these social
situations appear in the statistics of crime. Here criminal statistics
are no longer just factual reports of an agency's activities, but themselves come to play an active part in the process of law enforcement.'
(Wiles, 1975; 214).

Unfortunately, this statement is as methodologically unsound as it is
historically incorrect. In fact, it is a particularly good example of
the sociological technique of mysticism, whereby a hypothesis is posited,
illustrated (but not proven) and thereby transformed into a statement of
fact. Nowhere is any evidence cited that police manpower deployment did

vary between areas, and moreover, the implications of strategic use of manpower are not considered.

The professionalisation of the police in the nineteenth century was indeed largely a middle class response to the perceived growth of the 'dangerous classes'. However, such was the hostility shown towards the police that for some time their deployment in disreputable areas (the Rookeries) was restricted. For example, they might raid a house in pairs, and then retreat from the area. Thus to a certain extent they were deployed as a constraining rather than an invading force; they protected respectable areas, and only slowly infiltrated the slums. (Chesney, 1970; Dickens, 1858).

This highlights one of the problems of the discretionary policing theory. If police manpower is used selectively, it appears that certain criteria may dominate. For example:

(i) The police may respond to the public demand
(ii) The police may concentrate on those areas where offences
are committed.

Thus it could be argued that the police will be concentrated in more prestigious areas, or areas where offence rates are high. That these will not necessarily be high offender rate areas (i.e. areas where offenders tend to live) is an assumption which will be tested in chapter four.

Be this as it may. Cicourel's point is rather wider. He implies that not only will police manpower be concentrated in certain areas, but that police behaviour will vary between areas. Thus levels of suspicion will vary between areas: in problem areas, a wider variety of behaviour will be considered problematic. Or, as Werthman and Piliavin have succinctly stated in an article already quoted, residents of disreputable areas may more frequently be 'selected' as suspects. (Werthman and Piliavin, 1967).

The selective aspects of area policing in the British context are stressed in two recent studies of highly distinctive problem council estates. In their research in the Easterhouse district of Glasgow, Armstrong and Wilson (1973) argued that the offender rate for the area was boosted by the police concentrating resources in the area and inter- vening more readily in situations where there were some slight possib- ilities of offences occuring. More recently, Gill (1977) has reaffirmed this argument:

'In relation to the delinquent area, I would argue that because the police are a limited resource they define certain areas as delinquent and concentrate their resources in these areas. There are at least two stages at which such police discretion can be of significance in determ- ining high rates of official delinquency in such areas: (i) the decision as to what level of surveillance to give different areas; (ii) the decision as to what course of action to take with offenders from different areas' (Gill, 1977; 10-11).

As this quote illustrates, however, both Gill and Armstrong and Wilson, like Piliavin and Briar, put little emphasis on the detection process, except where this motivates police intervention on the street in ambigu- ous situations, and here Gill, to his credit, shows some evidence that,

30

the police records of 'Luke Street' residents are rather likely to include public order incidents.

On the other hand, there is no evidence that this pattern applies to high crime rate areas in general, (rather than extremely notorious estates) not indeed that the overall crime rate of such areas is significantly affected by such processes. Moreover, even if policework does vary according to area, the work of Wilson (1968) and Bittner (1967) indicates that this does not necessarily mean that discretion will tend to exaggerate area differences. It could in fact decrease them.

If we refer back to the previous four sections of this chapter, there are thus four levels of law enforcement which may operate to affect area crime rates:

(i) The discovery and reporting of crime: may vary either because the police are more likely to look for or because the public are more willing to report crime in certain areas.

(ii) Detection: the detection process; may vary according to area, due either to police use of the 'method of suspicion' in areas with which they are more familiar or, again, because of differences in public responses.

(iii) Police recordkeeping: may vary according to police definitions of the different areas and their residents.

(iv) Dealing with offenders: the handling of known offenders may vary if area of residence is considered by the police as a valid contribution to their image of the offender.

There are, then, clearly, a number of quite separate levels on which area policing can be considered. It is important to stress this because, as has been suggested, concentration on only one level, or indeed one part of a level, may give a wholly misleading impression of the influence of policework in the production of crime statistics.

These different levels, then, will be considered in more detail in chapters four to seven. Before then, however, it is appropriate to introduce the subjects of the research in more depth. Consequently chapter two is devoted to a description of crime (as measured in a variety of ways) in the areas of the study. Then in chapter three the focus turns to the role of the police in the areas, as expressed in their own words.

2 An Introduction to Sheffield and its Crime

CRIME PATTERNS IN SHEFFIELD

Although Sheffield is a city of some 500,000 people it is, as Baldwin and Bottoms have noted, perhaps distinct from other large cities in a number of respects. With its relative geographic isolation, domination by one major industry (steel), a stable population size and a low rate of geographic mobility, it is often referred to in cliche terms as 'the largest village in England' (Baldwin and Bottoms, 1976; 45-49).

Similarly, the crime picture is one which compares favourably with other cities. Apart from the industrial violence of the 1860s, the major claim to notoriety in the city was the gang warfare of the 1920s, when the Mooney and the Garvin gangs used violence to secure a hold on the rackets (Baldwin and Bottoms, 1976; 49-50). Indeed, local police mythology is still dominated by this violent period, with the story about the Chief Constable of the time who 'recruited illiterate six foot buggers to sort it out' (Field Notes).

Since then, however, it seems that, at least according to official records, crime rates for Sheffield are relatively low. A comparison of the six major English cities outside London, for example, reveals Sheffield as having a lower crime rate than Manchester, Leeds, Birmingham and Liverpool, and over the years a rate only slightly above that for Bristol. Similarly it appears that rates of mental illness, suicide and receptions into care of children are lower than might be expected (Baldwin and Bottoms, 1976; 51-53).

This, then, is the general picture. However the first stage of the Sheffield research provided valuable information on crime patterns <u>within</u> the city, and notably variations between areas.

Baldwin and Bottoms took samples of offenders and offences known to the Sheffield police from the police files for standard list offences, 1966. Concentrating on offender rates in different areas, there appeared to be clear evidence of a zonal patterning, with inner zones having higher rates than outer areas, and the results falling in line with the classic Chicago model (Shaw and McKay, 1969). However, when the census enumeration district (E.D.) was taken as the unit of analysis, it was also clear that the zonal model oversimplified the picture. For example, some areas on the periphery of the city (notably council estates but also some areas of rented accommodation) had relatively high offender rates.

Areas were distinguished, following Rex (1968), according to their predominant tenure type, i.e. owner occupied, privately rented or council rented (other areas which could not be so classified were called 'mixed' areas). According to this distinction, there was a clear difference initially, between the owner occupied areas, with unanimously low offender rates, and rented and council areas. However, even here the picture was far from simple - some council and rented areas had high offender rates, others low rates. As an attempt at distinguishing between them, regression equations were worked out for council and 'private' (i.e. rented plus owner occupied) areas separately, to see what variables were related to the varying offender rates.

The results showed that in the council areas social class was correlated with offender rate, but controlling for this no other variable appeared related. Thus, the adult male offender rate was related to the social class composition of the area (r = 0.51), as were, to a lesser extent, the female and juvenile offender rates.

However, whilst in the council areas social class seemed to be the only discriminatory variable, in the private sector its predictive value was less. Instead, a number of other variables, including the percentage of the population in rented accommodation, persons per room, and, significantly, a group of variables grouped tentatively into a 'social disorganisation' index, showed up.

The regression analysis revealed rather different patterns in the private and council areas. This was further exemplified in a comparison of offender rates in different tenure-type areas, according to the percentage of employed males in social classes iv/v. Taking council areas, the offender rate for social classes iv/v rose consistently as the percentage of the population in the areas in social classes iv/v rose; in privately rented areas, on the other hand, the relationship was curvilinear. That is, as the proportion of the population in social classes iv/v rose to 34%, the offender rate for social classes iv/v rose to 102, thereafter it fell. (Baldwin and Bottoms, 1976; 133).

This point is of considerable interest since it is relevant to the disorganisation/subculture debate. That is, there is some evidence here that 'disorganisation' (both in terms of the 'social disorganisation' index and the social class mix of the area) is related to offender rates in rented areas, whilst subcultural theories (but certainly not anomie theories) would appear more pertinent in the council sector.

Baldwin analysed the data for the council sector according to estate rather than enumeration district (E.D.), and carried out a number of comparisons. As with the E.D. data, there appeared to be a negative relationship between the social class composition of an area and the offender rate, but when Baldwin went on to compare estates in more detail, some interesting findings emerged.

In particular, the newer estates did not have higher offender rates than the older ones. This finding seems to contradict the theories of Mannheim (1948) and Jones (1958), since the most recently built estates might have been expected to be in a state of transition with no developed norms and values. On the other hand, there were apparent differences between pre- and postwar estates. The prewar estates had distinct patterns - offender rates were either high or low and consistently so over a ten year period. In contrast, postwar estates had generally intermediate offender rates.

One implication that might be drawn from this is that estates developed their reputations over a period of time, and that prewar estates had settled reputations, whilst for the postwar estates the situation was one of flux. In the long term, this raised the interesting question of whether it would be possible to record this process as it occurred.

However, with limited data at his disposal, Baldwin concentrated on comparing two prewar estates with contrasting offender rates, and carried out a small survey in the two areas (Baldwin, 1974 (i)).

This provided some interesting results. In particular three aspects might be noted:

(i) Although residents in the two areas differed, - as one might have expected - in their judgements of the offender rates of their respective areas, the difference was not excessive. For example, on the estate with the high offender rate, as many as 63.4% of respondents said that people on the estate 'get into trouble with the law' about the same as anywhere else, whilst 8.1% said people were less likely to get into trouble with the law. (See also Herbert, 1976). This could of course be a defence against criticism of the estate by outsiders. In fact, many residents accepted that the estate had a bad reputation, but blamed this on residents at the other end of the estate (according to Baldwin, the official data showed no such pattern) (see also Damer, 1976)).

(ii) Thus it appears that residents of the problem estate employed certain strategies to deny that the label applied to them. However, they were noticeably unwilling to blame differential policing for the reputation. Hardly anyone in the sample (which was of adults only) thought the police patrolled the area too frequently, and only 6.3% of respondents on the problem estate thought relations with the police were 'not very good' or 'bad'.

(iii) In contrast, Baldwin found that tenants were quick to blame the council for the state of the area. 56.3% of respondents said they had received unsatisfactory treatment from the council, notable over repairs either not carried out properly or left for some time. Baldwin therefore suggested that whilst there was evidence of negative labelling of the estate by the council - resulting in a self-fulfilling prophecy - there was no evidence of extra police activity in the area or of bad police-public relations.

It is of course, unnecessary to go into more details of the first stage of the project, which has been written up elsewhere (Baldwin and Bottoms, 1976). Nevertheless, it is important to note the considerations which bound the present stage of the research. In particular, the first stage revealed clear distinctions between areas of different tenure type and (in the council sector) different development periods. This raised the possibility that differences in recorded crime may be in some way due to different policing policies. To test this, the second stage focused on nine areas of contrast within the city of Sheffield.

THE AREAS CHOSEN FOR THE SECOND STAGE

The first stage of the research had suggested that comparison could be made according to the tenure type of the area, the offender rate of the area (for council and rented areas) and the age of the estates (for council areas). Therefore in the second stage, it was decided to concentrate on these variables, holding social class constant where possible. Nine areas were chosen, which may best be distinguished according to four groups:

(i) Prewar council estates: Three estates were chosen which lay adjacent to one another. One was, according to the 1966 data, an area with a higher offender rate (CHH) (1), another had a low rate (CHL) and the third an intermediate rate (CHM).

(ii) Postwar council flats: Two areas were chosen, again adjacent to one another. Following Baldwin's earlier analysis it was considered that postwar estates would generally have an intermediate offender rate, and originally only one was chosen. However, preliminary analysis revealed that the estate had a low rate, and so a second adjacent estate was also researched. Data for this second estate show that it had a high offender rate (CFH) compared with the first estate (CFL). (2)

(iii) Privately rented areas: Initially the choice of privately rented areas was considered a difficult one. During the 1960s and early 1970s a large part of the privately rented sector was either under compulsory purchase or had been demolished. Since it was envisaged that the research would continue until at least 1976, steps were taken to ensure that the areas chosen were likely not to have been demolished by that time. This precluded a large number of areas from consideration, particularly those which in 1966 had a high offender rate. An additional complication was provided by the composition of the E.Ds since it appeared that the E.D. boundaries cut across what seemed like 'natural areas', and this was particularly so in the privately rented sector. Eventually it was decided to choose three areas, two with high offender rates and one with a low rate. However, it later appeared that although one area had a high rate (RHH) and another a predictably low rate (R'HL) the second high rate area in 1966 had, according to 1971 data, a low rate (RHL). This was unfortunate, particularly because (for the reasons stated below) the remaining high rate area may be atypical as far as Sheffield is concerned.

(iv) Owner occupied areas: Since all owner occupied areas had low rates, only one was chosen. This was one of the areas with a relatively high proportion of residents from skilled manual occupations and was in fact the area in which I was living at the time (OHL).

The areas were chosen according to two principles. First, as far as possible, they were chosen so as to represent meaningful 'areas' to the people who lived there. Secondly, for council areas the unit of analysis was the estate itself; for all other areas it was the E.D. at the 1966 census.

In the following sections, the areas will be described according to the matched comparisons. However, before doing this it is important to note that quantifying variables for comparison is difficult. Data from the 1971 census is inappropriate (except as an approximation) since the E.Ds for that census do not coincide with the areas as defined in the survey. Similarly data from the 1966 census, although appropriate in some areas, is dated. On the other hand information from the interview survey (which was carried out as part of the wider project in 1975), (3) is extremely useful, except that the survey was not carried out in two of the areas (CHM, RHL).

The prewar council estates (CHH, CHM, CHL)

These three estates are located in the north of the city, being separated from one another by main roads and (on the CHL/CHH boundary) some shops and private housing. The high rate area was built in the 1920s, being one of the early council estate developments in Sheffield. Perhaps more than almost any other estate in Sheffield it epitomises the 'problem estate'. The offender rate was one of the highest in the city, and it was well known to local residents as having an adverse reputation. In contrast, both CHM and CHL were rather inconspicuous. Unlike CHH, neither of them had council-designated names; both were build in the interwar period at a date slightly later than CHH.

Walking through the estates, it is difficult to distinguish between them. All three estates are built on the sides of hills, with many of the roads crescent-shaped. On CHM and CHL the roads are narrower and tree lined, and the gardens are perhaps better kept than on CHH, but even this distinction is questionable and perhaps based on preconceptions.

In all three areas the housing was predominently two storey semi-detached or terraced, two or three bedroomed. Small gardens were encased in privet hedges. In the evenings, cars lined the narrow roads, since there were no garages.

The area of shops, which fell within the boundary of CHH and CHL, was a focal point for shoppers from the three estates as well as a wider area. Most of the shops were small-grocers, butchers, etc. - the sort that line any main road, but in CHL there were two large supermarkets.

In contrast, the estates themselves were almost devoid of shops. There were none within CHL and CHM, and only one or two corner shops on CHH.

Perhaps the most distinguishing feature to the newcomer was the shape of the estate. Whereas CHL and CHM were practically round, looked at on a map CHH more resembled a bone, with bunches of streets joined by a narrow bridge of housing along two streets. Unlike the other two areas it was the only one which gave itself to an easy division, with the SE block at least in practical terms separated from the rest.

Considering social variables elicited from the interview survey CHH and CHL were noted more for their similarities than their differences. 92.6% of residents on CHH and 89.3% on CHL had left school by the age of 15: 54.6% of residents of CHH and 50.0% of CHL were in social groups D/E; (4) 87.0% of residents of CHH and 81.8% of CHL had been born in Sheffield.

On each estate, the number of addresses where more than one household resided was very low, as was the percentage born in the West Indies, Africa and Asia. Approximately two thirds of respondents from each area were married, and household sizes were very similar. Only in two respects were there any notable differences between the areas - in CHL 65.6% of respondents were aged 45 or more, whilst in CHH 52.8% were: considering time of residence in the area, the proportions were very similar except that 13.9% of residents on CHH, and only 4.9% on CHL, had lived there for less than one year.

Taking the 1971 census approximations, the patterns of similarity between the areas is maintained. The percentages of males in the areas were similar at between 48-50%; the average household size was similar at between 2.79 - 3.10, the percentage of males over 19 married was similar at 71.6 - 76.1%. However, there is an indication that the social class composition of CHM might be slightly lower than CHH and CHL.

In conclusion then, one can say that these three areas are similar in a number of respects. Although there are some differences, the offender rate stands out as being the main distinguishing feature between the areas.

The postwar council estates (CFH, CFL)

To move from the prewar to the postwar estates is to inhabit a different world. To the resident, as well as to the researcher, the differences are extreme. CFL, and later CFH were high rise developments built in response to a housing shortage and urban redevelopment in the 1950s and 1960s. In close proximity of one another, they remain close enough to the city centre to prevent any feeling of insularity one might have on the prewar estates. Yet there is insularity of a different kind - one dictated by design requirements which sent these developments soaring skyward, a landmark for miles around, hidden only by more and more estates of the same kind.

Architecturally the estates are somewhat different. CFL is built in rows one above the other to a height of six stories. CFH is more varied, with some two storey rows, some rather taller blocks and one large block dominating the rear.

The shops in the two estates are moulded by the design principles. On CFL, the shops form a block in the centre of the estate, with some, adjacent to the block, encased in the ground floor of one of the residential units. In contrast, there are less shops on CFH, and these are all set into the ground floor of the tower block.

Despite these differences, to the outsider the estates are essentially the same. Movement along one level is restricted to a corridor along the outside of the building, with flats on one side only. No plain windows face out onto the corridors, but what sense of privacy this affords the transient is lost by the feeling that each corridor leads somewhere, that there is no way through the estate except on the ground level (even here, there is no way through the estates for the motorist). Movement vertically is either by steps up the outside of the buildings, or by lift.

According to the 1971 standard list offence files, the offender rate on CFH was some four times that on CFL. However, although the rate for CFL was similar to CHL, the rate for CFH was rather less than for CHH. Again, the areas were similar in a number of respects according to other social variables, but there were rather more differences than between CHH and CHL.

According to the interview survey, 87.5% of CFH residents had left school by 15, compared with 88.8% of CFL; 65.4% of CFH respondents were in social groups D/E compared with 59.9% of CFL; 78.8% of CFH respondents were born in Sheffield compared with 84.1% in CFL; practically all addresses in each estate contained only one household, and about two thirds of respondents were married.

On the other hand there were differences between the areas in household sizes, with CFH tending to include larger families (43.2% of respondents

37

on CFH lived in households with four or more members, only 25.1% on CFL); and more children under ten. Respondents on CFL tended to be a good deal older (65.5% in the 45+ age group compared with 35.5% of respondents in CFH); and there was some indication from the 1966 census that unemployment was higher in CFH (5.1 - 7.6% compared with 0% on CFL). Moreover, a higher proportion of residents on CFH had lived there a shorter time - 17.3% had lived there under one year, compared with 5.6% of CFL, whilst 26.9% had lived there between one and five years, compared with 18.7% on CFL.

There were then, differences in the populations of CFH and CFL. In particular, although social class differences were small, differences in the age structure of the populations, plus the variations in household size could exert considerable influence on the offender rates.

The privately rented sector (RHH, RHL, R'HL)

There were considerable differences between the three areas included in the privately rented sector. Of course, the first notable difference was in terms of their location. Whilst each council estate was close to the one with which it was matched, the three privately rented areas were considerable distances apart. To a certain extent this was made necessary by the difficulty in finding suitable areas, but it was accentuated by the slum clearance programme which tended to be directed at rather larger areas of privately rented accommodation, leaving aside smaller areas which were hedged in by private housing or shopping areas.

This apart, the high offender rate area was atypical in a number of respects. For example, it had the highest offender rate of any E.D. in Sheffield, and was notorious as a centre for prostitutes and to a lesser extent, drugs and illegal drinking clubs.

The houses were largely of the privately rented type - in 1966 68% of households lived in private accommodation and an approximation from the 1971 census put the figure at 70.6%. The houses were mainly Victorian terraced, rundown and generally in need of repair. A large number were sublet, resulting in a large proportion of single tenancies including a high student population. According to the 1971 census, some 44.7% of households were without an internal WC, 31.6% lived in less than four rooms, 17.5% were in shared dwellings and 60.5% were one and two person households. According to the survey, 30% of respondents were students; this was reflected in the high proportion in the younger age groups (67.7% aged 17-45) and unmarried (44.9%). Over a quarter of respondents had lived there less than a year, and over half less than five years. Excluding the students, 56.8% of respondents had left school by the age of 15 (a lower percentage than any area but OHL), but 48.4% were in social group D/E. The survey also revealed a comparatively high proportion of foreign-born respondents - 10.3% of respondents were Asians, and 5.8% had been born in Africa or the West Indies.

· RHL was similar in some respects to RHH. It was an area of rented accommodation bordering a main road out of the centre, and because of this was bisected by a shopping centre. To the East, the area was bordered onto mixed areas of owner occupied and privately rented accommodation, to the West it merged into the owner occupied belt, adjoining OHL. The 1971 census revealed that 6.1% of the population were born in New Commonwealth countries, 60.8% were living in privately rented

38

accommodation. Much of this property was made up of rather large terraced houses, sublet into flats: 71.4% of the households were without an internal WC, and 60.6% were one to two person households; however, only 13.4% had less than four rooms, and 7.6% were in shared dwellings (less than the 17.5% in RHH but rather more than in any of the other areas).

In contrast R'HL was an area of two parts. To the West, bordering a main road into the city, the housing was terraced and poorly kept – small and similar in appearance to RHH: however, Eastwards the area contained a number of semidetached houses, many owner occupied. In 1971, just over half of the households lived in privately rented accommodation (52%; however by 1975 at the time of the survey, it seemed that a slight majority of the houses were owner occupied, with a large minority privately rented). At the 1971 census 57.3% of households were without an inside WC, and 57.9% were one to two person households. However, only 3.0% had less than four rooms, and 1.6% were in shared dwellings, indicating that by and large houses rented were not subdivided.

Data from the survey indicated that 77.3% of respondents had left school by the age of 15 (higher than RHH), 36.2% were in social groups D/E (lower than RHH), 15.1% were single (lower than RHH) and 39.5% aged over 45 (higher than RHH). (Despite this it also had a high proportion aged 17-34). In addition almost all respondents were English born (96.6%) and households were on average rather smaller than in any of the other areas except OHL. Only 27.7% of the population had lived there less than five years, and 45.5% had been there for at least fifteen years.

The owner occupied area (OHL)

The owner occupied area bordered RHL to the East and the rather better class owner occupied areas to the West. In 1971 83% of households were owner occupied and 15% privately rented. The 1975 survey revealed that the area was different in a number of respects from almost all of the other areas:

(a) Social group – only 13.3% of respondents were in social groups D/E and 38.1% were A/B. Only RHH of the others, with 11.6% had any appreciable number in A/B.

(b) Marital status – 79.6% of respondents were married, more than any of the other areas, although similar to R'HL (73.1%)

(c) Education – 50.5% had left school by the age of fifteen, a lower percentage than any other area.

(d) Place of origin – 53.1% of respondents were born in Sheffield (lower than any other area except RHH where the student population exerted some influence).

(e) Household size – on average households were smaller than in other areas, being similar to R'HL.

Residents of OHL contrasted then in a number of respects from the other areas. Although chosen because it had a higher percentage of manual households than many other owner occupied areas, it in fact still differed considerably from the council and rented sectors. To the passerby it also stood out as rather different. Houses were mainly semidetached, built in the interwar period. There were some terraced houses of the larger variety, and on the Northern fringe some fairly new houses on a small estate. Almost all the houses had gardens and these were generally neatly kept. Like many areas developed in the interwar period, OHL was almost devoid of shops. Only four were evident, and the focal shopping points were some distance away, downhill to RHL or uphill to the smaller but 'better class' shops on another through road. There was one pub in the area located near the central shops.

CRIME IN THE NINE AREAS - DATA FROM THE 1971 FILES

As has been noted already, the nine areas covered in the second stage of the research were matched according to their 1966 offender rates, and these were updated using data from the police standard list offence files for 1971. However, in building up a picture of crime in these areas, it is clear that there are a number of different ways of compiling the figures, even from just one source. Indeed here three basic measures were used, although even these were sometimes subdivided:

(i) The offender rate: This was based on the number of people who lived in each area who were judged by the police to have committed known offences, and was subdivided into a female rate, and two male rates (adult and juvenile).

(ii) The offence rate: This was based on the number of offences known to have been committed in the area. Again this was subdivided, first according to whether or not the victim was a resident of the area, and secondly according to whether the victim was individual or corporate (e.g. a shop).

(iii) The victimisation rate: This was based on the number of people living in each area who were the reported victims of crimes.

Even leaving aside for a moment the victimisation rate, the distinction between offence and offender data is crucial, especially where the two can be compared with respect to meaningful social areas. Other studies which have considered offender's residence and place of offence separately (and there have been many that have ignored it) have tended to work on a purely quantitative dimension, i.e. by measuring the distance between offender's residence and place of offence (Turner, 1969; Chappell, 1965). A small minority has gone further by analysing the data according to whether the place of offence and offender's residence are within the same geographical area. However, if this information is to be used meaningfully - either towards mapping the social network within which the offender organises his life or towards some critique of policing or reporting practices - it is surely vital that areas defined according to social rather than official criteria should be consi dered. On the one hand, the point is whether the offender has 'moved into alien territory' to commit an offence; on the other hand, whether the offence and offender are situated within an area small enough to be meaningful from the point of view of the patrolling policeman or the victim, whose decision to call the police may be one of a larger range of options where the offender is known to be a local.

Thus, it seems that many researchers who have implied that offence and

offender data can be used interchangeably have been guilty of an advantageous reading of the numbers game. Moreover, once this conclusion has
been made, it is suggested, they have gone on to draw rather wider conclusions than a rigorous consideration of the data would allow.
(Baldwin, 1974 (ii)).

The first stage of the Sheffield project contained a great deal of
information on the spatial factors of offence and offender data (Baldwin
and Bottoms, 1976; chapter 3) and its precision and detail does much to
undermine previous research.

The research findings were couched in terms of two perspectives - the
offender area of residence and the place of offence. Looking at a sample
of offences, Baldwin and Bottoms found that approximately half the crime
committed by known offenders took place within a mile of the offender's
home, and at the other extreme 20.2% was situated over three miles away.
However, within this general finding there was a great deal of variation
according to:

(i) Age of offender: with younger offenders tending to commit more
local offences.

(ii) Recidivism: there was no difference for adults, but for juveniles,
recidivists tended to travel further to commit breaking offences (the
lack of a clear trend here is clouded by the relationship between
offender rate of area and distance, see (iii).

(iii) Area offender rate: comparing ward data, it seemed that 'the
higher the rate of delinquent residence in any ward, the shorter distance
do offenders who live in the ward tend to travel when committing their
offences'. (Baldwin and Bottoms, 1976; 88).

(iv) Predominant tenure type of area: for adults, but not for
juveniles, it appeared that 'there is a consistent tendency for offenders
living in rented areas to travel less far to commit their offences than
those in either council or owner-occupied districts'. (Baldwin and
Bottoms, 1976; 89-90) - however, this difference may be largely due to
other factors, notably the location of council estates and owner occupied
areas on the perimeter of the city, further away from 'crime attracting'
areas than are the rented areas.

(v) Type of offence: with violence and sex offences being the most
'local' and shoplifting involving longer journeys.

These differences are based on the distance (as the crow flies) between
the offender's residence and the place of the offence, and in many
respects confirm previous research, although the examination is more
detailed here. However, while many differences were found, it is notable
that other differences were not. For example, it has already been noted
that recidivism and tenure type were only partially related to distance,
and significantly, other variables - social class and numbers involved in
the offence - showed no difference according to distance.

The authors then went on to consider factors related to characteristics
of offence areas. Data on the situation of offences had previously been
used to illustrate the extent to which offences were commonly committed
near to the city centre, and, certainly as far as three central wards

were concerned, there seemed to be a relationship between crime and opportunity (as measured by the number of industrial and commercial premises). Moreover, the zonal configuration of offence rates held not only for offences against corporations, but also for assaults in places of entertainment and public thoroughfares and a number of individual thefts indexes, suggesting that the numbers of people passing through an area might be as important a variable as the number of people living in an area. (Baldwin and Bottoms, 1976; chapter 2).

In contrast, when they considered the distribution of housebreaking offences, it seemed that the offence rate here was highly related to rateable value. Thus, for houses with rateable values up to £100, the rate per 1,000 dwellings varied between 5.9 and 6.6, for rateable values £101-£200 it was 23.4 and for rateable values of £201 and over it rose to 51.9. (Baldwin and Bottoms, 1976; 63). This startling fact that in one year one in twenty of high value houses is likely to be burgled is not considered further, although it is interesting that in contrast thefts in and around dwellings showed no association with rateable value (for a comparison with American victim study data see Boland, 1976 and Hindelang, 1976).

Given this wide consideration of offence variables, Baldwin and Bottoms give the topic far less attention in their chapter three (on the relationship between offence and offender data). However, having made a ward comparison of the percentage of offences cleared up committed by locals, an interesting conclusion is reached which is worth quoting in full:

'(A)s a general tendency, offences are most likely to be of a predominantly local nature where there are no major 'attracting' factors (i.e. where there is no large shopping, commercial or high class residential area nearby, as for instance on some large interwar council estates). Here crime tends to be of a petty nature, with offenders and victims commonly living in close proximity. At the other end of the continuum, in areas where the opportunities or the rewards for committing offences are greatest, offences tend to be committed by offenders who travel considerably further.' (Baldwin and Bottoms, 1976; 93).

From the point of view of the area of offence, three factors would thus appear to be related to the number of offences committed there:

(i)   The extent to which there are 'attracting' factors, such as shops, offices, or high status housing.

(ii)   The city centre dimension, which is related not only to the 'attracting' factor, but also to the extent of mobility of population.

(iii) The offender rate of the area. (Baldwin and Bottoms, 1976; 97-8).

This last factor receives perhaps less consideration than it could. However, using the original 1966 crime data (see Table 2.1) it is possible to consider the areal rates for breaking offences from individual victims according to the offender rate of the area. The numbers involved in each area are not surprisingly, extremely small, but Table 2.1 demonstrates that for council areas at least (and council areas tend to be further from crime 'attracting' areas) there is a significant relationship between offence and offender rates. At the other extreme, there is no hint of such a relationship for owner occupied areas, a point which substantiates the suggestion that these attract offenders from outside. Given this relationship, the rest of this chapter will be concerned with data from the nine residential areas and the relationship between different data.

Table 2.1

Relationship between offender rate of area and rate for breaking offences against individual victims, 1966 data.

Offender rate	Offence rate (breaking, individual victims)	
	Low (less than 10 per 1,000 households)	High (10 or more per 1,000 households)
Council areas		
Under 30	34	7
30 or more	12	10
total	46	17
$(x^2 = 5.96, P \quad 0.05)$		
Privately rented areas		
Under 30	23	9
30 or more	12	9
total	35	18
$(x^2 = 1.27, P \quad 0.10)$		
Owner occupied		
Under 15	41	16
15 or more	15	8
total	56	24
All areas (including 'mixed')		
Under 30	124	44
30 or more	27	22
total	151	66
$(x^2 = 6.28, P \quad 0.05)$		

INDICTABLE CRIME RATES FOR THE AREAS

Offender rates in the nine areas

The areas were originally selected because of variations in offender rates. Table 2.2 demonstrates not only how great were these differences, but also how they proved consistent for both adults and juveniles, and males and females.

Table 2.2
Offender rates in the nine areas

	CHH	CHM	CHL	CFH	CFL	RHH	RHL	R'HL	OHL
Total	96.7	46.6	32.4	76.7	22.2	141.5	25.5	21.9	5.2
males under 20	56.3	20.6	10.0	23.4	12.1	40.0	6.9	3.6	3.4
males 20 or more	26.0	9.6	10.0	26.0	7.1	75.4	13.7	10.9	0.9
females	14.4	16.5	12.5	27.3	3.0	26.2	4.9	7.3	0.9

Clearly the high offender rate areas have higher rates than the low
rate areas for both males under 20 and males over 20, and, with the
exception of the three prewar council estates, have higher rates for
females.

If we briefly consider data on offenders in more detail, a number of
interesting points emerge. Taking first data on social class and employment record (of adult male offenders), as expected known offenders from
the nine areas were overrepresented among the unemployed and semi- and
unskilled workforce. However there were no clear differences between
areas - that is, certain types of area did not appear to be distinct in
terms of the population of lower class or unemployed offenders therein.

Information on employment which is contained in police records may, of
course, be incomplete or invalid - for example unemployment may be the
result of arrest, not a precipitating factor. On the other hand, details
of prior convictions and offence type are more likely to be accurate. In
Table 2.3 offenders from each area have been compared according to whether or not they were known to the police at the time they were detected.
That is, if an offender was caught and his cases dealt with on two occasions in 1971, he would be counted twice, i.e. he might be a 'recidivist'
twice or a 'first offender' once and a 'recidivist' once. (It should be
noted that the definition of recidivism used in this study is a special
one, since it includes cases known to the police where a formal caution
was administered previously).

Table 2.3
Percentage of offenders known previously to the police at time of arrest

	Males -19	Males 20+	Total males	Females
CHH	64.6	80.8	70.3	20
CHM	50.0	71.4	55.2	8.3
CHL	44.4	37.5	41.2	30
CFH	73.7	71.4	72.5	23.8
CFL	25.0	71.4	42.1	(0)
RHH	61.3	77.4	71.4	17.6
RHL	57.1	66.7	63.6	(40)
R'HL	(75)	33.3	46.2	16.7
OHL	(0)	(0)	(0)	(0)

The table shows that in general males from high offender rate areas are more likely to be previously known to the police than are males from low offender rate areas. However, when age is taken into account, some inconsistencies appear - for males under twenty, the trend is not evident in the privately rented sector, whilst for males twenty plus it is absent in the council flats.

The data for females are based on rather smaller numbers, and appear somewhat inconsistent. However, the lack of any clear relationship between recidivism and areal offender rate is demonstrated if the area data are combined. For the three high offender rate areas (CHH, CFH, RHH) 20.8% of female arrests were of those previously known to the police: for the five low rate areas the rate was 24.0%. Moreover if the five areas with high female offender rates - CHH, CHM, CHL and RHH - are compared with the other four areas, 20% of offenders in each area were known to the police prior to their 1971 arrests.

It appears then, that for males, but not females, high offender rate areas tend to contain rather more offenders who are already known to the police than do low offender rate areas. On the other hand there was no evidence, once offender rate of area was controlled, that the proportion of recidivists in privately rented areas was lower than in council areas, a surprising finding of the first stage of the research. (Baldwin and Bottoms, 1976; 129-32).

The first stage of the research also found some differences in the types of offences committed by offenders from different areas. (Baldwin and Bottoms, 1976; 139-40). Here the areas were compared according to all offences committed by each offender. Each offence was generally counted once. If two offenders from one area committed one offence, it would be counted only once. However, in the small number of cases where offenders from different research areas committed an offence together, this was counted twice, once for each offender's area of residence.

In fact, there appeared to be little difference in the distribution of types of offences (5) committed by offenders from different types of areas. Although offenders from some areas appeared to commit proportionally more of certain types of offences, there are no consistent differences, either between high and low offender rate areas or between the privately rented and council sectors. For example, taking each offence type separately, it would appear that:

(i)   Thefts of and from cars make up a higher proportion of offences by offenders from CHL, CFH and CFL.

(ii) Shoplifting makes up a higher proportion of offences by offenders from CFH, CFL and R'HL.

(iii) Thefts (other) make up a higher proportion of offences by offenders from R'HL.

(iv) Breaking offences. Offenders from RHH seem particularly involved in housebreakings and offenders from CHH in other breakings - however, the third high offender rate area CFH has low proportions of its known offenders involved in both types of breaking offences.

45

(v) Fraud etc. Offenders from CHL and RHL are proportionally more
involved in fraud offences. However, in the latter area this
is due to one offender in particular committing a number of
similar offences.

(vi) Violence, damage and sex offences are relatively rare and are
unconnected with area type. This is particularly notable in the
case of violence offences, since the first stage of the research
found some difference between privately rented and other areas.
(Baldwin and Bottoms, 1976; 134). This could indeed, be taken
as an indication that RHH is rather different from many of the
high offender rate privately rented areas described in the first
stage.

Looked at from another perspective, it appeared that when offender
rates for each area were considered for specific offence-types, area contrasts were maintained with minor exceptions. For example, although both
postwar estates had relatively low offender rates for breaking offences,
in general high offender rate areas had higher rates than low rate areas
for individual offence-types.

Offence rates in the nine areas

Table 2.4 shows the proportion of offences committed in each area which
were against residents, nonresidents and corporate victims respectively:

Table 2.4
Offences committed in each area

Victim	CHH	CHM	CHL	CFH	CFL	RHH	RHL	R'HL	OHL	Total
Resident	43.4	60.0	31.8	56.1	36.4	34.9	45.2	31.3	84.6	41.0
Nonresident	4.4	4.4	14.8	4.9	9.1	33.0	21.0	12.5	7.7	16.9
Corporate	52.2	35.6	53.3	39.0	54.5	32.1	33.9	56.3	7.7	42.1
Total	100	100	100.1	100	100	100	100.1	100.1	100	100

Taking the areas together approximately 40% of offences were against
residents, 40% against corporate victims and just under 20% against non-
residents. However, these totals mask considerable variations, which are
not surprisingly, related to the nature of the areas. Areas with a
number of shops, offices, warehouses, etc. (CHH, CHL, CFL, R'HL) tended
to have a higher proportion of offences committed against corporate
victims, whilst areas where one might find a large number of people passing through who are not residents tend to have higher proportions of
offences against nonresidents. In this respect it is notable that all
three rented areas have relatively high proportions of offences against
nonresidents, whereas only one of the council areas had (CHL, an area
with supermarkets and a wide range of other shops). This cannot be
related solely to shoppers, and subjectively at least, three categories
of nonresident victim may be distinguished:

(i)   Those who go shopping in the area
(ii) Those who park their cars in an area
(iii) Those who frequent public houses and other places of
      amusement and entertainment (notably in RHH and RHL).

46

The extent to which the characteristics of the different areas affect
the offence rate was illustrated when a distinction was made according to
various offence types. Whereas some patterns seemed to be maintained
for different offence types (CHH and RHH have high rates for most offence
types and OHL has low rates for all offence types), there were also some
interesting differences.

For example, taking three areas, CHL, CFL and RHH:

CHL is an area with supermarkets and good shopping facilities which
tends to attract shoppers from a wider area; correspondingly recorded
shoplifting is considerably higher than in the other areas, and thefts
of and from cars are also comparatively frequent.

CFL has a number of small shops, not large enough to warrant employing
store detectives, but carrying larger goods (e.g. bicycles) which attract
breaking offences (the high vandalism rate here is a reflection of this,
since in most such cases, the incidents seem to have been attempted
break-ins).

RHH has comparative high rates for most offences except thefts from
shops (there aren't many), but its extremely high rate of thefts of and
from cars may reflect its proximity to the city centre, which makes it
a popular parking area, and in fact offences concerning cars account for
a large part of the high proportion of offences against nonresidents.

Because of the relationship between crime and opportunity, it is
relatively meaningless to develop an index of offence rate which incor-
porates all the variable features. Therefore, as an alternative, in
Table 2.5 two indices are given; first the offence rate per 1,000 households, (A), secondly the offence rate against individual residents per
1,000 households (B).

Table 2.5
Offence rates for the different areas

	CHH	CHM	CHL	CFH	CFL	RHH	RHL	R'HL	OHL
A	203.5	63.1	76.0	58.6	55.4	326.2	59.8	51.0	11.2
B	85.1	37.0	23.7	31.2	20.2	113.8	27.4	18.2	9.5

The contrast between lines A and B clearly shows how a mobile population (through RHH) and offences against corporate victims (CHH, CHL and
CFL) can distort the offence picture. Nevertheless, using index B it is
evident that area differences do exist which are not due to such factors.
Moreover, a comparison of the matched areas demonstrates the relationship
between the residential offence rates (B) and offender rates, with CHH
having a higher rate than CHM or CHL, CFH than CFL and RHH than RHL and
R'HL. On the other hand it is also notable that not only does OHL have
an extremely low rate, but also that CFH has a relatively low rate for a
high offender rate area. Whilst the rates on index B are consistently
similar for CHL, CFL, RHL and R'HL, the rate in CFH is very much lower
than that in CHH which is itself lower than RHH.

Areas were also compared to see whether the extent and seriousness of

crimes committed there varied, by considering the amount stolen and recovered in each property crime (see Mawby 1978 (i); 95-99). However in
neither case were there any consistent differences between areas, although the amount stolen did seem to vary according to whether the victim
was individual or corporate, and goods were some two to three times more
likely to be recovered where the victim was corporate, a difference at
least partly due to the influence of shoplifting offences where the offender was almost always caught in the act.

Police records also contain some information, however vague, on the
relationship between offender and victim (where an offender is known).
Although the proportion of offenders who were known to their victims for
offences cleared up is likely to be an understatement, (because of inadequate information) in fact where the victim was an individual the
proportion of such cases was fairly high, 37.8% taking all the areas
together. Once again, however, there was a great deal of similarity between areas with CHH and CHL being the only areas with different patterns,
in each case the proportions being lower.

In summary then, it appears that when opportunity factors are taken
into account, high offender rate areas have relatively higher offence
rates than low offender rate areas. However, although it was possible to
consider data on a number of other factors, like the relationship between
offender and victim and the amount stolen, what differences there were
showed little meaningful pattern.

Victimisation rates in the nine areas

In Table 2.4 data on offences in the nine areas were considered and
revealed a great deal of variation between areas in the proportion of
offences committed against residents, and in regard to offences against
residents compared with nonresidents. In Table 2.6 the data are reconsidered from the point of view of the victim, such that the extent to
which residents are victimised in their own areas can be analysed.

Table 2.6
The victimisation rate, according to place of offence

	CHH	CHM	CHL	CFH	CFL	RHH	RHL	R'HL	OHL
Offence in area (x)	85.1	37.0	23.7	31.2	20.2	113.8	27.4	18.2	9.5
Offence elsewhere (y)	27.4	13.7	8.7	36.4	11.1	15.4	13.7	8.5	7.5
Total	112.6	50.8	32.4	67.7	31.3	129.2	41.2	26.7	17.2
Ratio x/y	3.1	2.7	2.7	0.9	1.8	7.4	2.0	2.1	1.2

In fact, Table 2.6 demonstrates the relationship between victimisation
rates and offence rates. The relative victimisation rates are very
similar to the offence rates for offences against residents, largely due
to the high proportion of offences being committed in the area. Indeed,
the exceptions to this pattern are interesting. In the highest offence
rate area, RHH, the proportion victimised outside the area is very low

(the number of residents victimised inside the area being over seven times as high); in the lowest offence rate area, OHL, it is relatively high. On the other hand, the three council housing estates have very similar proportions victimised elsewhere.

The most atypical example is that of CFH, where in fact a small majority of victim-experience is elsewhere. This could be partly due to the proximity of the area to the city centre, but this does not explain the rather lower proportion in CFL which is adjacent, and it could well be that different patterns could have developed due to variations in population mobility or leisure pursuits between areas, an issue which may be clarified by the questionnaire survey (which is being analysed separately).

It can thus be seen that where the victim is an individual (or his possessions), the offence is highly likely to take place in his area of residence. Thus victimisation rates, as well as residential offence rates, vary according to the offender rate of the area in residential areas.

This point may be an obvious one, but if the relationship were not thus, a number of possibilities might follow. For example attitudes towards the crime problem, willingness to report incidents to the police, and many other variables might have been expected to vary not with area of residence but with experience of victimisation. The fact that the two variables coincide is a strong factor in predicting that areal variation will be per se important.

Intra-areal variation

However, before going on to consider the relationship between offence and offender data, it is pertinent to consider one other factor - the extent to which, within areas, offender rates vary. Of course there is considerable evidence in other research - notably that carried out in 'Radby' by Jephcott and Carter - that delinquency may be concentrated, for example into a street. (Jephcott and Carter, 1954). However, in a comparison of two council estates, undertaken as part of the first stage of the research, Baldwin found no such concentration within the one high offender rate estate (Baldwin, 1974 (i)). The question may thus be asked, for the nine survey areas - is there any concentration of offenders within the areas, and if so, is this a feature of low and high rate areas, or of low or high rate areas only?

Of course, the simplest way to demonstrate any concentration would be to use maps. However, this will not be done, since it would make identification of the areas by readers easier. Instead, in the chart below, each area has been considered separately, and details given of any concentrations.

In some areas the number of offenders we are considering is small, and caution is advisable. Nevertheless, it appears that in only one of the nine areas is there no indication of any concentration of offenders into one part of the area.

Concentration of offenders in each area

Area	Any sign of concentration	Unit of concentration
CHH	The SE corner of the area has an offender rate one and a half times that of the NW section.	Part of area
CHM	One road in the area has an offender rate three times that of the rest of the area.	One road
CHL	None.	-
CFH	One block had an offender rate twice that of the rest of the area.	Block
CFL	One block has a rate twice that of any other block. Parallelling this, one floor has a rate 160% that of the other floors together.	Block or floor
RHH	Half the offenders lived in one small section of the area, bounded by four roads.	Part of area
RHL	The area is divided by a main road. The section on one side of this road, dominated by rented accommodation, has a rate over twice that of the other section.	Part of area
R'HL	The southern end of the area with more rented accommodation, has a rate over twice that of the rest of the area.	Part of area
OHL	Although there are only a few offenders here, most live in the NW quarter of the area.	Part of area

In the privately rented and owner occupied areas, it could be argued that this concentration is not surprising - after all, our definition of the boundaries of the areas is based on census limits, not social reality, and indeed in two areas (RHL and R'HL) the high rate sections of the areas are where there is a concentration of privately rented accommodation. Nevertheless, it is also notable that in both high offender rate council areas, the medium rate area and one of the low rate areas there is some evidence of intra-areal differences. The question of whether there are similar differences in the offence rates will be posed in the next section.

The relationship between offence and offender rates

In the last four sections the extent of the relationship between offence and offender rates has been referred to a number of times, and this can be demonstrated by comparing the offender rate with the offence rate against residents (offence rate B) (Table 2.7).

50

Table 2.7

Comparison of offence and offender rates

	CHH	CHM	CHL	CFH	CFL	RHH	RHL	R'HL	OHL
Offender rate	96.7	46.6	32.4	76.7	22.2	141.5	26.5	23.1	5.2
Offence rate B	85.1	37.0	23.7	31.2	20.2	113.3	27.4	18.2	9.5

Clearly the relationship is a strong one, and using a Spearman rank correlation the two variables are significantly related at the 0.001 level of significance (r = 0.95).

However, this is not to imply that crime in each area is generally committed by locals. Therefore in Table 2.8 two further comparisons have been made, according to whether the offences committed by local residents were committed in their area of residence or elsewhere, and according to whether offences committed in the areas which were cleared up were committed by residents or nonresidents.

Table 2.8
Relationship between offence and offender rates

	CHH	CHM	CHL	CFH	CFL	RHH	RHL	R'HL	OHL
Offences by residents % committed locally									
Male	44.6	31.6	19.0	18.0	28.6	17.0	26.9	38.0	0
Female	50.0	6.7	27.0	0	0	32.0	40.0	17.0	(0)
Offences in areas (where offences cleared up) % committed by locals	61.5	47.8	20.0	73.7	25.9	39.1	42.4	31.6	(50)

The Table demonstrates the complexity of the relationship between offence and offender data, with the proportion of detected local offences committed by residents being in general greater than the proportion of resident's offences committed locally. However, although it is tempting to take this inference further by suggesting that offenders from an area tend to commit a large proportion of the offences in that area, but still commit a majority of their offences elsewhere, it is certainly possible that 'locals' are more easily caught than nonlocals, and that it is this which 'creates' the fit. Bearing this in mind it is necessary to con- sider the data in more detail.

First, the rather fluctuating proportions of local offences committed by female residents should be noted, and this has in fact been separated from the male rate for this reason. This variation is almost entirely due to the specialist nature of the offences committed by women. At any rate, for these nine residential areas, female offences tended to be either shoplifting (almost entirely a nonlocal offence) and meter thefts (by definition a local offence). Consequently the variation reflects the proportion of female offenders in the nine areas committing these offences.

Leaving this aside, the male offender data and the offence data may be considered together. The two sets of figures tend to vary independently with the relationship between them not significant (Spearman, r = 0.10). Generally there are three 'patterns' - some areas have a high proportion of offences committed by residents and residents generally committing their offences locally (CHH, CHM); one area had a low proportion of offences committed by residents and residents generally commit their offences elsewhere (CHL); on the other hand CFH has a low proportion of its offences committed by residents and a high proportion of residents committing their offences locally, and RHL has a relatively high proportion of its offences committed by residents and a low proportion of residents committing their offences locally. In conclusion there appeared to be no systematic variation, either according to offender rates, tenure type or 'opportunity'. Taking offences committed by residents, within the council housing sector it seemed that the proportion committed locally varies directly with offender rate, whilst in the council flats and rented sector the opposite tendency appears. Similarly taking offences in the areas, in the council sector a higher proportion are committed by locals in the high offender rate areas, whilst no clear differences emerge for the rented sector. In the owner occupied area, only two offences committed in the area were cleared up, but it is significant that none of the residents committed their offences locally.

Given the results of the first stage of the research (Baldwin and Bottoms, 1976; chapter 3), it might also have been expected that those areas nearest the city centre might have their residents committing a high proportion of offences elsewhere, but local crimes being committed by residents. However, whilst in CFH, CFL and RHH residents seem least likely to offend locally (excepting OHL), no pattern is evident for offences committed in these areas.

Apparently, then, there is little consistency in whether offenders commit their offences locally or not, or as to whether local offences are committed by residents or not. Nevertheless, high offender rate areas do appear to have high residential offence rates. In view of the findings of the last section concerning 'pockets' of offenders' residences within the areas it is perhaps worth considering whether similar pockets are present when offences are considered.

Concentration of offences in each area

Area	Any sign of concentration	Comparison with offender rate concentration
CHH	Concentration in SE of area, especially where offence is against house as unit or housebreaking offence.	Similar part.
CHM	Concentration (slight) in N of area, i.e. nearest part of area to CHH, CHL and shopping area.	Part of area, not same as offender rates.
CHL	Concentration (slight) in S of area, i.e. nearest part of area to CHM (not CHH) and shopping area.	Not relevant. Part of area.
CFH	If offences in or against the house are considered, the rate in one block	One block, same as offender rate.

(the high offender rate block) is
twice that elsewhere.

CFL	Although only seven offences were committed in or against the house, six were in the high offender rate floor.	One floor, same as offender rate, no variation by blocks.
RHH	No variation over area.	–
RHL	Concentration of offences in high offender rate side of area.	Part of area with higher offender rate.
R'HL	Concentration of offences in high offender rate side of area.	Part of area with higher offender rate.
OHL	Offences spread over area.	–

It can be seen that the relationship between offence and offender data
within area is in some areas at least in the expected direction. Whereas
in eight of the areas, offenders were concentrated in part of the area,
in seven areas, offences against residents (notably offences in or
against houses) were concentrated in certain parts of the area. In five
areas (CHH, CFH, CFL, RHL and R'HL) offences and offenders were concentrated in the same parts of the area; in two areas (RHH and OHL) offenders were concentrated in certain parts of the areas but not so offences;
in one area offences were concentrated in a different part of the area
from offenders; finally in one area (CHL) there was some evidence of
concentration of offences but not offenders.

Since the general pattern is for some concentration of offences and
offenders, the exceptions warrant further consideration. The two estates
of council houses are of interest in that offences were concentrated near
the edge of the areas. This is particularly notable since the edge in
each case borders the main road near the shopping area, not the side
nearest the high rate area. This pattern is similar to that described in
an American study of spatial aspects of burglary (Brantingham and
Brantingham, 1975). In each area, not only are more people (and therefore more potential offenders) likely to use this edge of each estate,
but it is correspondingly less protected against suspicious acts – i.e.
whilst a stranger walking through the middle of the estate may appear
conspicuous, one sticking to the perimeter (especially the busiest edge
of each area) is less accountable for his actions. This is of course a
tentative explanation, but if it is justified it may demonstrate which
factors mitigate against offences, at least by nonresidents. In this
context it is worth reporting that the effect of building a police house
on CHM has had no effect on offence patterns – rather than acting as a
deterrent to offences in its vicinity, it in fact is situated in the
section of the estate where more offences were committed!

Area OHL would appear more vulnerable, relatively, to offences in the
middle of the area precisely because it is less a single unit. People
living there, and perhaps nonresidents, do not see it as one area, and
access is encouraged by two comparatively well used roads running
through the area (the number of offenders and offences in the area are
also small). At the other extreme, RHH has such a high offence rate that
it is, for practical purposes, not possible to distinguish any section

as being under-victimised.

This section has stressed that whilst there is no consistent relationship between area of residence and where offences are committed, and vice versa, offence and offender rates seem to correspond, both on an inter-area and an intra-area level. It seems, indeed, that within the residential sector (of which these districts are representative) those areas which have high offender rates are also beset with high offence rates. Since it was also demonstrated earlier in the chapter that there was no consistent areal variation in the types of offence committed by offenders living in the areas, it might also be speculated that indices of crime and deviance other than the indictable rates, would be similarly distributed. This is considered in the next section of this chapter.

FURTHER DATA ON CRIME AND DEVIANCE, 1973 - 76

In order to build up as complete a picture as was possible of crime and deviance in the nine research areas, a variety of different sources were used. As has been described elsewhere (Bottoms et al., forthcoming; Mawby 1978 (i)) these included a self report study of juveniles and a victimisation study of householders from some of the areas. However in addition to these other records, kept by the police and the GPO, were utilised. Before considering the results of these analyses, it is therefore appropriate to spell out the sources in more detail, especially since in many cases such sources had not previously been used.

(i) The records

Nonindictable crime statistics, excluding motoring offences, were researched for offences committed in the nine areas or by offenders from the areas. While a good deal of effort goes into the compiling of reports on indictable crime (see chapters four and five), the same cannot be said of nonindictable data. Information kept locally is minimal, and national data are restricted. Although national statistics are compiled for nonindictable offenders, no separate records are aggregated on offences not cleared up, nor are the records kept in a self contained unit.

Two alternative procedures were used by the South Yorkshire police to deal with these offenders. On the one hand they might be summoned to appear before the magistrates; alternatively they might be arrested. Although a summons book is kept of all offenders in the former category, for those arrested the most available source of information is the arrest book in the substations, where no indictable/nonindictable distinction is made.

Given these difficulties it seemed that the only practicable solution was to limit the enquiry to data on offenders. This meant that, although data on offences in the areas is available, this is only the case where the offender is caught. In practice the distinction is a fine one, since most nonindictable offences involve public order crimes - soliciting, indecent exposure and drunken and disorderly behaviour for example - or technical offences, like under age drinking and owning a firearm without a licence. In such cases the discovery of a crime simultaneously involves the discovery of an offender, so by definition few crimes are discovered but not cleared up. The major exception to this is minor vandalism. Although all vandalism is indictable according to the legal

54

definition, only vandalism costing over £25 is recorded in the standard list of crime statistics. All minor vandalism may be categorised as within the nonindictable statistics, but, since little appears to be cleared up, data here are restricted.

Focussing then on nonindictable offences which were cleared up, the year 1973 was chosen for the research, this being the earliest year for which police records were available, but at the same time being one for which all cases had been completed. With no satisfactory frame or filing system available, the most effective means of constructing area patterns was by systematically going through each police officer's official file for 1973.

This created certain difficulties. Although permission for the researcher to go through the files personally was originally given, complaints from one sub division caused it to be revoked. Instead, in this one division only, all nonindictable material was taken from the files by a police sergeant and sorted on an area basis by the researcher. This may not have increased the error, but it does raise some doubts - the researcher was in no position to see how carefully the material was sorted.

One further problem existed for soliciting offences. The police took the view that, since two cautions for soliciting were mandatory before an arrest could be made where the offender was not a 'known prostitute', in such cases no offence had taken place - although the girl was taken to the station and fingerprinted. They therefore declined access to the records surrounding those girls who were cautioned rather than charged, and this incompleteness must be taken into account.

The arrest form used by the police for nonindictable incidents was by no means as complete as the one used for indictable offences. The details on the latter form could, with witness statements, run to some dozen pages, but in contrast information on nonindictable arrests usually filled one page, and even here details were sometimes omitted. The situation for summary offences was even less desirable, since the record was contained in a ledger, with one line being given to each suspect charged.

Drug offences, were not recorded under the indictable or nonindictable systems, but were kept in separate files in the Drug Squad Office. The police treated the information with such care that I was not allowed access to the files, and Professor Bottoms carried out the search. Despite this initial caution, the records were extremely informative, being as comprehensive as the indictable data, and moreover, because of the nature of the Squad and the fact that more recent records were being used (1974-76), Professor Bottoms received a great deal of help from the officers responsible.

Incident forms. With the exception of drug data, it would appear that records of crimes not included in the standard list file were kept in a fairly haphazard way. However, in March 1974 the Chief Constable introduced a system of incident forms, whereby any report or complaint made by a member of the general public, personally or by telephone, would be written out on a separate sheet, known by the police (because of the colour of the form) as a 'yellow peril'.

This method of compiling information was universally disliked by the police, mainly because it involved more paperwork and because the classification system used to order the files was far from discrete. Nevertheless it had the explicit intention of cutting out the desk sergeant as a discretionary agent in the recording of reports, and if carried out conscientiously should provide a more reliable source of information.

The only way of testing this would be to list the type of minor incident likely to be recorded on a 'yellow peril', and then count the numbers under the old system, where a log was used, and the new system. This was not practicable in the present research. However, it is probable that the yellow peril data is fairly accurate, for at least two reasons. First, it is clear that when an incident is first reported it is difficult for the police to estimate its precise seriousness - for example a complaint of a domestic dispute may involve serious injury - so an incident form is likely to be completed to 'cover' the recipient of the call in case the matter turns out to be serious. Secondly, the forms were intended as a filed record to which to refer should repeated incidents occur, and failure to find evidence of a previous complaint could seriously embarrass an officer-in-charge.

Despite these qualifications, the completeness of data classified in this way is open to doubt and this point should not be ignored. However. with this qualification in mind it is pertinent to consider the types of information available from the incident forms.

When a member of the public makes a complaint or report of any kind, it should be recorded on an incident form. If the investigating officer judges that a crime has been committed, and, in the case of nonindictable offences, an offender has been caught, the incident form would be replaced by one of the forms described earlier. In other cases it would remain on file.

These cases would seem to fall into five categories:

(1) Disputes - where a member of the public asks the police to intervene in an ongoing dispute, for example between relatives, neighbours or restauranteurs and customers.

(2) Nuisances - where the police are called in by a member of the public to help get rid of some nuisance - instances of this kind range from minor vandalism (not cleared up) through litter and garden fires to ambiguous complaints of 'youths gathering' or 'children playing football in the street'.

(3) Obscene telephone calls - where the caller is not traced.

(4) Hoax calls - where the fire brigade is alerted a report is automatically sent to the police, so that an accurate picture of hoax fire or bomb calls is possible.

(5) Service requests - in addition to the incidents listed above, which involve some minor deviance, the police also receive a number of other calls, where members of the public request a variety of forms of assistance. These calls, both in Britain and America, have been documented elsewhere (Punch and Naylor, 1973; Meyer, 1974), and it was not relevant to the present research to consider them further. However, in

passing it is interesting to note that they included a wide variety of incidents - requests for 'no parking' signs, help with opening locked doors, searching for 'missing' neighbours to name but a few. Perhaps the most bizarre was the family who asked the police to check the house while they were on holiday, and to feed the pets when they did so - amazingly the police agreed to do this!

The incident forms are thus a statistic based entirely on requests to the police by the public, and are here used as a means of measuring the number of minor criminal or deviant incidents. The information available is unfortunately sparse, with little more than a brief description of the event, the complainant, the time of complaint, and the way the police handled it. Nevertheless, it is a valuable contribution to a review of a wide variety of records kept by the police and allows us some access to those incidents the police do not classify as crimes.

In addition to the police records, however, it seemed appropriate to consider crime data which were kept by other agencies and which would be omitted from police files. Therefore the GPO were approached and kindly agreed to allow access to records on TV licence evasion and kiosk vandalism.

TV licence evasion. The GPO includes a specialist department concerned with the discovery and handling of evasion. At the time of the research some changes in the recording of data were taking place due to computerisation, and this enabled the researcher to consider three types of data. The work of the licencing department has been considered elsewhere (Mawby, 1979 (i)), and here only one recorded source will be described, the prosecution files. These were books with single line entries for each case, in which were details on all those evaders who received the official caution prior to prosecution. In fact, not all of these were prosecuted, a few avoided the summons and more were formally cautioned as an alternative to prosecution, but in most cases the prosecution did follow and in all cases prosecution was intended when the entry was made in the log.

The details in the log were minimal - the method of discovery of the offence, the date, the type of TV set in use, the name and address of the evader and the court decision. However, for all those cases which were prosecuted more information was available in separate prosecution files which supplemented this data with further details of, for example, occupation, employment record and previous convictions for evasion. Because of the smaller numbers of licence evaders in the areas, all records were examined for a three year period, 1971-73.

GPO kiosk vandalism records. The research on kiosk vandalism has been published as a separate paper (Mawby, 1977 (i)) and will be referred to only briefly here. However, it is important to stress one point of contrast with the other data collected. Whereas the police data covered offences and offenders and the television licence records were an example of offender and offence being inevitably at the same address, by contrast the records kept by the GPO of kiosk vandalism are of offence data only. The GPO file vandalism data on separate cards for each kiosk in the district. The information collected included the type and cost of damage, the date it was reported, whether an offender was caught, and whether the police were informed. In fact, over the study period, 1973-74, in no cases in the nine areas was an offender caught (as far as GPO

57

records show), nor were the police informed of any of the offences, although some of them were technically indictable.

(ii) results

For these records, in contrast to the indictable material, it is evident that the relationship between offence and offender data varies considerably according to the nature of the incidents being recorded. Thus television licence evasion is a good example of where offence and offender are automatically located in the same area. At the other extreme so few cases of telphone kiosk vandalism are ever cleared up that offence data is all that is available in this case. (Mawby, 1977 (i)).

The incident form data can be treated as an example of the types of incident which neatly bridge the gap between offence and offender data, as becomes clear when the nature of the incidents is examined. If we concentrate on disputes and nuisance data, which formed the bulk of requests, it is possible to subdivide the data into five categories, as shown in Table 2.9.

Table 2.9
No-crime complaints made to police in the nine areas considered

		number	%
1. Disputes	(a) domestic	170	32.4
	(b) neighbours	40	7.6
	(c) miscellaneous	33	7.3
2. Nuisance	(a) by children	115	21.9
	(b) miscellaneous	107	20.4
3. Damage		54	10.3
Total		524	99.9

In disputes (domestic) and disputes (neighbours) it is fairly clear that the complainant is a local resident in most cases; however, the person against whom a complaint is made is not necessarily a local. Moreover, it is in many cases unclear who is in fact the 'offender' and who the 'victim'. Because of this the 'residence qualification' employed is that the incident takes place in one of the nine area, and that either offender or victim is a local resident. Disputes (miscellaneous) are rather different, in that they generally involve a resident and a non-resident, but again all cases included occur in the areas. In practice they commonly fall into two categories (a) disputes between individuals, (b) disputes between a local tradesman - or dosshouse superintendent - and actual or possible customers.

Nuisances are incidents which occur locally and involve a resident as the complainant. However, in many cases the 'offender' is either unknown (having disappeared by the time the police arrive) or is a nonresident. Similarly, incidents involving damage are rarely cleared up.

Because of the ambiguity, incident form data could well be included in the 'offence data' sections. However, since in many cases it is clear

that the 'offender' is also a resident, disputes (domestic) and disputes
(neighbour) will be treated as offender data and disputes (miscellaneous)
nuisance and damage categorised alongside offence data.

In contrast nonindictable crime data can be distinguished according to
offence and offender characteristics in the same way as indictable data.
An analysis of the data (Table 2.10) showed that there were five broadly
distinguishable categories - soliciting, public order (other than soliciting - generally drunk and disorderly and minor sex offences), vandalism,
technical (drinking) and technical (other). In Table 2.11 the data have
been recorded for offences committed in the areas and by offenders from
the areas, in order to demonstrate the extent of each subcategory.

Table 2.10
Nonindictable data: offender and offence data in each subcategory

	Offender data number	Offender data %	Offence data number	Offence data %
Soliciting	14	6.3	48	39.0
Public order (other)	98	43.8	33	26.8
Damage	18	8.0	3	2.4
Technical (drinking)	74	33.0	26	21.1
Technical (other)	20	8.9	13	10.6
Total	224	100.0	123	99.9

The numbers in each area are very small, but a glance at the totals
reveals contrasting patterns for different offences. In soliciting, and
technical (other) offences, offenders tended to commit their offences
locally; in public order (other), damage and technical (drinking) they
were unlikely to offend locally. On the other hand, for technical
(other) offences, local offences were likely to be committed by residents,
in public order (other) and technical (drinking) approximately half were
committed by locals, whilst soliciting offences were most frequently
committed by nonresidents. The case of soliciting is particularly striking, especially given its predominance in one area (RHH). It seemed that
girls who lived in the area were most likely to be arrested for soliciting near home, but that a majority of the girls who were arrested for
soliciting in the areas do not live there. This may be partly due to
prostitutes having business addresses in the area but living elsewhere,
but it also reflects the extent to which prostitutes need to work in an
area which is well known to potential customers.

The present analysis follows the pattern set earlier for indictable
offences, in that it seems that offences in areas are fairly commonly
committed by residents, but that residents frequently commit offences
elsewhere. On the other hand, it was also suggested that offence rates
tended to be high where offender rates were also high. In Table 2.12 the
various sources have been amalgamated to give a number of different measures of offence and offender rates.

With the exception of soliciting and drugs, where offenders lived
largely in only one of the nine areas (RHH), on every other offender rate
variable used there is a consistent difference between areas such that
the rate is: CHH   CHM   CHL, CFH   CFL, RHH   RHL/R'HL, with OHL having

59

Table 2.11

Nonindictable data: offender and offence data in each subcategory

	CHH	CHM	CHL	CFH	CFL	RHH	RHL	R'HL	OHL	Total
Soliciting										
% offenders offending locally	-	-	-	-	-	95.0	(0)	-	-	76.0
% offences by residents	-	-	-	-	-	39.6	-	-	-	39.6
Public order (other)										
% offenders offending locally	19.2	16.7	20.0	4.5	14.3	9.9	28.6	25.0	-	13.2
% offences by residents	71.4	-	33.3	33.3	-	23.5	-	-	-	45.5
Damage										
% offenders offending locally	-	-	-	-	-	-	-	-	-	5.5
% offences by residents	-	-	-	-	-	-	-	-	-	-
Technical (drinking)										
% offenders offending locally	16.7	0	37.5	0	0	0	-	0	25.0	21.7
% Offences by residents	35.7	-	50.0	-	-	-	-	-	100	56.3
Technical (other)										
% Offenders offending locally	-	-	-	-	-	-	-	-	-	67.7
% offences by residents	-	-	-	-	-	-	-	-	-	76.9

the lowest rate on every measure. Moreover exactly the same trend is evident from the offence data, with high offender rate areas having higher offence rates according to almost all the measures used. Here, again the most notable exception is soliciting which is even more markedly concentrated in RHH. However, in addition there is a less clear distinction on the total offence rate index (A), whilst in two respects the data veers from the pattern: 1. the nonindictable offence rate (police data excluding soliciting) is higher in CFL than in CFH, largely due to the low rate in the latter, 2. the kiosk vandalism rate in all the privately rented areas, especially RHH, is lower than in the council sector. (Mawby, 1977 (i)).

Further, whilst the rates in OHL are typically lowest (except for kiosk vandalism), the incident forms rate is comparable with other low rate areas, rather than being far lower, which is entirely due to the complaints of 'nuisance'.

Certainly some of these similarities or differences may be due to differential reporting or policing patterns, and this will be reconsidered in later chapters. Nevertheless, the main conclusion to be drawn here is to emphasise similarity. Not only is there similarity in offence or offender rates across a wide variety of indexes, including some recorded by agencies other than the police, but it is also clear that there is a fairly close correspondence between offence and offender rates, and this despite the fact that offenders not uncommonly commit their offences elsewhere and offences in the areas are commonly committed by outsiders.

Before going on to consider the implications of these findings, it is perhaps in order to follow up the consistency issue by analysing nonindictable and 'noncriminal' data with each area. Because of the small numbers involved for some categories, especially for data from some of the low rate areas, it is difficult to assess each index. The information presented below can therefore be regarded as a minimum indication of variation within areas.

Soliciting

RHH   Soliciting and the addresses of arrested prostitutes is concentrated in that part of the area with an above average offender rate.

Nuisances

CHH   There is no evidence of a concentration of complaints of nuisance in any part of the area.

CFH   Nuisance complaints in one block (that with a higher offender rate) seem to be slightly more frequent than in the rest of the area.

Disputes (domestic)

CHH   No intra-areal variation.

CHM   Parts of the area seem to be more prone to reported disputes. However, the area is slightly larger than that located as having a high offender rate - two central roads rather than one.

CFH   The high offender rate block has a rate twice that of the rest of the area.

Table 2.12

Various measures of offence and offender rates

	CHH	CHM	CHL	CFH	CFL	RHH	RHL	RHL	OHL
OFFENCE DATA									
1. Indictable (1971)									
Total offence rate (A)	203.5	63.1	76.0	58.6	55.4	326.2	59.8	51.0	11.2
Rate v. residents (B)	85.1	37.0	23.7	31.2	20.2	113.8	27.4	18.2	9.5
2. Nonindictable (1973)									
Soliciting	0.0	0.0	0.0	0.0	0.0	73.8	0.0	0.0	0.0
Rest of police data	37.5	4.1	3.7	6.1	9.1	29.2	3.9	3.6	0.0
Kiosk vandalism (incidents per kiosk, 1973–74)	23.3	19.0	15.5	32.7	20.0	8.5	15.0	11.0	9.0
3. Incident form data (1974)									
Disputes (other), nuisance, damage	73.6	43.8	23.7	47.1	23.2	101.5	28.4	19.4	13.8
OFFENDER DATA									
1. Indictable (1971)	96.7	46.6	32.4	76.7	22.2	141.5	26.5	23.1	5.2
2. Nonindictable (1973)									
Soliciting	0.0	0.0	0.0	0.0	0.0	15.4	2.9	0.0	0.0
Public order (other)	33.2	8.2	5.0	14.4	7.1	40.0	6.9	4.9	1.7
Other police data	49.1	12.3	10.0	19.0	10.1	15.4	6.9	4.9	4.3
TV licence evasion (1971–73) (Prosecution file)	62.0	19.2	10.0	44.0	19.2	36.9	16.7	20.7	1.7
3. Incident form data (1974)									
Disputes (domestic and neighbour)	79.7	32.9	25.4	53.7	19.3	49.9	16.5	13.1	2.1
4. Drugs data 1974–76	4.3	0.0	0.0	1.5	1.0	21.5	2.9	0.0	0.9

CFL   Although only nine families were involved in reported disputes, five of these lived in the row which had a higher offender rate although only some third of householders lived there.

RHH   There was some concentration of disputes in the high offender rate part of the area, although the area of concentration was slightly wider than for indictable offender data.

Television licence evasion

CHH   There was a concentration of evaders in the high offender rate part of the area.

CFH   The high offender rate block had a rate rather higher than the rest of the area.

CFL   The high offender rate floor had a rate three times that of the rest of the area.

R'HL   The high offender rate corner of the area had an evader rate four times that of the rest of the area.

These alternative sources of information suggest that in some areas, for certain types of data, there may well be differences within the areas which correspond to differences in the offender rates. Although the consistency of these differences is not as great, it must be remembered that in many areas the number of known incidents is small. Only in one area, CHH, does it appear that differences between parts of the area which show up on offender data are definitely not replicated by 'non-criminal' data, whilst in the two postwar estates, differences appear remarkably consistent.

It thus seems, at this stage of the analysis, that:

(i) There are consistencies between areal rates, both for different types of data (whether police of GPO data, indictable or nonindictable crime or incident form data) and for both offence and offender data.

(ii) In many respects these differences are accentuated by intra-areal comparison, especially in the high offender rate areas, but also in some of the low rate areas too (especially CFL and R'HL).

Looked at from this perspective alone, it would be easy to justify ignoring the differential impact of offence and offender rates. However, the analysis has also shown that, despite this consistency of overall rates, there is no apparent consistent relationship between being an offender from an area and committing offences in that area. This point, moreover, is of particular importance to a consideration of the processes behind the discovery and reporting of offences in different areas.

However, the area data described in this chapter are drawn from official records, kept, in most cases, by the police. Therefore, despite the degree of consistency, it is possible to argue that police recording practices are such as to influence area rates in ways which are hidden from a study based on the resulting records. Moreover, when in chapters four - eight the content of the records is considered more fully, quite clearly the wider arguments raised against the use of official sources, which were outlined in chapter one, are especially pertinent. It is therefore appropriate, at this stage, to reconsider the use of official statistics, in the light of the sources described in this chapter.

A NOTE ON OFFICIAL SOURCES

Numerous research studies of the police, which have already been cited, have stressed the importance of police discretion with relation to non-recording, both of incidents and suspects. This research is based, fundamentally, on the use of recorded data. One needs to ask therefore how far the results are invalidated by the extent of nonrecording and the ways in which incidents are described in records. Behind both these questions is a third one - why are some data recorded in the way they are? What purposes do they serve the police organisation? Bottomley and Coleman distinguish three 'organisationally relevant purposes'.

(i) As a basis of statistical returns which provide a picture of the crime situation.

(ii) As accounts of police activities, a demonstration to superiors that officers have honoured 'routine occupational obligations'. That is, 'writing up crime reports is part of, and a demonstration of 'good police work'.

(iii) As 'an important component of the process of mapping events and personalities into an ordered perceptual scheme' which may form the basis for future action, e.g. prosecution. (Bottomley and Coleman, 1976; 37-38).

In these terms, it is clear that nonrecording of incidents makes sense in a number of contexts - for example, where incidents are defined as not a relevant part of the crime situation or where police officers may see advantages in not placing themselves in a position of being accountable to superiors. On the other hand, equally clearly, nonrecording is less likely where there is a likelihood of the matter being raised again and where ones' activities may well be challenged (for example where there is a persistent complainant). Moreover at the initial stages of an inquiry records may possibly be kept as a basis for future action, where details are too vague to allow one to predict the likelihood of any future action.

These points are not, however, in any way conclusive and it must be accepted that any research which is dependant upon recorded data must be treated with scepticism. Nevertheless, two points should be stressed here as relevant to the Sheffield research. First one feature of local policy should be stressed. In 1974 the South Yorkshire Police introduced a new system of recording citizen reports, which, as already noted, had the explicit aim of cutting out the element of discretion at a station level. Although it is not possible to test out the extent to which the measure was successful, there are good reasons to suppose that it was in the interests of the police to record all incidents reported to them in the station for the reasons already given.

Secondly, though, attempts were made to collect other sources on crime which avoided this difficulty in many respects. As already noted, these included not only the use of records kept by the GPO, but also a self-report study of juveniles from three of the areas and a household victim study in seven areas. (Bottoms et al., forthcoming). As has been demonstrated elsewhere, the picture of police practices described in this book is in no way undermined by any of these findings and although no one method can be claimed as an indicator of the 'real' situation, it is suggested that similar findings from alternative methods with contrasting strengths and weaknesses lends considerable support to our faith in the present research method.

Having acknowledged the weaknesses inherent in any methods which do not focus on recording decisions as they occur, it becomes pertinent to consider the organisational context and personal priorities in which accounts are presented and aspects of behaviour come to be defined in particular ways. For, as Garfinkel notes in relation to psychiatric clinic records, information is recorded for reasons other than to present an 'objective' picture of the 'facts':

'In our view the contents of clinic folders are assembled with regard for the possibility that the relationship may have to be portrayed as having been in accord with expectations of sanctionable performances by clinicians and patients.' (Garfinkel, 1967; 199).

And again:

'From the point of view of patients and clinic personnel, populations are not merely accepted or turned away - i.e. 'selected' - on grounds of 'sex' or 'age' or 'socio-economic status' or 'motication' or 'diagnosis'. They are accepted or turned away on these grounds as 'good reasons'.' (Garfinkel, 1967; 212-13).

If we accept this position, it is easy to argue that records provide their own justification and that it is therefore impossible to use them as a means of questioning their own bases. For example, one could argue, following Douglas and Cicourel, that the police use their own definitions of 'real crimes' as a basis for selecting incidents which are recorded as crimes, and incidents which do not fulfil these 'commonsense requirements' will either go unrecorded or, in the Sheffield case, be recorded as minor incidents of a no-crime nature, and importantly described in such a way as to justify the label.

Two examples may be used to illustrate the point:

(i) In the case of violent incidents, where these are recorded as crimes, the police reports will tend to stress the extent of the injury so as to justify taking action; where these are recorded as minor 'noncriminal' incidents or nonindictable crimes where the police cannot act, information on injury will be minimised.

(ii) In the case of bicycle thefts, where these are recorded as crimes, reports may be written so as to stress the criminal intent (e.g. the bicycle had been resprayed), where they are 'no-crimed' the report may imply that the bicycle was misplaced rather than actually taken.

A pessimistic view of the utility of official statistics is easily gained from these examples. Nevertheless, in order to deal with the issue more systematically, it is useful to consider examples from the present study. In each case, these may be assessed in terms of the

extent to which the data allow for a greater understanding of the processes involved. There appear to be at least three relevant issues:

(i) The correspondence between the cases reported and those which
actually occurred. Obviously, records are only of help to us if they are
made. If no information is recorded, only physical presence at the time
of the incident can compensate. Nevertheless, there is good reason to
suppose that in at least one respect the records are complete, notably
where the incident is initiated by a complainant.

Where an incident is reported to the police, especially at the station,
it seems likely that it will be recorded, at least under some heading,
for one of two reasons. First, because the police may not know at the
time of the report exactly how serious the incident is - this is particularly the case for telephone messages. Secondly, because the complainant may prove a threat to the police if his complaint is lost and he
attempts to check up at a later date on what action has been taken.

Neither of these factors is operative where incidents are police initiated, or initiated on the beat rather than in the station. In such
cases the officer in charge is less constrained by other people, and may
decide on an informal course of action spontaneously with no requirement
to justify it to anyone later.

Thus it seems likely that the opportunity for discretion in the
statistics will be least in those cases which are reported to the police
station and most for that set of incidents where the police act proactively. Between these extremes, the opportunity for police selectivity will
be moderate in cases where an incident is brought to the attention of the
police on the beat (see, for example Wilson, 1968; Bottomley, 1973).

(ii) The correspondence between the incident which occurred and the
way it is categorised by the police. Whilst the incentive to record
incidents reported by the public is considerable, there still remains
considerable discretion over how they will be recorded. Evidence from
victim studies shows a difference between recorded and reported crime,
much of which may be due to the police 'redefining' the crime into a less
serious category.

In order to guard against bias created by this strategy, as wide a
range of police records as possible was covered in the present research.
This meant, in effect, that, if the incident was recorded at all it would
be covered by the research project. Take, for example, the case of
domestic disputes.

It has been argued (Pizzey, 1974; Select Committee 1975), that a large
proportion of domestic disputes are not recorded as crimes by the police,
even though they may fulfil the legal requirements of indictable crimes.
If this is so, they should be filed in the incident form data kept by the
police, rather than in crime reports.

However, if this point is taken further, and we wish to argue that
particular types of domestic dispute (e.g. in the present case, disputes
in certain areas of the city) are more likely to be handled as minor
'noncriminal' incidents than other types, this can be checked by comparing the rates in the different areas for indictable violence and for
'noncriminal' domestic disputes. If certain areas have higher rates for

'noncriminal' domestic disputes than we would expect, given the indictable data, this could support our argument – if not, it would appear that, even if the police use their discretion to redefine certain incidents as 'noncriminal', this does not affect variation between areas.

(iii) <u>The correspondence between the incident which occurred and the way it is described by the police</u>. This raises a third problem, the validity of the accounts made by the police. For example, continuing the discussion of the domestic dispute data, one could argue that the police are highly unlikely to classify an indictable offence as 'noncriminal' and then give a detailed account of the incident (e.g. details of serious injury) which allows their decision to be questioned.

This example illustrates Cicourel's criticism, and is therefore worth developing further. In the context of the present study, it will be argued that official records' details of how incidents come to be known to the police and how suspects were uncovered provide actual information of what happened, and are not merely masking operations.

Referring back to the article by Bottomley and Coleman in which a description of the purposes and routines under which files are assembled was given, two of the purposes suggested are of particular relevance here. That is, that the reports serve as accounts of police activities, and that they provide a background to developing police involvement in the case (which ultimately of course may culminate in a trial) (Bottomley and Coleman, 1976; 37-38).

Bearing these two requirements in mind, the form of police recording can be considered in the context of different situations. For example:

The discovery and detection process

(i) Situation where member of the public calls the police to the scene of a crime and the policeman is able to identify the offender using descriptions given to him by members of the public.

The requirement of being able to accumulate a picture of evidence for the court suggests that the officer in charge will record certain basic processes - like how the incident was brought to the notice of the police and most importantly, the information provided by witnesses, which could, indeed be crucial evidence if the case came to trial. Moreover, the first requirement, that police efficiency could possibly be measured, reaffirms this. At an early stage of my research, when the records were first explained to the research team, the Inspector in charge came across a case where a constable had been alerted to an ongoing crime by a passerby. However, no mention was made of the name of this person. The Inspector elaborated on this case as an instance of unprofessional recording by a none too bright constable, and pointed out that through not taking and recording the witness's name and evidence, the constable may have prevented a conviction being obtained, either because of lack of evidence to prosecute, or because all the evidence which could have led to an arrest had not been gathered.

On the other hand, where a conviction is more certain, for example where the offender admits his guilt, the officer in charge may have cause to mystify the proceedings. Notable, he may overemphasise his own initiative in the case. Whilst the organisational requirements are such that it would be difficult for him to claim that he <u>discovered</u> the offence, it might be possible for him to suggest in <u>his report</u> that he alone was responsible for clearing up the crime. Whilst a research method which relies on recorded data is vulnerable to such manipulation, it must be noted that this would not undermine all the results, but rather would suggest that the active role of the police would, if anything, be overstated in reports.

(ii) Situation where a policeman, acting on his own initiative stops and questions a member of the public, who is consequently found to have committed an offence.

This example is similar to those quoted in earlier critiques of statistics. (Cicourel, 1975; Bottomley and Coleman, 1976). For example, in some police statements phrases occurred such as 'he was behaving suspiciously'. Accepting that such statements are made (but leaving aside for the present time the frequency with which they are made), what are the implications for the use of statistical data?

It would appear that, on the levels adopted here - namely the agency involved in the discovery and detection processes - the effects are minimal. Whilst the mystification of evidence does mean that there is no way, in the present study, of discovering in these cases what the officer thought was suspicious about the offender, it does not preclude our being able to consider, subject to the constraints discussed in example (i) the nature of involvement in the discovery and detection process. Thus it can be deduced that the discovery and detection were police initiated, moreover, and that police attention was drawn to the incident due to the <u>behaviour of the offender</u>, rather than because evidence of an <u>offence</u> was clear. It therefore appears, from this and the previous example, that whilst the written records may be exercises in impression-management rather than accurate accounts, in terms of the discovery and detection processes such mystification is limited.

Justification for caution

If the officer in charge thinks that the offender should be cautioned, he will write his reasons for this. These may include, for example, a description of the offender, his home circumstances, etc. Two cautionary notes may be made here. First, clearly, there is no need to assume that the extent to which, say, home circumstances is mentioned is an accurate reflection of the home situation. Second, the reasons given may not be the ones actually believed by the officer in charge. Rather it seems likely that the justifications for cautions are, instead, a list of points which the officer in charge feels will have most impact on his superior, and that these will be couched in language familiar to his superior. In this respect, it can be argued that the points made <u>are</u> a good indication of how the police perceived the distribution of the various attributes among the 'favoured' group. What one cannot say is that those who are not recommended for caution are any different in these respects.

It is clear from the descriptions given that I would argue that, even without access to the ongoing decision making process, the recorded data is a useful source of information, even if it must be used with care and supplemented where possible, by other sources.

68

The need for these approaches is an indication that the difficulties of using police records must be recognised. However, the present section has contained a detailed account of critiques of these records and an explanation of some of the processes involved as these relate to the research in Sheffield for two reasons. First, because if the criticisms voiced by Cicourel and Garfinkel are accepted at face value, the credibility of the whole project is undermined. Secondly, and following from a rejection of this position, if we accept record keeping as a discretionary process, it is crucial that we should consider, instance by instance, the pressures involved in this process. If the recording process is a masking operation, it does not necessarily follow either that the entire process is masked, nor that it is impossible to estimate the extent and direction of difficulties which are created.

This point is particularly pertinent in the context of offence/offender rate distinctions. As noted in chapter one, some critics of police statistics have used their general criticisms of, for example, the effects of manning levels as though these would influence area offender rates. However, since, in this chapter, a number of distinctions have been drawn between offence and offender data, it is appropriate to conclude by considering the significance of these distinctions for a review of police discretion.

THE SIGNIFICANCE OF DRAWING OFFENCE/OFFENDER DISTINCTIONS

The distinction between where an offender lives and where an offence is committed is a vital one for any study of the social processes involved in the production of criminal statistics. In chapter one a number of social scientists were cited who claimed that areal differences in official statistics might be more the result of the reporting and recording processes than indicators of differences in residents' deviant or criminal behaviour.

If this were the case, we might expect the effect to be more pronounced with regard to offence than offender characteristics. That is, the model implies that differential policing or reporting may affect the distibution of known offences rather than offenders. However the initial finding of this chapter – that for residential areas those with high offence rates tend also to have high offender rates – seems, on the surface, to make this distinction less important. However, the results also showed that the fact that an area has high offender and offence rates does not necessarily mean that it is local offenders who commit local crime. Consequently if, as appears likely, the effect of differential policing is most pronounced on offence data, it would not exclusively influence area offender rates.

In terms of the information discussed thus far, this is of course conjecture, and it is a matter which will be covered more fully in later chapters. Nevertheless two other points should be noted here which fit this theory. First, it is clear that other nonpolice crime data, based on GPO records (and incidentally, data from the self report study also), reveal similar crime patterns. Secondly, area rates for police incident form records follow the same distribution, revealing no evidence that incidents in some areas are likely to be categorised differently from those in other areas.

Moreover, this whole question presumes a degree of knowledge on the part of the police which they may not even have. If offences are committed in certain areas, and offenders live in other areas, and if, moreover, the patrolling policeman has his involvement in detection curtailed by CID intervention, it is at least feasible that patrolmen have a rather vague idea of the offender rate of the area they patrol. In Sheffield, it seemed that in general <u>senior officers</u> had a clear idea of the high offender rates of CHH and <u>RHH</u> (although even here there was some confusion). However, discussions with the police who worked in the areas revealed a rather more ambiguous picture. It is therefore appropriate at this stage to turn from this somewhat complicated statistical description of the areas and their crime, and consider them from the viewpoint of the local police.

3 The Policing of Residential Areas: the Police Perspective

INTRODUCTION

The bulk of this research details the processes involved in the reporting, detection and handling of offences and offenders using official sources. However it seems appropriate to introduce this selection with a more general overview of the role of the uniformed police in these areas. Two sources of information will be used:

(i) Data from semi-structured interviews with police constables who worked in the areas.

(ii) Records kept by the researcher during a limited period of participant observation with the police in CFH and CFL.

Sheffield is divided into three police divisions, one of which is further subdivided into two. Three of the areas in the present study were policed from one division (CHM, CHL, RHH from X division), two more from a second division (OHL, RHL from Y division) and the rest from the third division (CFH, CFL, R'HL from Z_1, CHH from Z_2). However, due to boundary reorganisations in 1974, the areas were not necessarily in the same division in 1971 (the year of the indictable crime sample) as in 1975 when the interviews took place. In particular, CHM and CHL had previously been in Z_2 division (the same as CHH) and RHH had been in Z_1 division. Nevertheless, is seems that (according to the police) the overall pattern of policing remained constant over the period 1971-75, and the number of policemen involved in each area over this length of time was broadly similar.

The Uniformed Branch in Sheffield operate on three levels. First there is the area constable, next the area patrol car and finally the beat policeman. Beat policemen are confined almost exclusively to commercial and industrial areas and the main roads. A large number of officers were assigned to city centre beats, but only two foot beats coincided with the research areas. These were in the area RHL, where a foot patrol passed down the main road shopping area which bisected the E.D., and in areas CHH, CHM, CHL, where a foot patrol was used in the shopping area bordering CHH/CHL and CHL/CHM.

These apart the prevalent form of policing was the unit beat policing system, which developed from the Accrington experiment:

'In the immediate postwar years team policing had a vogue in Aberdeen, Salford and parts of Yorkshire and was tried out on an experimental basis in London, but fell into disuse. In 1966 the Police Research and Planning Branch examined a somewhat similar scheme for 'unit beat policing' which had had some success in two industrial towns in Lancashire - Accrington and Kirkby. A resident beat officer, with an intimate knowledge of his area, was supported by a mobile team equipped with a 'panda' car, together with a detective and another officer responsible for sifting and recording the information picked up by the team during the tour of duty.' (Wilcox, 1974; 146-47).

The working party set up by the Home Office in the light of the
Accrington experiment recommended the widespread adoption of the unit
system, at least in urban areas:

'Thus, in a typical urban area we think that the pattern of policing
might consist of foot patrols in the city centres, with the whole of the
inner and outer suburban areas divided into 'beats' - it is open to
question whether the old term should remain. Each of these beats would
be the particular responsibility of a single constable, who preferably
(though we recognise that in some large cities and towns this may not be
feasible) would live in his own area. Superimposed over this ground
system would be mobile patrols operating continuously day and night. The
beat man would be in radio communication with the patrols and with the
section headquarters, and he would have a large measure of discretion as
to the distribution of his working hours. In this way we should expect
to elevate the status of the beat constable in a way that would bring out
the best qualities of a policeman - self discipline, personal initiative
and discretion - and challenge and intelligence, as well as his maturity
and common sense, from the outset.' (Home Office, 1966; 118).

The aims of the system were clearly defined in an appendix to the report:

'1. To increase police efficiency
 2. To cultivate a better understanding with members of the public
     by:
     (a) closer contact with the men on the beat
     (b) swifter response to calls for assistance and complaints
 3. To increase and improve the information flow
 4. By combining resources to overcome the shortage of police
     officers
 5. To create a new challenge in the method of beat working
     particularly for the younger constables.' (Home Office,1966;139).

The emphases of the report are especially interesting for their implications on policing in different types of area. The report makes only two
distinctions - between rural and urban forces, and between city centres
and housing areas. Nowhere is any mention made of differences between
residential areas.

This uniformity is reflected in the implementation of the system in
Sheffield. The basic requirement is for an area constable to patrol a
beat of a particular size, and although where resources are tight area
constables who have been moved may be replaced more slowly in some areas,
variations in the extent of policing per 1,000 households are not great.

Thus CHH has one area constable whose unit is approximately twice the
size of the estate, and is backed up by a patrol car which covers two
units; areas CHM and CHL are covered by one area constable who also
includes a third estate in his area, and is backed up by a patrol car
covering two units; CFL has one area constable who also patrols some
nearby flats, and CFH has two area constables who also patrol nearby
flats, and all these areas are covered by only one patrol car which also
covers part of the city centre; one constable covers area RHH as part of
a wider area, and is backed up by a patrol car which covers two units,
and a similar situation exists in R'HL; areas RHL and OHL are covered by

one area constable although some of OHL falls in a different unit, and these two areas form half of a patrol car beat.

Two days were spent interviewing members of the unit policing system for the nine areas using a structured set of items to be covered (rather than a tight interview schedule). Most of those 'working' the areas, particularly as area constables, were interviewed, although due to manpower shortages no area constable was specifically assigned to CHM/CHL at the time of the survey. The following were interviewed:

CHH	area constable, who had previously worked in CHM/CHL
CHM/CHL	area constable for adjacent area (to the West) who was at the time also responsible for this area; area patrol car driver
CFH	two area constables
CFL	area constable
CFH/CFL	area car driver
RHH	area constable
R'HL	area constable and area constable of adjoining area
RHL/OHL	area car driver
OHL	area constable of part of area.

The information from the interviews covered three broad areas:

   (i)   The role of the police in the areas
  (ii)   Perceptions of the areas
 (iii)   Police styles in the discovery, detection and handling of incidents.

These three themes will form the basis for the remainder of this chapter.

THE ROLE OF THE POLICE IN THE NINE AREAS

The area constable and the panda patrol form part of a team. Perhaps then, inevitably, they tend to operate in different ways over and above the question of their mobility. The area constable is likely to be a constant face in the area - over a period of time he will get to know, and become known to, many of the residents. Although the fact that he does not live in the area - as was the case with all the area constables interviewed - limits the extent to which he 'belongs', perhaps the most notable feature of the interviews was the extent to which area constables stressed the function of their job to be contact with the public leading to an extensive knowledge of the area, mutual trust and respect:

'I make a point of getting to know people, whereas the beat constable just walks round - he's only there for a week or so - people would ask for me and know where I was. I call in at the schools, the community centre, one or two old people. It's really public relations work rather than policing - you're there when you're wanted. You're at a school and someone's broken a window and a word from me who they know is better than from someone else.

I like working there. I've made a lot of good friends .... I build up a working relationship where people would tell me things where they wouldn't anyone else, or wouldn't bother to ring up. I had an example last year where a woman from 'F' saw me on my first day back from holiday

73

and said 'we've had trouble with X' and they'll wait and see me rather
than complain.' (Area constable, adjacent to R'HL).

'I'm supposed to know virtually everything that goes on in the area
involving the police, and if I'm not on duty when it comes in I'd follow
it up later - like crime or damage. I'm continuation officer on school
liaison and have good contact with all the local schools .... My job is
to get out and circulate everyone in my area, especially the tradespeople,
and schools, and call on as many people as possible during the day ....
letting people know they have a policeman who takes an interest.' (Area
constable, CHH).

'It gives you closer contact, especially with the shops on CFL.
There's a lot of work with OAP's; you call on them. You keep in close
touch with the porters.' (Area constable, CFL).

The visibility of the area constable, combined with his slow progress
through the area, make him almost symbolically the reassuring figurehead
of prevention:

'The mere fact that a bobby's walking down the road will either stop
them doing it or make them think. It's surprising the reaction you get
with one of these on your head (pointing to his helmet) walking down the
road. They think there are plenty of bobbies.' (Area constable,
adjacent to CHM/CHL).

'It's the importance of letting people see you're there; patrolling
regular, letting people see you're about, it's a deterrent kind of thing.
It's persistent regular patrolling. You can see a gang off and they'll
be back in two minutes - persistent patrolling: to show 'em you mean
business.

You don't find many cases, but you do find the potential - like cars
unlocked and you can warn the owners, lead roofing loose and so on.'
(Area constable CFL).

Similarly the panda patrol officers made the same points, often with
similar phraseology:

'It's showing the flag. If people realise that there's someone in the
area, if people think the police are in abundance in a particular area
they'll think twice about doing something, won't they?' (Panda patrol,
CFH and CHL).

'Crime prevention - simply by being there - showing the flag is the
phrase we use'. (Panda patrol, CFH and CFL).

However, whereas both the panda patrol and the area constable see their
function as being present and visible, what they do while there tends to
vary. The car man is more likely to be on the lookout for suspicious incidents and to consider short term intervention a possibility. On the
other hand neither type of officer expects to be involved in the discovery of crime, much less being able to catch offenders in the act:

'Occasionally you come across things, if you're lucky. You come round
a corner and someone's breaking into a car. But it's luck. You might go
for weeks without finding one and then you're on your way back and drive

74

into one.

It happens. And if it does it's good and you get credit for it. It's a matter of keeping your eyes open. You've got to be a really slow criminal to do something when a black and white police car comes by. The idea of the marked panda car is that you're preventing crime by your presence.' (Panda patrol, CFH and CFL).

Instead the panda patrol is largely a reactive tool. The driver patrols his beat, keeping his eyes peeled for suspicious incidents he knows he will rarely find, waiting for instructions to be radioed to him from the station. When a message does come, he may compete with the area constable for the enquiry, but he is more likely to become operational-ised, largely because the area constable, working an eight hour day, is frequently off duty, but also because he is in most instances able to respond to the call within a matter of minutes.

In such circumstances it is almost inevitable that the area constable is left to deal with minor incidents which may have long term solutions, where speed is not of the essence but where local knowledge may be of help in restoring order and fulfilling a service role:

'I don't take a lot of crime complaints - a lot of petty sort of things, like washing being pinched, but burglaries, never.' (Area constable RHH).

'I deal with the more trivial sort of things. They'll pop out, 'I've been meaning to phone you up, I'm having trouble with the next door neighbours .... ' I think the area bobby's job is more domestic than the car beat driver.

The biggest problem, without a doubt, is the kids, 13-16s; and a typical night for me is chasing the kids. You get them out of one place they shouldn't be and then ten minutes later they're somewhere else. You get no respect from them. The other day I was told to fuck off by a fourteen year old lass.' (Area constable, adjacent to CHM and CIIL).

However, it would be a mistake to see the area constable's functions as ending there. Because of his knowledge of the area, he has a wealth of information to pass back to the station. Much of this is ongoing, a long term contribution to the data bank; the rest is related specifically to current enquiries, when his local knowledge may prove an asset to CID.

The function of the area constable as the gatherer of information is clearly stated:

'You get into conversations with people - bump into a lot of people - find out about things, especially damage, what's happening to offenders, about kids they're having a problem with .... ' (Area constable, CFL).

'Chat to criminals, prostitutes, drugs - prostitutes are very good for letting you know about absconders from girls' homes and things like that. I've not been there long enough to get reliable information regularly. We have very close liaison - all the police help each other - who's in prison, pinching and so on.' (Area constable RHH).

'Making contact with the public. Older people like to see a constable walking around and they like to stop and have a word about anything, and

I do mean anything! If there's any crime or anything they think you'd want to know about then they'd also tell you that. They'd say 'I don't know if you know anything about it, but the other night a white Cortina parked down the road and I don't know if he were up to any good'.' (Area constable, fringe of OHL).

Even where the area constable has been unable to provide information of a general kind, where he is brought in on a specific case his knowledge of the area may allow him to provide a lead, or discover a source of information.

'The best thing - you get to know all the likely lads, so if a job turns up and you've got a description, you probably know who to go to straight away.' (Area constable, adjacent to CHM, CHL).

'CID ask if I've got any ideas of this, a description or a name I might be able to pass on. I make enquiries and I haven't been there long enough to get a nucleus of informants. I ask the worried, the concerned people.' (Area constable, RHH).

'The other day I went to a house damage. They gave me a description of the lad and I knew who it was and went to his house. A car beat driver wouldn't know that .... I know the trousers he wears, the jumper he wears .... It's merely routine, petty nuisances, helping CID with your personal knowledge of people in the area.' (Area constable, adjacent to CHM and CHL).

'If it's a minor theft I'm brought in. If it's big CID are brought in from the first - it's up to them whether they bring you in or not. If it's not detected at the time then I get the follow up enquiries to do .... Keeping my eyes and ears open, talking to old people who are prepared to talk to us.' (Area constable, fringe of OHL).

The involvement of the area constable in the detection process implies that his knowledge of those living in the area, based as it is upon day to day policing and information passed down to him from his colleagues, is both sound and precise. However, there are good reasons for doubting this belief. For example, unlike the patrol car driver the area constable is less likely to be the first police officer at the scene of the crime; once there he may be excluded from involvement by other officers; if he is off duty he may never know of the crime, or at best only when it is cleared up. It appears, at least from the area constables' perspective, that their involvement is greatest in those cases where the crime is not quickly cleared up. At this stage, as the wider research indicates, their contribution will be minimised by two constraints - the fact that the majority of such offences are never directly cleared up, and the implication that offences are committed by locals. At best the area constable may have a vague idea of local 'notorious' criminals, backed by some feeling about the number of offences committed locally. Thus, whilst one of the area constables felt that co-operation with his colleagues was a two-way process, even he hinted that the reason for this was largely to prevent his interference; for the rest, a clear feeling of being disjointed was evident.

'I'm the permanent policeman there - it's my area. I get quite a lot of cover from the beat car, drugs and vice squads - could be anything up to half a dozen policemen in the area at one time .... There's so much goes on, drugs and things, that I think I can do a better job going in and getting bits of information and passing them back to the specialist departments. Then the specialists pass information back .... You've got to keep close liaison with drugs etc. to make sure we don't poke our nose in and spoil things for them, like when they're keeping observation on a place.' (Area constable, RHH).

'If it's put out to CID, and they get a detection straight away, I'm not informed of it, but very often CID go to the scene of a crime and they've got a good idea of who may have done it from the M.O. of the job. They then won't want us interfering, as they put it.' (Area constable, fringe OHL).

'Beat officers don't get very involved in the detection of crime. He hands over to CID, unless he comes across a crime taking place. Crime is just one small part of his job, and he's not a specialist in crime as are the CID of course.' (Panda patrol, CHM and CHL).

This does not preclude the area constable operating a 'method of suspicion' and indeed some of the quotes above illustrate this. Nevertheless, crime is only a small part of his job. The man who knows the area best, and thus might be expected to be the focal point for any operation of the 'method of suspicion' is frequently on the perimeter of the detection process. This in itself implies that police definitions of problem areas, as well as suspected offenders, may be less precise than might have been hypothesised.

POLICE PERCEPTIONS OF THE NINE AREAS

The idea of teamwork which was envisaged in the unit policing scheme is formalised in two information channels - the daily crime bulletin and the area log. In fact the crime bulletin is a divisional publication which lists crimes relevant to the wider area which have been committed recently and are as yet undetected. Because of this offences which are cleared up on the spot will not be recorded in the bulletin and the area constable may never know about them, or may know second hand from local gossip. In this respect his knowledge of offences committed locally (and of course reported) is bound to be limited. In addition, unless descriptions of suspects are so detailed as to provide him with clues, his ability to judge whether offences elsewhere were committed by offenders from his patch is considerably impaired; even where a local is arrested, if the incident was committed elsewhere he may not be informed; in this way his knowledge of offenders is limited.

The area log, being more specific, does provide more immediate information about his area. However, in practice the log is used for minor incidents (such as loitering by teenagers) which are considered suspicious or threatening, which may alert him to the possibility of trouble, but provides no accurate information on actual offences.

More generally, his perceptions of the area may lack any relative framework - his lack of precise awareness of the size of his area, let alone the opportunity factors which might distort the offence rate, added to his lack of awareness of the comparability of rates elsewhere, mean that his imagery is at best vague, at most dependent on 'reputations' which are handed down to him. Interestingly, the area constables

had a clear idea of problem areas in the sense that these were fairly
atypical areas where there was a lot of 'action', but such distinctions
were clearly polarised, being especially focussed on the transitional
areas of the city. More subtle distinctions - say between council
estates, or according to offender/offence criteria, were rarely made.

This said, it is also true that some officers did have a clear idea
of the state of crime of the area, even to the extent of noticing changes
over time. In order to put such perceptions in perspective the quotes
below have been taken in full and ordered in such a way as to show
whether contrasts between matched areas were or were not perceived as
such by the officers.

The private sector

'It's a diverse area - bedsitland of moving population - a lot of the
summonses have moved. Students, the rougher element - Irish in RHL - and
a better class of flats in I. You get burglaries over the whole area;
thefts, motor vehicle thefts - not large crime. There are a few in the
better class area but not many. We don't suffer too much from petty
complaints, like on council estates where neighbours are at each others
throats. There are some domestics, but not neighbours. The kids are a
nuisance everywhere - like for damage. There are problem families, but
not in specific roads - more in RHL.' (Panda patrol, OHL, RHL).

'It's a well to do area. A medium sized crime rate. Housebreaking and
thefts in good class houses - they get away with a lot. There's vandalism, but not bad - garden walls pushed down, paint spraying and so on.
Invariably crime that's committed in any area is done by an outsider -
all you can do is make enquiries with the neighbours to see if they saw
of heard anything.' (Area constable, finge of OHL).

'An ordinary, working class residential area - poorer; ready to come
down and waiting to be moved. Densely populated, busy, interesting. Far
more things happen - minor things - damage, always complaining. They
live on top of one another; the kids cause damage, the neighbours cause
disputes, squabbles and so on. It's not got a high crime rate, surprisingly enough. What there is is petty crime, 90% juveniles and little
children. Minor burglaries - not like Ecclesall. The worst part of the
area is 'East', the slums. They live there because they can't afford
anything else or because they spend it all in beer and whisky. Paying
the rent is the least priority. Some families keep cropping up, the
father, mother and three or four children. Domestic disputes and neighbour disputes are common, especially where the husband spends all the
money on booze and 'comes home and throws the wife out.' (Area constable
R'HL).

The man in area R'HL had in fact, a fairly good idea of the amount of
crime and the number of offenders, and correctly identified that part of
the area which had the most. However, he clearly saw this as a poorer
area than others he knew of (where he lived?) and his idea about the
number of disputes is not supported by the statistics. In contrast the
area constable from RHH, perhaps because he had become used to the area,
perhaps because much of the crime was not passed on to him, and inevitable because of his lack of experience, exhibited a total lack of awareness of the extremely high offender and offence rate of the area:

'It's cosmopolitan. The majority don't work, on the dole. The kids
play in the street. There's drugs and prostitutes, licencing offences
(parties in cellars and things like that); assaults. The rest, its petty,
meters, kids, petty burglary - like sneaking and pinching tins. Take
away the drugs, prostitution and assaults and the rest of the reported
crime is not great. There are few domestic disputes, low compared with
other areas. Little pockets of communities, keep themselves to themselves and although they don't socialise with themselves they don't cause
trouble.' (Area constable, RHH)

The prewar council estates

The contrast between these estates is not only not recognised, but even
denied. The area constable for CHH, who had previously worked in CHM
and CHL, while aware of the reputation of the area was eager to repudiate
it. On the other hand, the area constable who was looking after CHM and
CHL saw no difference between these two areas, and, like the panda patrol
man, who covered these areas and other estates, contrasted them with the
better areas to the North West:

'It has a name, crimewise, troublewise. A large proportion of people
are known to the police in the area. It's different from CHM or CHL
because there are more people on it, but there are not proportionately
more criminals. CHM and CHL have no reputations because there are fewer
people living there. Whereever you go there's a council estate with a
name, that's got a lot of people on them who are criminals. I've never
been one to go on to an area and say this is a bad area. The problem on
CHH is youngsters causing damage and annoyance. Few crimes are committed
on CHH, CHM or CHL. It's got a name because of criminals who live on the
estate, not the crime committed there. Very little drunkenness. There
are domestic disputes and neighbour disputes, but not a lot where we get
called in. No pockets of problem residents. Damage, minor burglaries,
gas meters. Minor thefts. A few problem families, especially large
ones, with kids of various ages to our notice, but few and far between.'
(Area constable, CHH).

'Lower working class people, the remnants of Blackacre and things like
that - 50% anti-police- you knock on the door and they don't want to
know, you take the kids back and they think it's your fault. To the West
its council housing, but they take some care .... CHM and CHL are about
the same .... Gratitude's a lot of it, you walk down the street on CHL
and its curtains raised and looking out. They don't take as much care
of the gardens, and things like that .... The crime rate? It must be
high, higher than West.' (Area constable, CHM, CHL and West).

'From dealing with incidents it seems that more incidents you get
called to come from the bottom end (CHM, CHL) - I mean families that you
deal with of a criminal nature or a social nature .... They're a different class of people at the bottom end - less co-operative, more and more
people who are anti-police. Then CHM is slightly worse, especially B
Road - a small tightly knit group - the rest of the area is more open ...
You have your local families around CHM/CHL, domestic disputes, on yes,
weekends - Thursdays, Fridays, Saturdays, without any question. That's
all over my beat. They can be anything, you know, from an argument over
a fence to someone assaulting someone.' (Panda patrol, CHM, CHL and
West).

The council flats

Here, in contrast the variation in the opinions of the different officers
was particularly noticeable. While one area man had a very clear idea of
area differences and was able to distinguish both intra-areal differences
and changes over time, the other officers tended to make little distinction between the area, a feeling confirmed during the participant observation period:

'When the flats were built they were more or less ordinary working
class families. Over the years you get more problem families, problems
with children - the ordinary respectable man wants to get off CFH. I've
noticed a big difference in the last two to three years, it's going downhill rapidly. A lot won't work, they're common criminals, drunks, wife
bashers. I do believe a stranger coming to Sheffield who goes on the
housing list can walk straight into a flat on CFH. The main problems are
little bits of kids .... you get some burglaries, meters done, a series
with the same culprit - not much, not serious. Hooliganism with children.
If you're walking on the ground floor you can get a bottle on your head
or anything - you get complaints about this from others too. There's a
lot of vandalism, but its minor. The newsagent has had burglary and
damage. There are one or two hard cases. On B row you get rougher
people, like domestics, burglaries all over the city, and warrants for
nonpayment of fines.' (Area constable CFH).

'I like working in the area - it varies. You know where you are with
the people - they're working class. I'm working class and you know where
you are with them - not like Totley or Dore where they're more standoff-
ish. A nice area once you get to know. The ne'er-do-wells were put in
C Street and D Street, where they've all got records and don't work. In
CFH the majority are working people. Not many offences - the main one
vandalism, one or two violence, especially domestic assaults. There are
spates of burglaries caused by juveniles kicking the door in and taking
what they can, otherwise it's not that bad compared to the crime figures
they keep issuing (from other areas). There's vandalism, especially
around the shopping area - street lamps, graffiti, dropping bottles on
cars. There are one or two families whose names always seem to be cropping up. The real criminals who live on the area go and do it elsewhere
- the burglaries we have on the flats are, as I say, kids.' (Area
constable, CFH).

'It's not a high crime rate area, it's low. CFH is worse, conditions
are rougher there. There are no pub problems. Bad vandalism, especially
lights, flowers, lamp standards. There's little window damage unless its
part of another crime. Very few domestics - two in two years.' (Area
constable, CFH).

'As far as I'm concerned it's a hell hole. There's no community spirit.
CFL is best, X Street is particularly scruffy, CFH has a high standard of
criminals, I don't know why it should be, more so than CFL or X. I like
working it. It's the only bit of my area with people on it. That to me
is policing. It doesn't compare with RHH, P, Q, where you've got modern
housing and terraced lodging houses, a lot of coloured and Irish - it had
everything there I joined the force for - it had trouble, problems,
your coloured pub, Chinese chip shop; you never knew what each day could
give you; adventure, it had everything I joined the force for.

'CFH has offences against dwellings. It had a spate of doors kicked
in, taking valuables away. It's like a concrete jungle, no chance of
catching them. Thefts of cars or things from them - you get service
roads go under the flats. Everyone's overlooking them but nobody's close
to them - you get a lot stolen from these particular roads. Offences? -
there's more problems - crime - on the city centre side of the beat.
There's an awful lot of broken windows - places like the community
centre, the caretaker's office .... there's a shop in CFH they actually
have the windows boarded up like you'd have in Belfast. The shop next
door, a newsagent, he had his windows broken and small stuff taken about
six times - finally we caught them.

They're more scattered problems on CFH and CFL than on Blackacre, where
you get one particular cul-de-sac that's a community. I don't think
there's any community of any kind on CFH or CFL. There's a group of 17-
20 year olds from the CFL area are going to be the criminals of the next
few years - big time shoplifters, jewellery, clocks, TVs. You've hit the
nail on the head with domestic disputes - it's just starting now with the
warmer weather - the kids going out to play. It's no worse, but with
people living close together it makes a small disturbance much worse.
Where the kid goes home and says Tommy's hit him, so his dad goes around
and thumps Tommy's dad.' (Panda patrol, CFH, CFL)

It is easy to read through the comments made by the area constables and
patrols and discover a great deal of information which fits the statistical information which was gathered. On the other hand, a lot more is
very evidently not in line with it, and constables may have conflicting
ideas about the same areas.

This is not to scorn the 'local knowledge' developed by the units, but
to undermine the precision of its factual base. Policemen do not have at
their disposal statistical information on relative offender or offence
rates, and to expect them to have precise knowledge is naive. Whilst
this may well lead to amplification where an area is given a name without
a great deal of empirical justification, it does not mean that areas with
contrasting crime rates will necessarily be treated differently. All too
evident in the interviews and general research was the feeling that, from
the point of view of police manpower, the place of the offence was a more
important, and perhaps, more readily available, piece of information than
relative offender rates, although even offence based evidence is imprecise, as was previously noted. More especially, given the ambiguity of
the definitions given of their areas by the unit police, it is perhaps
relevant to consider in more detail their role in the detection and handling of crime, before going on to consider the statistical information.

THE ROLE OF THE UNIFORMED BRANCH IN THE DETECTION AND HANDLING OF CRIME

The role of the area constable in generally gathering information has
already been considered (in section 'The role of the police in the nine
areas' of this chapter). More specifically this may be distinguished on
three levels:

    (i)   Getting to know locals who are a good source of information
    (ii)   Passing back information on disreputable residents or new
           residents
    (iii) Referring information on local offences.

81

Ultimately this is the foundation for Matza's conception of the 'method of suspicion' (Matza, 1969), and it is indeed sometimes tempting to read only the role of the police into this construct, a temptation sometimes accepted by the police themselves:

'Persistent offenders - the same names keep cropping up. It's no reflection - I'm far from brilliant but take a break in on B row and they had one name, well I could say 'I should think so and so's involved'. You know the ones, and until they satisfy you, you keep on; where have you been, what'd you do - you know, you can tell.' (Area constable, CFL).

However this is to ignore the fact that the source of the information may be a local resident. Two area constables, whilst agreeing on the role of the informant, disagreed on the extent to which he supplemented police intra-communication:

'It's public relations - general local knowledge - getting to know who lives in the area and what they're doing - local thieves and vagabonds etc. Through this - getting to know people and getting information - little in themselves, but pass on to CID, the collator - and it may be useful. Something crops up and you think back and string things together and ring CID, and tell them, 'did you know two crooks have palled up, changed their car and that'. The whole idea of the area bobby is to get to know people, and they know you and come to you and know where to find you. Say someone with a criminal record moved into my area - I pass on car numbers etc. and if it's owned by another crook that ties them together. The collator will then feed back information to the area policeman. It comes out in general conversation - in the general drift of their conversation - something they say you have to cotton to - someone moved in down the street, I don't know who he is but he doesn't seem to work, big car, etc.' (Area constable R'HL).

'An old woman might tell you something of use and you pass it on to the detective concerned. Very often someone's neighbour will bring something to your attention and you've got a crime. I'm a bit of a talker and I encourage people to talk to me. If you've been to a particular flat, you do make use of the public - you let them know your particular difficulties and they might give you a little bit of assistance without turning into copper's narks.' (Area constable CFH).

What emerges from this is that the area constable, far from having a clear idea of possible suspects, is far more attuned to the key information gatherers in the area. This may inevitably lead to his being able to identify possible suspects, but it is based on second hand reputations passed on to him by key local figures. The art therefore, is not so much knowing who might have committed the offence, but rather knowing who to ask for information. A system evolves where the constable in the general course of his work, concentrates a lot of his time on the area talkers - the shopkeepers, the elderly, the lonely:

'I visit the shops - its surprising what you get to know - you say 'what about old so and so?' .... They get to know you and build up a friendship and they'd rather tell you than anyone else. Not so long ago a lad who lived on the area - we knew he was doing some burglaries - I knew the shop and he told me, I mean, where to go, and he passed me on to someone else and gradually it build up a picture and told us where the stuff was going to and now the lad's inside.. (Area constable, adjacent to R'HL).

Or, to cite the classic, rather unflattering quote:

'You usually get one Ena Sharples on the block - no need to go to those houses, they'll know nothing; if Mrs. So and So doesn't know, nobody will.' (Area constable, adjacent to R'HL).

' .... by the residents on the area who see something, don't think its important enough to ring in, but if they see me they'll tell me - like 'I've seen X up the road with a box of chocolates'. With the lads themselves, you get one or two will tell you about someone at school .... Older people, especially retired ones - of course they have less tolerance towards the kiddies than the younger ones. They're more forthcoming, they feel that by passing on bits of information they're becoming involved.' (Area constable, CHM, CHL and West).

' .... other residents, people who might have been in the street at the time, - postmen, milkmen. You get to know they're the sort of people, especially in the older streams, who are in the habit of noticing what goes on; you get to know these people, and pick their brains. Sometimes its indirect and you find they're telling you something.' (Area constable, CHH).

Information may be passed on by the area man, but originally it is introduced by people from the area itself. Similarly, with detection the constables quoted cases where, by their own initiative alone they had been able to clear up an offence:

'You see somebody and by the way they dress or conduct themselves you become suspicious of them - the age old example of the man in the mucky raincoat in the playground.' (Panda patrol, CHM, CHL and West).

'You keep your eyes open for kids off school in the shopping area, around vehicles. Question kids off school .... I caught a boy on the spot for being around in school time. That's suspicious circumstances leading to clearing up a burglary. You can see when they're up to something, the way they drop their hands, their mannerisms, they start whispering, something like that ....' (Area constable, CFL).

Such comments were sometimes made, but the overall impression was that they are uncommon examples of 'real detection'; hung onto like a dream or created as a myth which ensures police expertise. If this is so, it seems that sociologists and criminologists, in radically criticising policework, have undermined the myth rather than the reality. Here it seems that for their definitions of problem areas and problem residents the uniformed branch are dependent on information. Such information, whether from the police organisation or the area itself, is by no means complete, leading to ambiguity, uncertainty, and incorrect perceptions. Conversely, with regard to when such information is translated into actual situations, i.e. in the defining of certain residents as 'suspects', the overwhelming impression is one of the dependency of the constable on the eyes and ears of the community. If this is so, it is to the area itself that we must look for the processes involved in the reporting and detection of offences:

'Much crime is cleared up due to members of the public at the time, not by the policeman on patrol. By the time I get it (i.e. what is not cleared up at the time) its twenty-four hours gone - its dead crime. When it's dead its very hard.' (Area constable, R'HL).

THE HANDLING OF OFFENDERS

What the officers say they do is by no means a reliable indication of what they do do. However it provides a basis for hypotheses - about the reporting and detecting of crime - which may form a corrective to the emphasis that has been placed on the role of the police alone.

Whilst information from police files will be used in subsequent chapters to test these hypotheses, it is, nevertheless, possible to conclude this chapter by considering one other aspect of policework which is, by its nature, not available for testing in any other way in the present research - namely the role of the police in deciding which situations should be officially recorded and which should not, or more specifically, the extent of police discretion over the use of informal action against offenders.

In fact, the unit officers denied that much crime was processed out of the system. Where it was, the nature of the offence was stated as the prime deciding factor:

'So and so had two bob pinched off them, and if you can resolve it and take them home to their parents you do - and minor complaints, but not others like vandalism.' (Area constable, CFM).

Incorporated into this consideration of the offence is an appreciation of the complainant's wishes:

'I report a crime to CID via headquarters - always. They're strong on formal reporting .... Say there's damage to a door - I'd question kids personally - if I found the offender I'd make it official, but only if the complainant desired.' (Area constable B, CFH).

'You always make out a formal crime report for indictables. But where the complainant's guarded - it depends on the victim - it happens quite regularly that no form is filled in for non-indictable.' (Area constable, RHH).

Similarly, it is within the context of the seriousness of the offence that the offender may be judged:

'I'd use informal means if I caught someone for vandalism - especially if it was the first time or they hadn't done any damage.' (Area constable, CHM, CHL and West).

'With minor things - milk thefts etc. - I'd proceed, but if it were kids I'd tell the victim and ask if they'd like official action or not .. .. Have they done any more besides this? - if they have I'll make it official, if not go round and see the person if they deny it do something. You can usually get somewhere seeing them with their parents. You know you won't get anywhere going to court, it frightens them to death. It builds up a respect, they say 'they're not so bad, policemen'.' (Area constable, adjacent to R'HL).

'I may use informal methods, but if there's wilful damage I'd have a word with the parents. It depends on background, home, attitude of parents, like if they're hanging around in the pub till late at night.' (Area constable CFL).

Thus it may be that where offenders are defined in terms of their moral or motivational characteristics, the official statistics (even including official cautions) may be limited, although even here it seems that this would occur only for minor offences. On the other hand, when the offender's characteristics were mentioned as important, it was notable that not one of those interviewed related this to area characteristics. Indeed, the only time in which the question of procedure was phrased within an area context related back to an urban/rural distinction remin- iscent of Cain's research (Cain, 1973). At no time was an intra-city distinction made along the lines suggested by Bittner (in terms of it not being worth bothering about minor crime in problem areas). (Bittner, 1967):

'I like working there. I enjoy it, using a placid country bobby approach. My experience is that everyone caught doing anything wrong is taken to the police station and things are sorted out there, even if they're under age. In a country force I was taught that you sorted it out on the spot and you took him home and sorted him out in front of his parents and then made your report. I try to do things as a country bobby and sort things out .... Now that was a typical country policeman type of working. You suspect a crime. I would have taken him home first and no report would be made. You've got social responsibility - I'm in the Youth Club at P church, and a school manager at Q First School. Through this I gain the friendship of youngsters at the 12-15 age, pot- ential trouble makers. Take some incidents - a milk bottle smashed, a traffic cone kicked across the avenue. If I hadn't have known them I would have had to knock 'em off to get authority.' (Area constable, CHH).

The rural force example is an apt one. The area constable concept, based as it was upon the rural ideal, brings with it a tremendous potential for the use of informal methods of dealing with offenders. Despite this, there was no evidence, albeit in this very limited methodological context, that it was used either for indictable crime (other than milk bottle thefts) or differentially.

CONCLUSION: POLICE INTERVENTION IN RESIDENTIAL AREAS

In this chapter two themes have predominated. First, the question of the reputation of each area, from the point of view of the area constables and panda beat patrols, has been raised. Second, the issues surrounding the discovery and detection of offences have been examined. In the first case, it seemed clear that the police had, for various reasons, rather vague or conflicting ideas of the reputation of the area they covered; in the second case, the extent to which the police were dependent upon the general public has been stressed.

In the context of the police presence in residential areas, these find- ings make sense. However, in concluding this chapter, use will be made more specifically of the (admittedly limited) time which I spent on panda patrol. The patrols involved covered CFH and CFL and a portion of the city centre. The following notes, taken at the time, cover four such patrol periods - one a four hour morning patrol, the other three three hour evening patrols.

Example 1 : 8am - noon

We drove around the city centre area. The patrolling officer explained that this was a good idea at this time of the morning, because when the traffic build up began it would be practically impossible.

8.30   Passed a car park. The driver noted that the man on duty was a stranger and ordered him to stop whilst we drove round to the entrance and parked. He was questioned and his credentials were checked, but everything was in order, - the regular watchman was on holiday.

8.50   Radio call that a shop alarm was sounding. Drove to shop at fast speed, dissecting traffic by driving down centre of road with sirens blaring. The alarm call proved false - as had been suspected, it had been set off by employees unlocking in the morning. Spent the next forty minutes parked watching the girls go by to work.

9.35   Followed car with no front number plate. Took particulars then directed driver, who was a stranger, to his destination.

9.45   Radio call requesting lift for D.C. to another part of the division.

10.10   Radio call re factory alarm. Competed with two other cars as to who arrived first - we won, for which the driver was justifiably proud. Again a false alarm.

10.25   Went back to watching girls go by. Woman came to car and enquired about procedure for making statement re the then current murder enquiry and was directed to headquarters.

10.32   Member of public asked for directions.

11.40   Radio call to transfer a prisoner from one station to another.

11.45   Radio call to deliver message to resident in CFL about accident to spouse.

12.00   Radio call about grass fire. Responded, but it appeared to be a false alarm.

Example 2 : 8pm - 11pm

8.00   Visited house on CFH to give new information to victim of car theft, which had been covered that afternoon.

8.30   Pedestrian made enquiries about making a statement to do with the murder enquiry.

8.50   Checked up at house on CFL re son who had jumped bail - rather sympathetic chat with his sister.

9.00   Called in at service station. Dealt with three girls who complained about a boy with an airgun and two women who gave new information about a purse they had originally reported stolen – in each case, note made in area log for attention of area constable.

9.50   Checked perimeter of CFL for stolen cars. The constable suddenly stopped his car and jumped out. He had seen a teenager lying in the grass bordering the estate, which he thought suspicious 'at this time of the day'. We went up and the officer questioned the boy, who explained his presence was due to 'too much to drink at dinner time'. However, the officer was slightly suspicious because the boy had a holdall. He there-fore, with permission, checked the contents of the holdall, and checked the boy's home address over the personal radio. This done we left the boy.

A few minutes later, we were passing the same spot when the officer saw the boy walk towards the road, without the holdall. This was seen as significant – the officer thought the boy had stolen the bag and had now panicked and dumped it – more likely he thought the boy had found a left-luggage ticket and checked it in, and had been in the process of emptying the bag when disturbed. He questioned the boy, again, more thoroughly and established that he had previous convictions for burglary. He therefore went back with the boy to where he had left the bag and questioned him minutely about its contents – for example, make of after-shave, collar size and make of shirt. Since the boy answered all his questions correctly, he let him go, saying he had nothing to go on, and if the bag was reported missing he knew where to find him.

10.20   Stopped car which appeared to be driven strangely. Driver ex-plained that he was short of petrol and coasting down hills – we followed him to the nearest garage and left him there.

10.50   Radio call re pub fight in city centre. Raced some three cars and a dozen or so foot beat men to the scene, but when we arrived every-thing was quiet and there was no sign of the victim or offender. We searched the area but to no avail.

Example 3 : 8pm – 11pm

8.00   Radio call to enquire at hospital. It appeared that a casualty case had given the wrong address and we attended the hospital to clear up the matter and let his relatives know – he had left without giving any more information and the matter dropped.

8.20   Radio call to go to the City Baths re a car reported stolen. Arrived and took details from owner. Searched area in case she had left it somewhere else and forgotten. Gave her a lift to the station to make a formal report and handed over case to CID.

9.05   Radio call to bring in drunk arrested by another constable.

9.20   Checked car parks and cars parked on perimeter of CFL.

9.40   Signalled to by two boys who reported a flood in an empty shop near CFL. The driver eventually broke open the door (used number one key) and turned off the tap which had been turned on, presumably by an intruder. Questioned our helpers, who said who they thought might have done it, but the driver didn't bother to take the matter any further.

10.50 Radio call about trouble at pub. Youths had left pub with glasses
in hands. We followed and caught up with them walking down the road –
they were told to take the glasses back and apologise to the landlord.

Example 4 : 8pm – 11pm

8.00   Radio call to go to Registry Office where alarm had gone off. Met
five foot patrol constables there and checked for break in. Appeared to
be a false alarm.

8.40 Stopped outside garage to check on two youths who appeared to be
acting suspiciously outside a garage. They explained their presence to
the driver's satisfaction and we left.

8.55   Drove around CFL and CFH. Man from CFH complained that kids were
constantly breaking his windows. He said he had made a complaint but
nothing had been done and that the police were never in the area. He was
treated with some hostility, and his claim that he did not know who had
done it was accepted with scepticism – 'He's the sort thinks the police
should be spending all their time on the flats. He could help us by
finding out who they are, getting a look at them, asking around. You
know as well as I do, if I go after them they'll scarper'.

9.50   Radio call to support ambulance which had been called to an
accident on CFL. A boy had fallen off a wall – we took his name and
address and ensured that his parents knew what had happened.

9.55   Radio call to deliver a stolen vehicle form to a constable.

10.00 Pub call – all quiet on arrival – waved on by two constables who
were already on the spot.

10.05 Heard alarm bell ringing at shop. Stopped and investigated.
Waited for owner to arrive and switch it off. Searched for signs of
entry, but eventually decided it was a false alarm.

   Although these notes cover only four short periods of car patrol in
two of the survey areas, they add significantly to the material from the
interviews, particularly on three points.

   The beat patrolman's routine is a largely uneventful one. There is,
therefore, a tendency to make it more interesting by pursuing what
Maureen Cain calls 'easing behaviour' (Cain, 1973). Given that the
patrolman has a wide area to cover, he therefore had discretion over
which bits of the area he should concentrate on i.e. which bits are likely to be most interesting.

   In making this decision it was striking what a negligible part CFH and
CFL played in the patrolman's thoughts about excitement. In the interviews it was notable that in comparing residential areas the only ones
which were mentioned as involving a great deal of potential action were
some of the privately rented areas. Only one council estate elicited
this response. The patrol car for CFH and CFL had, in getting to some
parts of CFH, to go out of its beat onto Blackacre, and a number of times
the drivers commented on the potential for action which Blackacre had
held in 'the good old days'. By comparison, patrolling the two high rise
estates was mundane, routine, and consequently avoided where possible.

Thus it is notable that very little time was given to patrolling the areas, even though the officers knew of my interest. Instead, they concentrated on the city part of their area, where, they implied, a beat could be spent more fruitfully. (Not only were there more crimes, there were also more girls).

Central to the concentration on action were two sorts of incident which were fairly common - alarm calls and pub fights. In the latter case, involvement in an ongoing pub fight was interesting, enjoyable, and eventful, and therefore not surprisingly, a radio call was usually responded to by every available man - indeed, in such cases a further call might be made to inform other officers that no more help was needed!

However, the potential for action was not the only reason for the ready response to calls to pub fights. In many - perhaps most - cases, even a speedy response was too slow, the action being over by the time the police arrived. In addition, alarm calls were also a signal for speed, even though the police considered them to be false. Rather, it seemed that one form of easing behaviour was the race itself - the ability of a patrolcar to reach the scene of complaint before anyone else, the thrill of accelerating down the centre of the road in the rush hour, of speeding round the 'Hole in the Road' (2) at sixty miles per hour, sirens sounding (see also Holdaway, 1976).

Thus it appears from what was an admittedly short period of participant observation that the police did not consider CFH as an exciting area to patrol, one where 'action' was possible. This confirmed the impression gained from the interviews with area constables and patrolmen. In general, it can be said that the uniformed police avoided residential areas where possible; that where they were involved in patrolling these areas their perceptions of the offence and offender rates of the areas was vague, largely relative and rarely in line with a labelling perspective of policework. In discussions surrounding the discovery and detection of offences and offenders, moreover, it appeared that the police were rather more concerned with acting as receptive vessels to public complaints, and organising their area in terms of 'people who could give information', than they were actively engaged in proactive policing. The method of suspicion, was, it is true, cited, but even here the role of the public seemed most important.

The picture of crime, and the areas in which the police worked, which is created by the informal interviews and participant observation seems at times to contrast vividly with the one described by other researchers. This view is however, that of the police reacting to the presence of the researcher. The following chapters consider the matter from another angle - that of the information recorded by the police and general public in their statements concerning incidents defined as crimes.

4 The Discovery and Reporting of Crime

INTRODUCTION

In previous chapters the emphasis placed by other studies on the role of
the police in the 'crime production' process has been criticised on two
counts - first, in terms of the interest shown in distinguishing the
crime discovery from the offender detection processes; secondly, in the
common failure to appreciate differences between where known offenders
live and where the offence takes place.

In this and the following chapter, I shall therefore focus on the
discovery and detection processes as logically distinct entities. However, whilst in the context of the discovery and reporting of crime, area
differences might be anticipated in terms of where offences occur, when
we consider the detection process we might anticipate differences between
areas of residence of offenders. Consequently, the focus in this chapter
will be on offences committed in the nine areas and in the next chapter
offenders living in the nine areas. In each case, however, comparable
material will be included where it supplements that being discussed.

Before considering the data in more detail, it is perhaps apt to describe the source, since there are good reasons to believe that variations between different police forces may be considerable.

The 1971 recorded crime files on standard list offences were used. The
South Yorkshire police operate a two fold classificatory system in recording indictable crime, and in this respect differ considerably from
the Hull police at present being studied by Bottomley and Coleman (1976).
The basic information is recorded by the officer in charge on a crime
sheet. This is checked by the statistics department, who might for
example modify it by recording it as a 'no crime' or by counting two
reports as a 'continuous offence' and therefore only one crime. It is
then given a number and filed as part of the official crime statistics.
This form, although only a single sheet, does contain a good deal of
information relevant to the researcher. For example, a note, however
brief, is made of who discovered the crime, how it came to the notice of
the police, how and when it was discovered and reported and (if an
offender was caught) what grounds the police had for suspecting him.

In addition to this information the police keep more detailed information on each case. This is kept primarily as evidence for court, should
proceedings ever arise, and includes a detailed statement by the officer
in charge of his involvement in the crime, and original witness statements. This enables one to fill in much detailed information not contained on the crime report.

Clearly this information is kept for official purposes and not for
investigating sociologists, with the subsequent disadvantage that some
data are incomplete - for example the colour of the offender or by what

means the offence was reported - whilst other information is unknown. One particular example is the vagueness of estimates of when the offence took place. However, one advantage is that all these reports were written before the research was conceived, thus eliminating the danger that reports were 'window dressed' for the benefit of outsiders.

AGENCIES INVOLVED IN THE DISCOVERY AND REPORTING OF CRIME

Following stress on the role of the police in the discovery of crime, Reiss' work may be seen as correcting the more extreme examples of over-generalisation. Using the term proactive policing to define incidents discovered by the police, and reactive policing to describe incidents reported to the police by complainants, Reiss has demonstrated that the majority of police activity is reactive. (Reiss, 1971). Indeed, British evidence from Hull (Bottomley and Coleman, 1976) and the views of the police in Sheffield described in the last chapter, support this.

Unfortunately, although this distinction is useful as a tool in any criticism of studies overemphasising the role of the police in the creation of official statistics, it is of little help to an analysis of the precise agents active in the reporting of crime. Although Bottomley and Coleman, following Sellin and Wolfgang, make a slightly more detailed breakdown, by distinguishing within the complainant group between the victim, his representative, and others, this again is imprecise. (Bottomely and Coleman, 1976); (Sellin and Wolfgang, 1964).

In the present study, no prior categorisation was employed. Instead, the reporting agent was in each case described in full on the coding schedule, and only after the data was collected for the indictable statistics was a post hoc categorisation employed. In all seven categories were ultimately employed.

The victim

An offence was defined as reported by the victim when it was reported to the police either by the victim or by someone acting on behalf of the victim in a private capacity. In each case, a commonsense definition of the victim was used, rather than a material one. For example, in cases where money was stolen from gas meters by an intruder, the victim was defined as the house occupier, whereas in fact the Gas Board may have actually lost by the action. Similarly, where an employee used his firm's van in his own time, and this was stolen out of working hours, the employee, not the employer, was defined as the victim.

The representative of the victim was defined as someone acting directly on behalf of the victim on his explicit or implicit instructions, excluding those employed specifically as law enforcement agents. In most cases, the representative as here defined was an employee, for example, a shop manager; in other cases, a victim might ask a neighbour to call the police on his behalf.

The private law enforcer (PLE)

Distinct from this were offences reported by people employed specifically to deal with offences. Most of these, as one might expect, were store detectives, who were thus distinguished from shop managers and assistants

- but other organisations, notably Securicor, were sometimes cited.

The witness

An offence was defined as reported by a witness, when the complainant was a third party to the offence, not involved in the offence or directly related to offender or victim. In many cases the distinction between a witness and a representative of the victim was a fine one, and the decisive factor was that the witness was acting entirely on his own initiative. For example, when an offence of housebreaking was reported by a neighbour, this was defined as reporting by a witness; however, where the neighbour discovered the offence because the victim had specifically asked him to check the property, the reporting agent was defined as the representative of the victim. Here four typical offences which took place in the research areas and have been defined as witness reported, are included as illustrations:

Case 1. Mrs. X noticed that the side entrance window of the house next door was open. She knew her neighbours were away on holiday and called the police, who confirmed that a burglary had taken place (CHL).

Case 2. Mr. Z heard the sound of breaking glass. He looked out of his window and saw a man walking away from a shop further down the road. He could see that the shop window was broken, so he phoned the police (RHL).

Case 3. Mr. Q heard a sound of breaking glass and looked out of his window. He saw three youths running away from a nearby shop. He did not report the matter at the time, but later noticed five or six youths hanging round the shop which had a broken window, and subsequently called the police (CFL).

Case 4. Miss R was walking down the road when she noticed two men fighting in a side road, one of whom appeared to be nearly unconscious. She called the police from a nearby phone kiosk (RHL)

An alarm

Alternatively in some cases no decision to report was made by anyone at the time of the offence. Rather, the report was 'made' by an alarm, sounding either at the place of the offence or directly to the police station.

The offender

A rather different reporting agent was the offender himself. Also in this category, which must be kept distinct from indirect reporting (see below), were incidents reported by a close relative of the offender. Most of the latter cases were where parents reported their children's shoplifting to the police. In addition there were a few cases reported by the offender, where he did so in a complainant capacity and did not admit his guilt until a later stage. The most common examples of this were meter thefts reported by the house occupier, which were later ascribed to the occupier or a member of his family.

The police

Offences were defined as discovered by the police themselves where the police, through their direct intervention on patrol, discovered offences. In practice this generally meant that the police discovered the offences by one of three approaches - through seeing some result of the offence (for example a broken shop window); through seeing the offence actually taking place (for example a man breaking a window); and through questioning a member of the public in such circumstances that an offence was brought to light which was not initially apparent (for example questioning a man with a cut head where interrogation might lead to the discovery that the cut was made in the commission of an offence). All these instances, however, must be kept separate from those discovered indirectly by the police. A number of examples are included of offences in the research areas which were discovered directly by the police:

Case 1. A householder who was going away on holiday asked the police to keep observation on his house. While making a routine check one morning the police discovered signs of a break-in (OHL).

Case 2. The police found a car with lights on and the door insecure. A routine check revealed that it had been stolen (RHH).

Case 3. A police officer saw a boy riding a bike which appeared to be hand painted. He questioned him and the boy admitted that the bicycle was in fact stolen (RHL).

Case 4. The constable went to the offender's home on another matter. While there, he noticed a danger lamp in the room. He questioned the offender about this and he admitted stealing it (R'HL).

Case 5. A policeman on patrol saw two men on the roof of a block of flats. He investigated and caught the offenders in the act of stripping lead from the roof (CFH).

Case 6. Police on patrol found signs of a break-in at a shop on X road. As they were touring the area later they saw some youths leaving another shop acting suspiciously. They were chased and caught, and later admitted the two burglaries (CHH).

Case 7. A police patrol stopped a car which was being driven erratically on suspicion that the driver was drunk. Subsequent questioning revealed that the driver had stolen the car (CFL).

Indirect reporting

A number of offences are not discovered by or reported to the police at the time they are committed, but are discovered at a later date when the police, having caught an offender regarding another incident, question him about previous offences (included here are also cases where absconders are caught and routinely questioned). Where he then admits other offences, it is often the case that these have been reported to the police already. However, in some cases, no record of the offence is known to the police, and it is only recorded at this point. This situation has been defined here as indirect reporting, and is analytically distinct from both offender reporting and police discovery.

Thus seven different ways in which offences came to the notice of the police were distinguished. In Table 4.1 the data from the nine areas have been combined to give total proportions in each category. As can

be seen, by far the largest proportion of offences committed in these
areas, 74.6% were reported by the victim. A further 2.8% were reported
by a private law enforcer, 6.4% by a witness, and 1.5% by alarms. Only
0.7% of offences were reported by the offender. This left 8.7% reported
indirectly and only 5.3% discovered directly by the police.

Having described this overall distribution, it appears logical to
exclude from further analysis all those offences reported indirectly and
deal with the remaining 91.7%. Of these, 81.7% were reported by the
victim, 3.1% by a private law enforcer, 7.0% by a witness, 1.6% by an
alarm, 0.8% by the offender, and 5.8% by the police.

These then were the aggregate statistics for the nine areas. The
rest of this section will take the analysis further by considering the
main reporting agents in more detail and analysing differences in their
importance in different types of area and for different types of offence.

Table 4.1
Agent reporting offences committed in the nine areas,
1971 standard list offence file

	Total		Excluding indirect reporting
	n	%	%
Victim	504	74.6	81.7
Private law enforcer	19	2.8	3.1
Witness	43	6.4	7.0
Offender	5	0.7	0.8
Alarm	10	1.5	1.6
Police	36	5.3	5.8
Indirect	59	8.7	-
Total	676	100.0	100.0

POLICE PROACTIVITY IN THE DISCOVERY OF OFFENCES

Although this, like other studies, has confirmed the extremely small
part played by the police in the discovery of offences, this is only a
partial denial of the applicability of the amplification model to indictable statistics. For example, Armstrong and Wilson (1973) implied that
extra police patrolling in the Easterhouse area of Glasgow led to an
increase in crime found in that area, and this might still be so even if
proactivity were minimal, if it were also variable between areas.

The matching of areas in the present study allows such a hypothesis to
be rigorously tested, although the evidence from the preceding chapter
makes it seem unlikely, given that high rate areas did not appear to be
patrolled more frequently, or by a wider variety of personnel (RHH
excepted). Thus there seemed no reason why there should be a larger
proportion of police discovered offences in some areas.

It is possible, taking the nine areas, to consider the offence and the
offender variables separately to the extent that two area - RHH and CHH
- stand out as having higher offence rates than the other areas. Thus,

in comparing the data from the nine areas, any differences in reporting methods between RHH, CHH and CFH might suggest different policing policies in high offender rate areas; differences in RHH and CHH alone might suggest differences in high offence rate areas.

One further distinction may be made here. One area (RHH) contains many of the features of the classical 'zone of transition' including a transient population, bedsitter accommodation etc. Not only are offence and offender rates both high, but other, nonindictable offences, are most commonly committed here and by local residents. For example, prostitution and drugs are particular features of the area, with the result that extra policing of the area, by policemen on plainclothes duty, with special reference to soliciting, and by the vice squad, is considered necessary. It might therefore be hypothesised that offences committed in this area alone might be discovered more often by the police, due to the number and variety of personnel employed in the area.

To test these various hypotheses, data on each of the nine areas were considered separately. The result was that although the proportion of offences discovered by the police varied between areas, from 1.8% in CHL to 17.8% in R'HL, there was no consistent trend between areas with varying offence or offender rates. Indeed, when the privately rented sector alone is considered, there were significantly more offences discovered by the police in low offence/offender rate areas (RHL and R'HL combined) than in the high offence/offender rate area (RHH) (χ^2_1 = 10.34, P < 0.01). Moreover, a similar, but insignificant trend in the same direction arises between the two council highrise estates (χ^2_1 = 1.13, P > 0.1). Within the areas of council housing the trend is in the other direction, but not only is the amount of proactivity minimal in each area, it is also likely that the difference is created by the high proportion of shopliftings reported in CHL, rather than by any difference in policing policy.

It therefore seems that none of the hypotheses relating to differences between residential areas is confirmed. However, this does not mean that police proactivity does not vary according to other criteria, and an attempt was made to test a number of other hypotheses concerning differences according to victim type and offence type.

First a distinction was made according to the victim of the offence – that is whether the victim was corporate or an individual, and for the latter, between local residents and other individuals. Although reporting agents for residents and nonresidents were similarly distributed, a significant difference exists between patterns for individual and corporate victims. In particular, police discovery is approximately three times as great for offences against corporate as opposed to individual victims. Combining reporting by victim and PLE agencies, a comparison of offences against corporate and individual victims shows a highly significant difference (χ^2_3 = 44.56 P < 0.001) (Table 4.2).

It seems plausible that there are at least two reasons for this difference:

(i) It may be that police carry out more checks on corporate property than on individual property. For example, whilst shops are likely to be routinely checked for signs of break-ins, private houses are not.

(ii) Since many offences against corporate victims take place at night,

95

when no agent is on hand to notify the police, a considerable time often exists during which the offence may be discovered by the police, before the victim or his representative arrives on the scene.

Table 4.2
Reporting agent according to victim type

| | Victim | | | |
| Reporting agent | Individual | | Corporate | |
	n	%	n	%
Victim/PLE	337	92.3	186	73.8
Witness	16	4.4	26	10.3
Police	11	3.0	25	9.9
Other	1	0.3	15	6.0
Total	365	100.0	252	100.0

Each of these explanations is connected to a third one, the inability of the police to discover offences due to the imposition of public defin- itions of privacy. This may be examined more fully if variations in proactivity are contrasted for different types of offence. There were a number of offences - shoplifting, meter thefts, violence and sex offences - for which no examples of police proactivity occurred in the sample, whilst police discovery of housebreaking occurred only once. In contrast, police proactivity was rather more common in cases of thefts of and from cars (9.8%), and for fraud (9.5%), and especially damage offences (29.4%).

These differences suggest that the situation of the offence may be an important determinant of police proactivity. The police patrol public places - roads, carparks, shopping precincts for example. Their right of entrance to more private places - houses, gardens etc. is limited by law as well as practical considerations. Consequently the police are most likely to discover those offences which are most apparent to them in their routine patrols. Of these, the most public are property damage, particularly the smashing of large display windows in shops, and the discovery of car thefts, where the car is taken from the street. On the other hand, since the police have no cause to enter private homes or shops, they are unlikely to discover thefts from houses, housebreakings, sex offences and shopliftings. The exceptional case of police discovery of a housebreaking may be used as an illustration - police discovery only occurred because the police were invited to check the premises; had they not been asked, it seems likely that the offence would have been reported by a neighbour or the victim when he returned from holiday.

This instance of where the police discovered an offence which would otherwise have been hidden because of the privacy of the place where it occurred, illustrates the difficulty the police encounter in acting pro- actively in private places. In general, the police are only likely to discover offences when these take place in public places (or private places visible from public places) and then only when there is no victim on hand to report the offence immediately.

Given this distinction, it might be argued that area differences are hidden because of the different types of offence, or different types of victim, between areas. To test this, areas were considered separately according to whether the victim was corporate or an individual victim.

96

However, far from modifying the conclusions reached earlier, the data confirm that differences between areas were if anything in the opposite direction to those hypothesised. This is especially evident for offences against corporate victims, where the three high offender rate areas have lower proportions of offences discovered by the police. When these three areas are compared with the five low offender rate areas, this difference is, moreover, significant (χ_1^2 = 5.08, P< 0.05) (Table 4.3).

Table 4.3
Police discovery by offender rate of area
(corporate victims only)

| | Offender rate of area | |
	High	Low
Police discovery	10	15
Other direct discovery	133	77
Total	143	92
Percentage police discovery	7.0	16.3

It seems therefore that the role of the police in discovering crime is related to the immediate situation of the crime, rather than to the actual residential area in which it takes place, with if anything lower offender rate areas having higher proportions of police discoveries.

However, it is possible to take the area comparison further by considering the precise ways in which the police discovered crime in the different areas. Since only 36 such cases were found extensive analysis is prevented (for a more detailed analysis of offences committed by offenders from the areas, see 'The offender sample' this chapter).

For police discoveries of offences in the areas four means of discovery could be distinguished. In 50% of cases, the police discovered signs of the offence, for example a broken window; in 16.7% of cases they saw the offender actually commit the offence; in 27.7% of cases police interrogation of people revealed offences which were not apparent at the time of intervention, whereas in 5.6% of cases an offence was revealed by a routine technical check. Of these the first two might be defined as 'offence based' discoveries and the third an 'offender based' discovery. If the differential proactivity model were applicabel, it might be hypothesised that 'offender based' discovery might be more common in high offender rate areas, where the police might be expected to be more on the look out for suspicious characters, and 'offence based' discovery methods might be relatively more common in other areas.

On the contrary as is demonstrated by Table 4.4 the opposite seems to be the case. In the high offender rate areas, 7.7% of police discoveries were 'offender based' compared with 39.1% in other areas, a provocative but not significant difference (χ^2 = 2.66, P> 0.10) (which, given the small numbers, is not surprising).

Whilst this confirmed the lack of variation between areas in the expected direction, it seemed likely that differences between different offences might be revealed for this small sample of police discoveries.

97

Table 4.4
Police discovery method, by offender rate of area

	High offender rate areas	Other areas	Total
Police discovered signs of offence	69.2	39.1	50.0
Police caught offender in act	23.1	13.0	16.7
Questioning of people revealed offence	7.7	39.1	27.7
Routine technical checks revealed offence	0	8.7	5.6
Total	100.0	99.9	100.0
n	13	23	36

Therefore, the most common offences, theft of and from cars and breaking offences, were distinguished from other offence types. The results clearly demonstrated that breaking offences which were discovered by the police were likely to be found after the offence has taken place, whilst thefts of and from cars were most likely to be discovered by the police interrogating persons they define as acting suspiciously.

Evidently then, not only is the likelihood of police proactivity dependent upon the offence type, but also the way in which the offence is discovered by the police also varies with offence type. Breaking offences involving corporate property are easiest for the police to discover afterwards, notably because the offence is evident and unambiguous. On the other hand, thefts of and from cars are particularly difficult to discover unless they are seen in progress, or unless the offender acts suspiciously after committing the offence, and thereby gives the trained policeman the excuse for intervening. This will be reconsidered later when the way offences are cleared up is discussed.

However, undoubtedly the most striking conclusion of the present section is that the role of the police in the discovery of crime in these residential areas is minimal, and that variation between areas does not fit the amplification hypotheses. Once this is appreciated attention inevitably turns to the role of the victim in the reporting of crime, for he is, as we have already shown, the main reporter of crime in these districts.

THE REPORTING OF CRIME BY VICTIMS AND PRIVATE LAW ENFORCEMENT AGENTS

When indirect reporting is excluded, 81.7% of offences were reported by the victim or his representative and a further 3.1% by a private law enforcer. The latter figure was low, as might be expected, in residential areas where facilities for shoplifting were slight and the employment of store detectives minimal. This is illustrated by the fact that almost all reporting by private law enforcers happened in one area, CHL, where two supermarkets employed store detectives. Since in both cases the store detectives were employed by the company and rotated between the various branches in the city, clearly the number of shoplifters caught was related directly to the distribution of store detectives. The crime files indicated district patterns, with no offences of shop-

lifting recorded for the area for a number of weeks, followed by a batch
of arrests on the same day.

The importance of the deployment of store detectives for the number of
offences reported is one aspect of a wider issue - the discretionary
power of the detective in carrying out her daily duties - and has been
covered in detail in an earlier study in Chicago. (Cameron, 1964).
However, one factor which has often been overlooked in studies of this
kind with one notable exception (Hindelang, 1974), is the discretionary
power of ordinary shop employees. In the sample here, for example, only
46.9% of shopliftings were reported by store detectives, a further 40.6%
being reported by ordinary staff in shops where no detectives were operating. This inevitably raises questions about differences in the
decisions made by store detectives, who are employed as specialists, and
other shop employees, who are not governed by the same terms of reference
or the same criteria of success - questions which have been raised, but
not answered, elsewhere.

This apart, consideration of the role of the victim is dominated as
the previous sections indicated, by the individual/corporate victim
distinction. As Table 4.1 showed, whereas over 92% of offences against
individual victims were reported by the victim or his representative,
less than 74% of crimes against corporate victims were reported by the
victim or a private law enforcer. To some extent this is due to the role
of the police or witnesses in discovering many offences before the victim
was aware of the situation, but perhaps the most important reason is the
converse of this. That is, in the case of certain offences - meter
thefts, various other thefts, housebreaking, violence and sex offences,
for example - the situation in which the offence takes place is such that
unless the victim informs the police they are unlikely to find out in any
other way.

Variations in victim reporting according to victim type and offence
type make distinctions between areas difficult. However, given the
importance of the role of the victim, it is possible to argue that differential decision making influences the offence rates in different areas.
For example, in descriptions of high offender rate areas various theories
of anomie, criminal subcultures, etc., have been used to account for the
crime rates. However, if such theories are true, and a dissociation from
'straight' society does exist, one might expect eagerness to call the
police to be less evident in such areas. Thus it might be hypothesised
that crime statistics underestimate the amount of crime in high offender
rate areas relative to low offender rate areas. If this is true, a
relatively smaller proportion of offences in high offender rate areas
would be reported by the victim.

In fact the analysis revealed that for all offences in the nine areas
precisely the opposite was the case. Victim/PLE reporting was proportionately greater in the three high offender rate areas than in the five
low rate areas (χ^2_1 = 8.82, P < 0.01). However, where type of victim was
controlled for, the distinction disappeared. Where only crimes against
individual residents were included, in all areas a large majority of
crimes against local residents were reported by the victim, and there
were no appreciable differences between high and low offender rate areas.

Thus, when data was considered for the two reporting agents - police
and victim - where differences between high and low offender rate areas

99

might be expected, the only differences found were in the opposite direction to those hypothesised. On the other hand, distinctions according to offence type and victim type were highly significant. In the light of these findings, it is therefore interesting to consider the role of the witness, statistically the second most important reporting agent in these residential areas.

THE ROLE OF THE WITNESS IN THE REPORTING OF CRIME

Perhaps no issue has received less attention from criminologists than the role of the witness in the reporting of crime. Police concern over the role of the general public is illustrated in current advertisements to the public regarding the need to report vandalism, but is also common when leads are needed in the investigation of a serious crime.

Police awareness of the general reluctance of the public to become involved is illustrated in an American controlled experiment of shoplifting, where the authors showed that, even when directly confronted, a significant number of shoppers refused to co-operate in the arrest of a blatant shoplifter. (Steffensmeier and Steffensmeier, 1977). On the other hand, as Chatterton has shown recently, looked at in terms of the actual proportion of all incidents reported to or discovered by the police, the role of the general public (other than the victim) is not insignificant. (Chatterton, 1976).

Data from the offence sample confirms this: 7.0% of offences reported directly were reported by members of the public, slightly more than were discovered by the police. Although this is obviously due to numbers (that is, there are rather more members of the public as potential witnesses than there are patrolling policemen) it does appear that the role of the witness is numerically important enough to warrant considerable investigation.

It seems probable that witnesses will be liable to see the same sorts of crime as the police, i.e. those which are publicly visible and those which are not immediately apparent to the victim. Thus witnesses were far more likely to report offences against corporate victims than offences against individual victims (Table 4.2) and were particularly involved in reporting damage and breaking (other) offences (13.8% and 35.3% respectively). On the other hand, they also reported violent offences relatively often (17.2%), and were under-represented in reporting thefts of and from cars.

There appear to be three important issues concerning the role of the witness in reporting crime:

(i) Witnesses, using their discretion as to whether a complaint to the police is necessary, are likely to report certain types of offences more than others. Here violent offences appear as an example of offences judged as serious by outsiders. (See McClintock, 1963, for a relevant discussion).

(ii) Because of their position, for example as neighbours, witnesses are more likely to discover offences committed in privacy than are the police. In this context they were more likely than the police to discover housebreaking, and some of the violent offences reported by witnesses were domestic incidents which neighbours heard through the walls of their homes, but which the police would be unlikely to discover themselves.

(iii) On the other hand, because of their authority and training, the police were more likely to discover some offences than were witnesses. In particular, witnesses were noticeably under-represented in the reporting of offences from and of cars, a particularly public type of offence. Two reasons may be suggested for this. On the one hand, these offences may not be immediately obvious to a member of the public, whereas a police officer is trained to look for particular relevant features. On the other hand, as was shown earlier, the police have the authority to check up on car ownership, by routine investigation of suspect driving for example, in a way that is closed to the general public.

There are, then differences in the extent of witness reporting between different types of offences. However, it is also relevant to consider whether there are differences between different types of area. This has rarely been considered by criminologists, but has been indirectly discussed by Newman (1973). (Mawby, 1977 (ii)). In his research on the relationship of architectural design and crime, Newman uses the term 'defensible space' which is reducible to two foci - the visibility of public areas (corridors, doorsteps and streets, for example) such that offences committed there may be seen by passers-by or neighbours, and the feeling of community responsibility leading to increased motivation to care for (including 'police') such areas and report suspicious incidents committed there.

Newman dogmatically asserts that 'defensible space' is a major determinant factor in explaining different offence rates, and comparing high rise developments with other types of housing design he concludes that the former have higher offence rates because of their poor defensible space qualities.

Unfortunately, despite the promising hypotheses Newman develops, his own methodological inadequacies prevent them being rigorously tested. (Bottoms, 1974; Mawby, 1977 (ii)).

The present research allows it to be tested more systematically, since areas were matched on both design features and offender rates. It was shown in an earlier chapter that offence rates in the different areas were related to the opportunities for crime in those areas and the offender rates in the areas, and this to some extent undermined Newman's theory. However, another way of testing the theory is to consider the role of the witness, not as a deterrent but as a reporting agent. That is, if high rise developments include space which is less defensible one might expect a lower proportion of offences there to be reported by witnesses.

However, the proportion of offences reported by witnesses in the two areas of high rise developments was higher than in any of the other areas. Comparing these with the conventional council estates (CHH and CHL, compared with CFH and CFL) the difference is significant (χ^2_1 = 9.95, P < 0.01).

Moreover, further consideration shows that this difference in witness reporting between areas is entirely due to differences in the reporting of offences against corporate victims. While the traditional housing areas tended to have slightly, but insignificantly, more offences against residents reported by witnesses, the flats had relatively more offences against corporate victims reported in this way. (χ_1^2 = 19.78, P$<$0.001). Some of this difference is undoubtedly due to the frequency of shoplifting (hardly ever reported by witnesses) in area CHL, but even when CHH and CHM are compared with CFH and CFL, the difference is highly significant (χ_1^2 = 16.85, P$<$0.001).

Here then is conclusive evidence that witnesses were more likely to report offences in the areas of high rise development than in the conventional design areas. However, far from undermining Newman's theory, it may in fact be explained using the concept of defensible space. In both areas of high rise development, the shopping precinct was situated in the middle of the complex, surrounded and overlooked by blocks of flats. Consequently any offence occurring there could, potentially, be viewed by any number of residents from their windows. The most extreme example of this occurred in CFL, where one offence of malicious damage (a shop window was smashed) was reported by no less than four residents of the flats overlooking the shop.

This degree of visibility contrasts markedly with the conventional shopping areas. Areas CHH, CHL and RHL all had shopping facilities, but these were either separate from residential quarters, or overlooked only by a small number of houses, with the result that the number of potential witnesses was diminished.

This said, it is worthwhile considering other aspects of the defensibility hypothesis, to see why area differences do not follow defensibility features. As has been demonstrated earlier, a great deal of the crime committed, at least in these residential areas, was committed in private, giving little opportunity for public overviewing. Housebreaking is a good example of an offence which straddles the public/private distinction. Although the initial entry, which may take but a few seconds, is in theory public, most of the offence takes place in the privacy of the home. The time period when a witness may see the offence take place is limited. However, it is evident that even here the extent to which entry is strictly visible to the public is problematic. Double loaded corridors - an example of Newman's - are relatively private, with few potential witnesses, but in a similar way suburban gardens, fences, etc., (not to mention darkness) present a barrier which limits the degree of visibility. That is, while some offences take place in visible territory (thefts of or from cars, shoplifting, shopbreaking, malicious damage) others do not, and a crude analysis of crime rates in total ignores this.

While on the subject of differences between areas, it is also pertinent to consider one other aspect of variation in witness reporting. It could be argued that public co-operation with the police in high offender rate areas is considerably less than in low offender rate areas. If this were the case, one might expect a lower proportion of witness reports in high offender rate areas. Indeed, as reported earlier, comparing just two areas, one earlier study had in fact found this to be the case. (Maccoby, 1958).

In fact, the overall impression from the data was that the high rise flats were distinct from the other areas, but apart from the exceptionally high rate of witness reporting in CFL, areal differences according

to offender rate are varied. Similarly, a control for victim types
failed to produce any consistent picture. The role of the witness, like
that of the victim, does not then appear less pronounced in high offender
rate areas.

The whole of the present analysis has demonstrated, more than anything
else, the importance of the offence situation in determining the reporting agent. Differences according to offence and victim type stand out,
but variations between areas (except in the case of witness reporting in
the council sector) are slight.

At this stage, however, the analysis has been limited in two respects.
First, a detailed consideration of police discoveries was impossible due
to the small numbers involved. Secondly, the focus on offences in residential areas limited wider area comparisons. It is therefore useful to
widen the scope of the inquiry at this juncture to include an analysis of
data from the offender sample.

THE OFFENDER SAMPLE

If we consider the offender sample in terms of the agency responsible for
the discovery or reporting of crimes committed by residents of the nine
areas, it is immediately evident that there are some differences of
emphasis. Taking all offences, some quarter were reported indirectly,
a rather larger proportion than for the offence sample. Moreover, when
these were excluded, the proportions reported by private law enforcement
agencies, or discovered directly by the police, were rather greater than
in the offence sample, and the role of the victim correspondingly reduced.
(Table 4.5).

One of the reasons for the difference is the fact that the offender
sample, by its very nature, is restricted to offences which were cleared
up, and the relationship between reporting agents and detection rates
will be postponed to the next chapter. Two other reasons, however, which
can be considered here, are the nature of the offence and the situation
where the offence took place.

Table 4.5
Agent reporting offences commited by offenders
from the nine areas, 1971 standard list files

	Total		Excluding indirect reporting
	n	%	%
Victim	249	43.1	58.5
Private law enforcer	57	9.9	13.4
Witness	30	5.2	7.0
Offender	10	1.7	2.3
Alarm	9	1.6	2.1
Police	71	12.3	16.7
Indirect	152	26.3	-
Total	578	100.1	100.0

103

In the last sections, the relationship between reporting agents and victim and offence type was clarified, and it seemed that offences against corporate victims and offences such as damage and thefts of and from cars were more likely to be police discoveries, and thefts from shops were often reported by private law enforcers. Since offences of these types were more frequent for the offender sample, the importance of police and private law enforcer discoveries is not surprising. Moreover, within the offender sample a similar pattern emerged. The police were more likely to discover offences against corporate victims (21.0%) than individual victims (11.2%) ($\chi_1^2 = 7.33$, P < 0.01), which is particularly striking given the number of shoplifting incidents in the corporate victim category. Similarly police discoveries tended to be proportionately higher for some offences than for others — for example taking all direct discoveries which were down to the police, these accounted for 31.3% of thefts of and from cars, 27.4% of thefts (other) and 22.2% of breakings (other). This pattern was broadly similar to the offence data, except for thefts (other), where the higher proportion of scrap metal thefts in the offender sample (an offence frequently discovered by the police) was responsible for the greater police role.

In previous sections, however, one of the most striking findings was the lack of a relationship between the area where the offence took place and the discovery/reporting agency. Here, two possible area links can be considered, in terms of where the offender lived, and where the offence took place. Not surprisingly there was no relationship between area of residence of offenders from the nine areas and discovery/reporting agency. However, when offences were considered according to whether they took place in one of the nine residential areas, the city centre or elsewhere, there was a highly significant difference.

Table 4.6

Agent reporting offences committed by offenders from nine areas, according to place of offence, 1971 standard list offence file

	Own area		City centre		Elsewhere	
	n	%	n	%	n	%
Victim	95	76.0	47	41.2	107	57.2
Private law enforcer	4	3.2	43	37.7	10	5.3
Witness	11	8.8	7	6.1	12	6.4
Offender	6	4.8	0	–	4	2.1
Alarm	1	0.8	0	–	8	4.3
Police	8	6.4	17	14.9	46	24.6
Total	125	100.0	114	99.9	187	99.9

As can be seen from Table 4.6, victim reports were most common in the nine areas and least common in the city centre, private law enforcer reports dominated the city centre figures, whilst police discoveries were least common in the nine areas and most common elsewhere. Taking the four most common discovery/reporting agencies only, there were statistically significant differences between offences committed in the nine areas and the city centre ($\chi_3^2 = 52.62$, P < 0.001), the nine areas and elsewhere ($\chi_3^2 = 19.54$, P < 0.001), and the city centre and elsewhere ($\chi_3^2 = 47.89$, P < 0.001).

Differences between offences taking place in the nine areas and the city centre are perhaps easy to explain. On the other hand, the distribution for offences committed elsewhere stands out, especially since police discoveries are apparently more common here than for city centre offences. This difference is however, entirely due to the influence of private law enforcement agencies in the city centre – if these are excluded the distribution for city centre offences and offences elsewhere is similar (χ_2^2 = 0.74, P< 0.60). Nevertheless, the distinction between offences committed in the nine residential areas and those committed either in the city centre or elsewhere is one which warrants further attention.

As reported in chapter three the Sheffield police operate an area constable system in residential areas, backed up by foot and car patrols. An area constable is assigned an area of an average 600-800 households, and a panda car patrols two such 'patches'. However, foot patrols are not considered necessary, given a manpower shortage in most residential areas, and are assigned to the city centre and commercial and industrial areas. Foot beats are only likely to intrude into residential areas where these are bounded, or cut in two, by main roads, shopping centres, etc. For example in RHL footbeats cover the main shopping area which bisects the area, but not the residential side roads. In contrast the city centre is covered by a number of foot patrols, particularly at night, but gets no more car cover than do the residential areas.

The low proportion of offences committed in the nine areas which were discovered directly by the police is thus easy to understand. However, the rather different distribution for the 'elsewhere' column seems to suggest rather more police proactivity in other types of area. Although a detailed analysis is impracticable, at least two reasons for the high proportion of police discoveries come to mind. First, whilst some of these offences were committed in other residential areas, a number of others were not, being located in areas of derelict housing, commercial and industrial districts, out of town shopping areas (subject to foot patrols) etc. Secondly, these offences include numerous metal thefts, especially from derelict property, where, as noted above, the role of police discoveries was fundamental.

It therefore appears that police deployment of manpower may affect how offences are discovered. This suggests, referring back to the last chapter, that an increase in police patrolling in problem residential areas might lead to increased police discovery in those areas. However, because residential area patrol patterns are so similar no such variation exists.

Before leaving the subject of the discovery of offences, it is relevant to reconsider, for the offender sample, the means by which the police discovered offences. As is evident from Table 4.7., not only were police discoveries more common for the offender sample, but in addition the means of discovery is distinct. In particular, a greater proportion of police discoveries were due to the offender being caught in the act, and a lower proportion due to the police discovering the offence, and if the three main methods are compared, the difference is significant (χ_2^2 = 13.28, P< 0.005). Evidently then, the increased role of the police in discoveries of offences committed by the offender sample is reflected in their role being more immediate to the committance of the offence.

Table 4.7

Police discovery method, by offender rate of area of residence

	High offender rate areas	Other areas	Total
Police discovered signs of offence	20	15.4	18.3
Police caught offender in act	44.5	38.5	42.3
Questioning of people revealed offence	28.9	42.3	33.8
Routine technical checks revealed offence	6.7	3.8	5.6
Total	45	26	71

The other interesting fact to emerge from Table 4.7 is that when police discoveries are compared according to the offender's area of residence, 'offence based' discoveries are slightly more common for offenders from high rate areas, although the difference is not statistically significant. On the other hand, corresponding to the offence sample data, there were differences according to offence type. Police discoveries of thefts of and from cars were commonly the result of the police questioning people acting suspiciously, whereas the discovery of breaking offences was largely due to the police seeing signs of a break-in. In the offender sample, however, a further distinction arose within the theft (other) category, with metal thefts usually discovered by the police catching the offenders in the act and the remaining thefts (other) largely resulting from the police questioning people behaving suspiciously. The case of metal thefts is an interesting one, since it covers a group of offences which involve a high degree of visibility. Three examples may be cited:

Case 1. The police officer saw the offenders leaving some derelict property carrying a heavy box between them (RHH).

Case 2. The police watched two youths coming out of a derelict house carrying heavy boxes (CHH).

Case 3. The police constables saw the offender on top of a private tip in the possession of scrap metal (CHH).

Consequently in such cases the role of the police as discovery agents was particulary great, and for police discoveries the most likely method was for the police to catch the offender in the act. Given that scrap metal thefts are highly visible and not infrequently involve an 'absentee victim', they perhaps best illustrate the extent of, and constraints on, the role of the police in the discovery of crime.

However it is notable that the role of the police in the discovery of crime was greater for the offender than the offence sample. One of the reasons for this was that when the area of offence was considered on a wider basis than was possible for the offence sample, (which was by definition limited to the nine residential areas) it was evident that police direct discoveries were more likely in some areas than in others. Whereas residential areas, whatever their offence or offender rates, did not seem to vary much in terms of proactive policing, it was notable that crimes committed elsewhere involve more police direct discoveries. Even then though, the importance of police patrols in discovering city centre crime should not be taken out of context, and here the role of store detectives (accounting for over a third of all crime reports) reveals the discretionary potential of at least one other agency.

CONCLUSION

Analysis of offence and offender material confirms the impression to be gained from other research, namely that – at least at the discovery and reporting stage – the role of the police as proactive agents is minimal. An attempt has been made, however, to take the issue further by considering in more detail the other agents involved in reporting crime. Clearly the victim stands out in this respect, but in addition stress has been placed on the role of private law enforcers (especially for city centre crime) and witnesses, a group commonly ignored.

Having described the variety of reporting agents, much of the chapter was concerned with considering the different types of situation in which these different agents were commonly involved. In this respect, the results echo Stinchcombe's (1963) emphasis on the privacy element (although here the focus is on the visibility of the offence rather than the offender) as well as focusing attention on the nature of the victim. Thus police discoveries varied according to whether the victim was corporate or an individual, and according to offence categories. An areal analysis was however, more ambiguous. On the one hand, it seemed as though police proactivity was minimal in residential, as opposed to other types of area. On the other hand, differences between different types of residential area were slight, the exception being in the case of witness discoveries (see 'The role of the witness in the reporting of crime' this chapter).

In order to stress the similarity between different residential areas, it is possible to consider the data in another way, by asking what the offence rates in each area would be if only specific reporting or detection agents' data were to be considered.

For example, in Table 4.8 the offence rate (total and for local residents only) has been considered according to whether the discovery reporting agent was the victim/PLE, the police, or another agent.

Table 4.8
Offence rate in each area according to each reporting agent

	CHH	CHM	CHL	CFH	CFL	RHH	RHL	R'HL	OHL
Total offence rate									
Victim/PLE	151.5	52.1	62.3	37.7	29.2	286.2	41.2	41.3	8.6
Police	7.2	1.4	1.2	2.6	7.1	9.2	3.9	9.7	1.7
Other	21.6	5.5	5.0	7.8	11.1	15.4	4.9	3.6	0
Offence rate where victim is a local resident									
Victim	70.7	30.2	21.2	26.0	16.1	109.2	25.5	15.8	7.8
Police	0	1.4	0	1.3	3.0	1.5	1.0	1.2	0.9
Other	7.2	1.4	2.5	2.6	0	1.5	0	1.2	0

Two important conclusions may be drawn from this Table. First, it is notable that victim reported incidents dominate the statistics, and not surprisingly, correspond to the overall offence rates. That is, differences between areas are considerable, with or without police discovered offences.

Secondly, the relationship between rates according to the discovery agency is extremely tenuous. This is what might have been predicted, according to a labelling model. However, a closer examination reveals that the differences are not in the expected direction. In previous sections of this chapter, data was discussed which demonstrated at least a tendency for police discoveries to be proportionally greater in low offence and offender rate areas. Given the small number of police discovered offences anyway, the data also reveal that areas with relatively high rates of police discovered offences are not consistently those with high offence rates. Taking all offences committed in the areas, police discovered rates show area R'HL as having a rate similar to RHH, and CFL a rate similar to CHH. Similarly, taking offences against individual local residents only, CFL has the highest rate.

At first sight this finding would appear to fit the pattern already developed. For example, if the number of offences discovered by the police is so small, and moreover, unrelated to the offence rate of the area, it is not surprising that their judgement of area offence rates is imprecise.

On the other hand, it does not correspond to the most obvious explanation of lack of variation of police discoveries in the expected direction. Given that the number of police in each area is approximately the same, and that offence rates in some areas are higher than in others, it could be argued that the police are unable to cope with the increased number of opportunities for crime discovery in some areas. That is, one could hypothesise a constancy in the rate of police discoveries per population in each area. However, this does not appear to be borne out by the data. Although we are considering very small numbers, there is no evidence whatever of a constant rate of police discovered offences.

In respect of area differences in reporting patterns, there is therefore a degree of variation which is perhaps unexpected. Nevertheless, the results must be seen in perspective, and it is appropriate at this point to consider the crime data from a later stage in the process, in terms of the detection process.

5 The Detection of Crime

INTRODUCTION

If the discovery and reporting of crime were to vary on an areal dimension, we might have anticipated differences according to the area in
which the offence took place, rather than according to offenders' areas
of residence. That is, the various processes involved might be expected
to influence offence other than offender rates. On the other hand, the
implications of other writings lead us to accept that at the detection
stage we might find differences according to different types of offender,
and clearly in this case the area of residence of offenders may be
important alongside other factors. Therefore the first sections of this
chapter will concentrate on the offender sample, and then at a later
stage data from the offence sample will be used.

As has been stressed throughout chapter four, although members of the
public, through their decisions to call the police, determine to a large
extent the distribution and numbers of offences recorded, this does not
mean that the discovery of offenders is similarly determined. Therefore,
in the same way to that developed in the last chapter, the agent responsible for the detection of the offender, and the 'method' employed, have
been classified using information from the police records. (Table 5.1).
In all, eight different categories were distinguished:

(i) Indirect detection. As might be expected from previous research,
the data was dominated by one detection method, indirect detection; that
is, offences which were cleared up due to routine questioning of offenders who had been caught for other offences. In all 39.6% of all offences
by offenders from the nine areas were cleared up in this way. This is
particularly interesting since it contrasts with the 26.3% of all offences in the offender sample which were reported indirectly. Since no
offenders were originally located due to indirect detection (by definition) these cases will be excluded from all other comparisons in this
chapter.

However before passing on it is interesting to note two distinct
patterns in the indirect detection data, in terms of area of residence of
offender and offence type.

Taking first the offender characteristics, there was a clear and
significant difference in the proportion of offences cleared up individ-
ually according to the offender rate of the area in which the offender
lived. Of known offences committed by residents of the three high rate
areas, 43.8% were cleared up indirectly, compared with 29.5% of offences committed by those from low rate areas ($\chi^2 = 8.02$, P < 0.005). This
difference is especially notable since there were no area differences for
indirect reports from the offender data, nor for either indirect reports
or detections from the offence data. Moreover there was only a slight
indication that offenders from high rate areas committed more offences
that those from low rate areas. It therefore seems as though the police

may be more likely to attempt to 'clear their books' when they are faced
with offenders from disreputable areas, possibly because such offenders
are regarded as 'better bets'. On the other hand there is no indication
that in so doing the police concentrate on clearing up local crime in
this way.

Secondly, however, it is interesting to consider the distribution of
indirect detections between different offence types. Housebreaking
offences were most commonly cleared up by indirect detection, with as
many as 70.4% solved in this way. Other high proportions so cleared up
were thefts of and from cars (56.8%), breakings (other) (49.4%) and fraud
(43.9%), whilst meter thefts (12.5%), violence (5.9%) and sex and damage
offences (each 0%) were uncommonly detected indirectly. This broadly
fits other research which has considered indirect detection.

Moreover, a comparison of indirect detections with indirect reporting
illustrated how police use of TICs (offences taken into consideration) to
clear their books is related to specific crimes. Some offences, like sex
offences, damage, violence and meter thefts, were rarely either reported
or detected indirectly. Others like house breaking, theft of and from
cars, breaking (other) and fraud were likely to be both reported and
detected indirectly.

(ii) <u>Victim cleared offences</u>. In total 16.1% of offences were cleared
up due to the role played by the victim and when indirect detections were
excluded this figure rose to 26.6%. Detections were included in this
category only if the victim appeared to be the sole agent responsible for
detection. Borderline cases were included in the 'unknown' category or,
in some cases, in the police detection category.

Table 5.1
Detection methods for offences committed by
offenders from the nine areas, 1971 standard list files

	Total		Excluding indirect
	n	%	%
Victim	93	16.1	26.6
PLE	56	9.7	16.0
Witness	18	3.1	5.2
Offender	18	3.1	5.2
Obvious	19	3.3	5.4
Police	131	22.7	37.5
Unknown	14	2.4	4.0
Indirect	229	31.6	−
Total	578	100.0	99.9

Offences were usually described as victim detections in two sets of
circumstances. Most commonly, the victim, in reporting the offence to
the police, told them who the offender was, or, particularly in cases of
violence, pointed out the offender to the police when they arrived; in
about a quarter of the cases, the victim caught the offender and 'presented' him to the police at the time of reporting. Many cases of shoplifting fell into this category, but it was not unusual for private
individuals to catch offenders in this way. In one striking case (from
the offence sample) an old lady in area RHL caught a burglar by locking

him in the cellar.

In general though, offences of this kind were cleared up because the victim knew who the offender was. However, in a few cases, the victim, though not personally knowing the offender, was able to give such a precise description of the offender that an early arrest was easy. Examples like this included those where the victim took the car number of the offender as he drove away.

(iii) Offences cleared by Private Law Enforcers. Just as a number of shopliftings were cleared up due to shopkeepers detaining the culprit so a number were due to private law enforcers. In all, 16.0% of all directly detected offences were cleared in this manner. Indeed, nearly all offences (in the offence sample) reported by private law enforcers were cleared up and this was almost entirely due to the offender being caught in the act and detained. The exceptions to this were when an offender was caught but subsequently ran off, when the police were called in as a secondary measure, and where security guards disturbed burglars who escaped.

(iv) Obvious offenders. A similar, but slightly less clear cut, means of detection has been called here 'obvious detection'. What is implied here is that the reporting of the offence automatically defines the offender, although nowhere in the evidence is any formal identification given. The most common of these offences is meter theft by the tenant or occupier, where the theft is discovered by the gas or electricity board. Thus a routine report is made to the police, and it is clear to all parties who the offender is, but no precise details are included on this process.

Although most cases in this category were of meter thefts by residents, another possible inclusion is some cases of fraud, where discovery of the offence itself automatically implicates the offender. Again, it appears that the detection method is similar to victim detection, but the slight difference has precluded this type of categorisation. In all, 5.4% of direct detections, were categorised in this way.

(v) Offender detection. A rather different category is provided for those cases cleared because the offender (perhaps accompanied by some relative) gives himself up. Only a few cases - 5.2% of direct detection - fit this category, but it is distinctly different from other methods and so requires separate analysis.

Detections were defined as due to the offender himself in three sets of circumstances. First, in a few cases, the offender actually gave himself up spontaneously to the police. It seemed the motive here was generally a wish to spend a few nights in the shelter of a cell.

Secondly, and more commonly, the offender was in some cases brought to the police station by a relation. In most cases this involved parents who, discovering petty shoplifting by their children, brought them to the station so that the police could give them a talking to. In one exceptional case a boy (from CHH) was reported by his sister when she saw him put lighted paper through the letter box of a house in the area.

Finally, in the offender sample only, a small number of cases were included in this category where an offender from one of the research

111

areas was identified when a co-offender, not from one of the areas, named him. This was justified on the grounds that the study was concerned with how offenders from specific areas were located, and consequently it seemed most relevant to classify the sample offender's detection pattern, rather than that of his co-offender.

(vi) <u>Witness detection</u>. As with victim detections, witness detections usually occurred in two sets of circumstances. First, when the witness caught an offender in the act, and secondly when he named the offender to the police. In fact of all directly detected offences, 5.2% were witness detected, of which the majority were due to the witness either naming the offender or describing him with such accuracy that no further 'detective work' was necessary.

(vii) <u>Detection by unknown methods</u>. Before considering police detections, it is perhaps useful to briefly refer to those detections where the detection method was not apparent from the files. In some cases this was simply due to the fact that the detailed case material was missing; in others it was because the detection agent was ambiguous. The clearest example of the confusion here comes from a case in the offence sample:

'Mr. A saw a boy taking his bicycle, and although unable to catch him was able to give the police a description. Following enquiries, the police interviewed the suspect at his home and took possession of the stolen bicycle. They then organised an identity parade at the boy's school, at which Mr. A was able to identify the offender.' (RHH).

This case illustrates the combination of factors - a description given by the victim, used by the police to identify a suspect. However, it is particularly interesting because it is exceptional. In most cases, the primary agent in the detection process is easily identifiable.

Other examples where there is some doubt include a number where the descriptive evidence starts at a point where a suspect has been identified. That is, the file statements chronologically <u>began</u> with the interviewing of a suspect. For example, the officer-in-charge might begin his statement with .... 'I had cause to interview X at his home. I said, 'X, I have reason to believe you were involved in ....''

It could be argued that such arrests <u>might</u> be due to police officers using their discretion to interview 'known tearaways'. However, were this the case, it would seem likely, given that the report is an exercise in impression management, that such 'local knowledge' (or use of initiative) would be noted in this report. On the contrary, it seems more likely that these interrogations followed routine questioning of locals (i.e. witnesses) coupled perhaps with a knowledge of which local offenders fitted the description. Nevertheless, given this element of doubt, it seemed most practical to include such cases as 'unknowns'.

(viii) <u>Police detection</u>. This means that, of those crimes detected directly, between 58.5% and 62.5% of offences were cleared up because evidence <u>given to</u> the police led them directly to the offender. This does not mean that the role of the police in such cases is superfluous - clearly the police know how best to elicit such information - for example, which local residents are most likely to have seen something suspicious. This was confirmed in the interviews with the area constables (see chapter three).

However, the important point here is that the vast majority of crimes cleared up in these areas were done so because of knowledge of the situation provided by members of the public. This means, conversely, that the potential for 'police discretion' or more specifically Matza's 'method of suspicion' was operative in no more than 41.5% of offences, and indeed only 37.5% of direct detections were attributed to the police. Before considering the distribution of clear up methods between areas, it may however, in view of Matza's theoretical assertions, be best to consider police detections in more detail, and ask how precisely the police directly cleared up offences. It proved possible to divide police detections into three groups:

(1) <u>Caught in the act</u>. Offenders were defined as caught in the act where the police intervened in a situation which was clearly an offence, and in so doing caught the offender. This included three sets of circumstances. First, the police in some cases saw the offender actually commit the offence, i.e. the offence was discovered and detected by the police simultaneously. Secondly, the police might be called to the scene by a member of the public and on arrival be able to arrest the offender in the act, i.e. the offence was reported by a member of the public, but was ongoing when the police arrived, allowing an arrest to be made on the spot. Thirdly in some cases the police originally discovered the offence and, upon investigation, disturbed the offender.

(a) Police summoned to scene

<u>Case 1</u>. Mr. B, a butcher, heard 'suspicious' noises in the shop next door and phoned the police. They arrived and caught the offender in the act. (CHH & RHH).

(b) Police attracted to scene by evidence of offence, then caught offender.

<u>Case 2</u>. A policeman on patrol found a broken door to a cafe. He went inside and through into an office complex, where he disturbed the offenders. (CHH).

<u>Case 3</u>. A policeman on patrol found a shop window smashed. He went inside and was looking around to see what stock had been taken when he heard a noise outside. He hid, and the offenders climbed back into the shop. He arrested them on the spot, and enquiries revealed that they had originally stolen some goods and had returned for a second haul. (CHH).

(c) Police saw offence take place.

<u>Case 4</u>. The youth was walking down the road quite clearly and openly carrying a pint beer glass. (RHL).

<u>Case 5</u>. The PC watched the offenders try to open three cars and arrested them when they succeeded in gaining entry to a fourth car. (CFH).

<u>Case 6</u>. The offender was seen by the constable in the grounds of the school carrying a claw hammer. (CFH).

<u>Case 7</u>. A policeman on patrol saw the two offenders, who were the worse for drink, take two safety lamps from roadworks on the boundary of RHL. (RHL, OHL).

(2) <u>Policework</u>. In a number of cases, the police cleared up offences due to their expertise, or to the special knowledge or techniques available to them - for example, by the use of tracker dogs, fingerprints, routine checking of the records of scrap metal dealers, and some fraud detections. Also included in this category is the 'detective fiction' favourite, routine interrogation of suspects, i.e. those cases where there are obvious suspects and questioning of these revealed the offender.

Case 1. An anonymous caller reported a break in at a shop on CFH. Police arrived but found no one. However a police dog was brought to the scene and followed the scent to the offender who lived nearby. (CFH).

Case 2. A policeman in Walsall noticed a fairly new car with hand painted number plates. These did not seem to be in keeping with the car, and dated it as rather older than it looked. He stopped the car and found that it had been stolen in Sheffield and the plates changed. (RHL).

Case 3. A policeman on patrol noticed that a parked motor scooter was displaying a licence which appeared to have been altered. He waited and confronted the owner when he returned. He admitted stealing the licence, and subsequently also admitted stealing the scooter. (CHL).

(3) <u>Police discretion</u>. Finally, a number of offences were cleared up in a way which might, using the terminology of Cicourel, Matza, etc., be properly called the use of discretion. In all, three distinct areas in which discretion was utilized might be distinguished. First, when an offence was discovered or reported at night when few people were about and it seemed that it had only recently been committed, the police used their discretion to question pedestrians near the scene of the crime. Secondly, the police might attempt to clear up known crime by routinely questioning people with known records or notorious reputations. Finally, and most commonly, the police might discover offender and offence simultaneously by questioning those whom they defined as acting in a suspicious manner. This categorisation is distinct from 'caught in the act', in which cases the police had clear evidence that an offence had been, or was being, committed.

Because the use of discretion has been emphasised so much in some of the literature, it may be appropriate to cite here a number of examples which have been categorised as such:

Case 1. A PC on patrol in the city centre in the early hours of the morning noticed two boys. They ran off when they saw him, and he followed, when he caught them he searched them and found money which they admitted taking during a burglary. (RHL).

Case 2. The boy was walking down the road rolling a new tyre. The policeman questioned him and he admitted stealing it. (CHL).

Case 3. The offender was seen on waste land near some derelict property throwing a knife. When the policeman approached he ran away. When subsequently caught he admitted stealing the knife <u>some months previously</u>. (CHH).

Case 4. The boy was seen by a policeman near the Cathedral carrying an ornamental sword. He was questioned, but denied stealing it, saying he had bought it. He was allowed to go home, but was subsequently arrested when the Cathedral authorities reported the sword missing. (CHL).

Case 5. The offender was tottering down the road in an obvious state of drunkenness when he was stopped by a policeman, who then noticed he had a beer glass in his coat pocket. This, it was ascertained, had been stolen. (CHM).

Case 6. The offender was questioned when he was seen riding a child's bike late a night. (CFH).

Case 7. 'He was of an untidy and dirty appearance and I went to him and saw something bulky inside of his coat pockets.' Questioning revealed that the offender had stolen ten packets of spearmint from a cafe he had broken into. (CHL).

Case 8. A police constable on duty in the shopping precinct noticed a girl standing nearby who appeared to be wearing two dresses. He questioned her and she admitted stealing one of them. (CFH).

Case 9. The police questioned two youths who were walking down the road. Reason for suspicion - they had in their possession an umbrella in a 'suspiciously new condition'! (CFH).

Case 10. A policeman stopped a group of boys on the perimeter of RHL and questioned them about local crimes. In the course of the conversation one of them admitted that a pen he was carrying had been stolen by another boy. (OHL).

Case 11. 'At 5.35pm on Tuesday 21st September, 1971 M was interviewed at B police station in connection with another matter from which he was eventually eliminated. During that interview it was put to M that information had been received about the theft of metals from the Wincobank and Tinsley area of Sheffield and when cautioned and told that it was believed he may know something about the matter, M replied, 'It's a bit back since I pinched any metal.'' (CHH).

In Table 5.2 the methods used by the police in direct detection have been detailed. As can be seen, 42.7% were the result of the offender being caught in the act, a further 22.9% followed routine policework, and 30.5% in some way involved the use of discretion. Of these well over half were cleared up due to police interrogation of people they defined as acting suspiciously, and only six involved the police directing their attention at suspects with 'reputations'.

In all then, police discretion accounted for a minority of all offences cleared directly by the police. It must, however, be stressed that this does not mean that the police do not regularly attempt to clear up crimes in this way, the point made by Werthman and Piliavin (1967). Police records are unlikely to detail police questioning of suspects which were fruitless, except in those cases where a fairly serious crime was committed and no offender caught and where the officer in charge wished to show his superiors that he had made every effort to make an arrest. The point that is being made, by contrast, is that, even if the police often use the 'method of suspicion' it is not this method which contributes significantly to offender statistics.

This said, it is important to note that there are no grounds for

Table 5.2
Police detection method for police direct detections

	n	%	Total category %
Caught in act			42.7
1. Saw offence first	3	2.3	
2. Saw offender commit offence	32	24.4	
3. After called to crime	21	16.0	
Policework			22.9
1. Tracker dogs	2	1.5	
2. Metal dealer tracing	5	3.8	
3. Fingerprints	4	3.1	
4. Technical	9	6.9	
5. Questioning suspects	10	7.6	
Use of discretion			30.5
1. Persons 'acting suspiciously'	25	19.1	
2. Person with 'reputations'	6	4.6	
3. Against those near scene of crime	9	6.9	
Unknown	5	3.8	3.8
Total	131	100.0	99.9

rejecting the point made by Matza that 'the method of suspicion' might be a lever towards a self fulfilling prophecy that is, that constant police harrassment of known offenders might stimulate crime as a counter response. Even if no statistical link is demonstrated, Matza's rhetoric is no less telling:

'To be stopped, frisked or interrogated for suspicious behaviour is not harrassment and, in the terms suggested here, it falls short of being subjected to methodical suspicion. But what of the suspicious person, a category known to police but not to court or federal commission? Is the juvenile who uttered these words subjected to harrassment?

'Every time something happens in this neighbourhood, them motherfuckin' cops come looking for me! I may not be doing nothing, but if somebody gets beat or something gets stole they always be coming right to my place to find out what's going on.'' (Matza, 1969; 194: see also Parker, 1975).

Examples have already been given of the use of police discretion towards people defined as acting suspiciously, or as being natural suspects. The fact that in many cases such a modus operandi is taken for granted as proper, leading to a refusal to accept protest from the suspect as legitimate, is well illustrated in the following quotation from a sergeant in Sheffield:

'This bloke who was down at the station tonight – he's an example of the lack of co-operation the police are up against. One of our lads was up CFL this afternoon and he saw this lad with a transistor radio, so he went up and asked him where he got it – that's all – just asked him,

116

polite like, and he answers back like he's no right to be asked, and now his father's down there complaining.'

Despite the cases which have been quoted which suggest that the police have, in some cases, no grounds at all for questioning a possible suspect, the number of examples which can be given is small. In only six cases from the offender sample was an arrest made where the basis of police discretion appeared to be the prior criminal history of the suspect. Instead, the primary definition of 'acting suspiciously' was commonly based on two sets of circumstances:

(i) An incongruous situation: where someone was not acting according to status, or where he was in a place at a time when he should be elsewhere (e.g. boys out at night; youth lying alone in grass at 9.0 pm).

(ii) Driving cases: car drivers are open to police discretionary questioning for at least three reasons. First, the law allows the police opportunity to stop cars on routine matters, e.g. breathalyser and tyre check, and then ask more searching questions. Secondly, the police have the facilities to check with headquarters about stolen cars, or, in the case of recently licensed cars, are able to check up on ownership details. Finally the police are able to make certain inferences from the performance of a car. Thus a car being driven by a 'novice' is easily detected and some arrests follow routine questioning of drivers handling their vehicles strangely.

Although the numbers are small, a breakdown by offence type demonstrates the point adequately. While 55.1% of breaking offences directly detected by the police were due to the offender being caught in the act (most being cases where the police were called to the crime), 59.1% of police direct detection of and from cars were due to use of discretion, particularly against persons acting suspiciously. Looked at another way, 32.5% of clear ups due to discretion were thefts of and from cars.

This discussion of the detection process appears to confirm the findings of chapter four, namely that the role of the police is less significant than many have supposed. Indeed, the records at times appear to echo the comments made by the police in the interviews described in chapter three, in focusing attention once more on the role of the public as informants.

The data thus seem to undermine labelling theory, in so far as this implies that police activity is a <u>direct</u> cause of different crime patterns. In the following section the analysis will be continued with differences in detection methods considered according to the different areas within which offenders lived, and according to offence and victim characteristics.

VARIATIONS IN DETECTION METHODS: THE OFFENDER SAMPLE

It is crucial to a labelling perspective that different types of offender - whether measured by social class or area of residence - have different chances of being caught, and that one reason for this is the operation of the 'method of suspicion' whereby police knowledge of possible suspects allows and encourages them to lean on the underprivileged or those with dubious reputations.

It has already been shown that although police knowledge of high offender rate areas varies considerably, most policemen would pick out CHH
and RHH as districts with a reputation, and as one sergeant put it, speaking of CFH, 'You university people, to try to tell us why people like
that commit crime, we know why, it's because they're all scrubbers up
there'. (Field notes).

From this, it might be hypothesised that police detections would be
proportionally more frequent in the high offender rate area samples than
among offenders from other areas. Detection methods in each of the areas
have been distinguished in an attempt to test this theory. However,
although there was variation between areas, there was no consistent, or
appreciable trend. For example, excluding OHL, where the numbers were
small, the highest proportions of police detections were for offenders
from CHL, CHH and RHL respectively, the lowest for CFL and R'HL. Similarly, comparing the three high offender rate areas with the five low rate
areas revealed approximately the same proportion of police detections in
each (37.2% and 38.8% respectively).

On the other hand, detection methods varied according to the place of
the offence (Table 5.3). The police detected only 26.3% of offences in
the offender's own area which were detected directly compared with 27.5%
in the city centre and 52.3% elsewhere. In fact there is a significant
difference in police detections between 'own area' and 'elsewhere'
(χ^2_1 = 16.08, P < 0.001), and 'city centre' and 'elsewhere' (χ^2_1 = 15.87,
P < 0.001), but not between 'own area' and 'city centre'. However, this
is almost entirely due to the prevalence of shoplifting among crimes
cleared up which were committed in the city centre. Thus, private law
enforcers accounted for 39.4% of detections in the city centre, but only
4.2% in 'own area' and 6.2% 'elsewhere'; of all other crimes cleared up
in the city centre some half were due to police detections i.e. about
the same proportion as 'elsewhere').

Table 5.3
Detection methods for offences committed
by offenders from the Nine Areas, according to area of offence

Offence	Own area	City centre	Elsewhere
Victim	33.7	20.2	26.9
PLE	4.2	39.4	6.2
Witness	6.3	3.7	5.5
Offender	6.3	3.7	5.5
Obvious	18.9	0.9	0
Police	26.3	27.5	52.4
Unknown	4.2	4.6	3.4
Total	99.9	100.0	99.9
n	95	109	145

The counter influence of shoplifting is once again demonstrated in
Table 5.4 where detection methods are compared according to victim type.
Overall, the police contribution is similar for corporate and individual
victims - however, if shoplifting is excluded the police detection
contribution to offences against corporate victims rises to 57.1% which
is significantly higher than for offences against individuals (χ^2_1 =

7.86, P < 0.01).

This pattern is clearly illustrated when offence types are distinguished. Whilst the police were rarely responsible for direct detections of
shoplifting, meter thefts, and sex offences, they were over represented
in the detection of thefts of and from cars, thefts (other) and breaking
(other).

Table 5.4
Detection methods for offences committed
by offenders from the Nine Areas, according to victim type

	Individual	Corporate	
		Total	Excl. shoplifting
Victim	37.8	18.4	10.6
PLE	4.1	24.9	0.9
Witness	5.4	5.0	8.0
Offender	5.4	5.0	5.3
Obvious	2.7	7.5	13.3
Police	39.2	36.3	56.7
Unknown	5.4	3.0	5.3
Total	100.0	100.1	100.1
n	148	201	113

The results so far seem to indicate that police detections vary more
according to offence characteristics than according to differences related to offenders' residence. However, even if the lack of any
correlation here is accepted, it could still be argued that there are
offender variables which are important, but that residence is not one of
them. In order to test this possibility, detection data was reanalysed
on an individual basis, for males only (given the small number of
females and specialist nature of their offences). That is, each time a
male from one of the areas was caught directly for an offence during
1971, the detection method was coded.

Overall this gives us a slightly different picture to the one already
developed, which is based on how offences were cleared up. It has the
advantage that indirect detections are omitted, by definition. On the
other hand, the offender detection category is increased drastically,
since the number of offenders arrested because they were 'shopped' by
co-offenders is clearly greater than the number of offences cleared up
due to the offender himself. This apart, the chief differences are an
increase in the importance of police detections and a decrease in victim
and private law enforcer detections (Table 5.5).

Within the overall picture, however, we might expect to find certain
differences according to the characteristics of different offenders. In
particular, three variables can be tested, namely the record of each
offender, the age of each offender, and the number of offenders involved
in the offence for which the offender was caught. Each of these variables has been considered separately and the results are included in
Tables 5.6 - 5.8.

Table 5.5
Detection method by which each male offender
from the Nine Areas was caught directly

	n	%
Victim	68	21.9
PLE	23	7.4
Witness	19	6.1
Offender	37	11.9
Obvious	16	5.2
Police	134	43.2
Unknown	13	4.2
Total	310	99.9

Table 5.6
Detection method for each male offender, according to age

	Under 17	17 - 20	21 and over
Victim	15.4	14.0	31.5
PLE	8.9	5.3	6.9
Witness	9.8	3.5	3.8
Offender	22.0	8.8	3.8
Obvious	0.8	5.3	9.2
Police	36.6	57.9	43.1
Unknown	6.5	5.3	1.5
Total	100.0	100.1	99.8
n	123	57	130

Table 5.7
Detection method for each male offender,
according to offender's record

	First offender	Recidivist
Victim	27.3	18.5
PLE	8.3	6.9
Witness	5.0	6.9
Offender	13.2	11.1
Obvious	4.1	5.8
Police	38.8	46.0
Unknown	3.3	4.8
Total	100.0	100.0
n	121	189

Table 5.8
Detection method for each male offender,
according to number of offenders involved

	Alone	Group
Victim	34.2	11.0
PLE	6.2	8.5
Witness	5.5	6.7
Offender	2.8	20.2
Obvious	8.9	1.8
Police	37.7	48.2
Unknown	4.8	3.7
Total	100.1	100.1
n	146	164

A glance at the tables suggests that there are some notable differences
in detection methods according to these variables. To test each one, a
chi - squared test was used comparing police, victim, offender and other
detections, although this was supplemented by additional tests for certain items where the numbers made a larger test impracticable. Taking
each Table separately, it appeared that:

(i) Age of offender was significantly related to detection method
(χ^2_6 = 32.76, P < 0.001). In particular victim detections were most
common within the 21+ age group, police detections within the 17-20 age
group, and offender detections within the under 17 age group. Offender
detections were most unlikely for the 21+ age group. In addition,
comparing witness detections with the rest, these were more common for
offenders aged under 17 than for older offenders (χ^2_1 = 5.76, P < 0.02).

(ii) Offender's record was not significantly related to detection
method (χ^2_3 = 4.24, P > 0.20). Police detections were slightly more
common for recidivists, but the difference was insignificant, even when
police detections were compared with all other detections grouped
together.

(iii) The number of offenders was significantly related to the detection method (χ^2_3 = 41.28, P < 0.001), although this was partly due to the
inevitable link between offender detections and group offences. However
when offender detections were excluded, the difference remained significant (χ^2_2 = 19.02, P < 0.001) with victims over-represented for
detection of lone offenders, the police for group offenders.

The relationship between victim detections and age and number of offenders is not surprising, given that victim detections are more likely where
the offender is known to the victim, for example where the offence develops from a continuing relationship. On the other hand the over-representation of witness detections for young offenders suggests that witnesses
may be more willing to co-operate with the police where the offender is
young, perhaps because they are less fearful of retaliation, perhaps
because they see young offenders as particularly in need of care or
control. The distribution of offender detections is also notable since
it reveals a low degree of 'grassing' among older offenders, but in

contrast implies the ease with which the police are able to persuade young offenders to inform on co-offenders. (The difference is magnified due to young offenders being more likely to be involved in group offences, but even considering only group offences the difference is significant.)

However, perhaps the most interesting differences surround the police detection category. On the one hand, there is no evidence that "known offenders" (in this case as measured by recidivism) are more likely to be caught due to police detection methods. On the other hand, the police are more likely to directly detect offences committed by groups of offenders and offenders aged 17-21.

One qualification must, nevertheless, be added here. The difference in police detections according to the number of offenders is entirely due to instances where the police catch offenders in the act having been summoned to the scene by a member of the public. If these cases are excluded, police detections fall to 32.2% for lone offenders, and 36.6% for group offenders. It therefore seems that the role of the public is more likely to be at the reporting and detection stage for individual offenders, but where more than one offender is involved the public are more likely to call the police but not intervene personally. On the other hand, if police detections following a citizen report are excluded, the age difference remains. For the under 17 age group other police detections accounted for 25.2% of direct detections, for the 21 or more group 33.8%, but for the 17-21 age group a staggering 56.1% (χ_2^2 = 17.02, P < 0.001). Although this difference may in part be due to the types of offence committed by offenders of different ages, it also seems probable that police interventions are more common for the 17-20 age group, which according to other research might be seen by the police to provoke the greatest threat to law and order.

This individual analysis thus provides some evidence of differential policing as far as offenders of different ages are concerned, but no difference according to record or, to some extent, the number of offenders involved. Remembering that from the offence-based analysis residence did not appear to discriminate between detection methods, there is therefore little evidence to support earlier theories of policework. It is, however, appropriate at this stage to return to the offence-based data and consider the sample of offences committed in the nine areas.

VARIATIONS IN DETECTION METHODS: THE OFFENCE SAMPLE

As is evident from Table 5.9, the detection methods operative for the offence sample varied somewhat from those for the offender sample. Although the proportion of indirect detections is similar at 40.1%, excluding these the proportions of police (29.8%) and private law-enforcer (9.4%) detections are lower and the proportions of witness (8.3%) and obvious (13.8%) detections are higher than for the offender sample. However, given the distinctions found for the offender sample according to place of offence and offence type, none of these differences are unexpected.

In addition, a comparison of detection methods according to victim and offence types reveals a similar set of findings to those discussed earlier. First, taking victim types, it seems, from table 5.10, that police detections are most common for crimes against corporate victims (excluding shoplifting) and least common for crimes against individual victims (who are residents of these areas), although these differences are only slight and not statistically significant.

Table 5.9
Detection methods for offences committed in the
nine areas, 1971 standard list offence files

	Total		Excluding indirect reporting
	n	%	%
Victim	51	16.9	28.2
PLE	17	5.6	9.4
Witness	15	5.0	8.3
Offender	7	2.3	3.9
Obvious	25	8.3	13.8
Police	54	17.9	29.8
Unknown	12	4.0	6.6
Indirect	121	40.1	-
Total	302	100.1	100.0

Table 5.10
Detection methods for offences committed in the
nine areas, according to victim type

	Individual Victim		Corporate Victim	
	Resident	Nonresident	All	Excluding Shoplifting
Victim	43.4	38.5	17.6	12.3
PLE	0	0	16.7	5.5
Witness	5.7	15.4	7.8	6.8
Offender	3.8	0	4.9	2.7
Obvious	9.4	3.8	18.6	26.0
Police	28.3	34.6	29.4	39.7
Unknown	9.4	7.7	4.9	6.8
Total	100.0	100.0	99.9	99.8
n	53	26	102	73

Secondly, it seems that detection methods vary according to offence type, with differences generally the same as for the offender sample. For example, offences most likely to be police detections were thefts of and from cars, thefts (other), housebreaking and breakings (other); at the other extreme sex, violence, shoplifting and meter thefts were rarely detected by the police themselves.

What then of differences in detection methods between areas with differing offender or offence rates? Although some differences are caused by the prevalence of particular reported offences in some areas − for example meter thefts in CHH and shoplifting in CHL, these apart the data show surprisingly little variation. Particularly interesting is the lack of any significant differences in police detections between areas, either comparing high with low offender rate areas, or by matching

123

areas. For example, for the three high offender rate areas, 28.4% of direct detections were police detections, compared with 31.2% for the other areas. This finding substantiates that mentioned in the previous section, when a lack of offender based police detection differences was commented on.

However, even if the police directly clear up no more crime in high than in low offender rate areas, it might still be argued that the ways in which they discover offenders vary between areas. Thus, it might be hypothesised that the police more often use their discretion in clearing up offences in high rate areas. In table 5.11 the different methods employed by the police have been distinguished for high and other offender rate areas separately. It is immediately apparent that whilst detections due to policework are similar in the different areas, the police are more likely to catch offenders in the act in high rate areas, and more likely to clear up the offence by discretion in other areas. Moreover, when these two methods are compared, the difference is significant (χ^2 = 3.99, P < 0.05) despite the small numbers involved.

Table 5.11
Police detection method according to offender rate
of area where offence committed

	High offender rate	Other
Caught in act	48	27.6
Use of discretion	20	44.8
Policework	24	20.7
Unknown	8	6.9
Total	100	100.0
n	25	29

This finding is fascinating, since it appears to contradict all the assumptions made by contemporary deviancy theorists. However, it is possible, following the argument presented in the previous section, to account for this variation.

It has been suggested that discretion is often used by the police because they define a situation as incongruous. In an area with a low offender rate it is therefore possible that "suspicious incidents" might stand out more than in areas with high offender rates, where they are more likely to be defined as normal. This would fit Bittner's description of the slum as an area where much marginal deviance goes unchallenged by the police because they assume such behaviour to be normal in these areas. (Bittner, 1967)

On the other hand, it is possible that the police might respond to citizen complaints more quickly when these come from high offender rate areas than when they come from low offender rate areas, thereby catching more offenders in the act in the former. Another possibility is that complainants in high rate areas call the police at an earlier stage than those in low rate areas.

Clearly the evidence available is not sufficient to resolve the issue. Nevertheless, once again the findings do not fit the pattern that had

originally been expected. It thus appears that whether we consider
offence or offender data, all reported offences, all detected offences,
or only police detections, there is no evidence to suggest (let alone
demonstrate) that police involvement in any way creates differences in
crime rates between different residential areas.

THE CLEARING UP OF INDICTABLE CRIME

In chapter two, overall detection rates were considered for crime in
each area, and, in line with the above findings, there appeared to be no
clear pattern which distinguished some types of residential areas from
others. The offence data, however, allows this analysis of detection
rates to be taken further, since it is possible to compare detection
rates according to different reporting agents, and to contrast detection
rates and methods for different types of crime.

If the relationship between reporting agents and detection rates is
considered, a clear pattern can be distinguished (see table 5.12).
Although 81.7% of all offences in the areas were reported by the victim,
less than seventy per cent of all solved offences were so reported.
Similarly, although the police only discovered 5.8% of offences recorded,
they had discovered about ten per cent of all offences which were cleared
up directly.

To put the data another way; of all crime reported by the victim, only
33.1% was solved, compared with 57.1% of witness reported incidents,
60.0% of alarm calls, 72.2% of police discoveries and 94.7% of reports
by private law-enforcement agents.

Table 5.12
Reporting method according to whether or
not crime cleared up (and by offender)

	Solved	Unsolved	Solved	Unsolved	Total%	Total
Victim	69.2	91.1	33.1	66.9	100	504
PLE	7.5	0.3	94.7	5.3	100	19
Witness	10.0	4.9	57.1	42.9	100	42
Alarm	2.5	1.1	60.0	40.0	100	10
Police	10.8	2.7	72.2	27.8	100	36
Total %	99.9	100.1	-	-	-	-
Total	241	370	39.4	60.6	100	611

To a large extent differences between non-police reporting agents
depends on their commitment to report. Whereas victims are likely to
report crime which is "cold", witnesses are more likely to report crime
which is ongoing, or where the offender is known, and private law-
enforcers and store detectives in particular, are unlikely to report
crime unless an offender has been detained. On the other hand, the high
proportion of offences discovered by the police which are cleared up is
clearly related to the fact that they are more likely to discover crime
which is ongoing.

In table 5.13, the detection rates for each offence types are considered. It can be seen that whilst in the sample as a whole the detection rate was 45.2%, variation between offence types was large. As might be expected, high rates were recorded for meter thefts, and shoplifting and low rates for property offences like thefts of and from cars, house-breakings and malicious damage. This broadly agrees with national statistics and the pilot survey conducted by Bottomley and Coleman (1976) although categorisation in the present research allows for more meaningful distinctions. (See also Baldwin, 1972)

Table 5.13
Detection rate for each offence type

		% Detected
Theft	Cars	28.1
	Shops	95.1
	Meters	100
	Others	41.0
Breaking	Houses	25.7
	Other	39.9
Other	Fraud	76.5
	Violence	86.7
	Sex	61.5
	Damage	17.6
Total		45.2

Why are there these differences? One possible link is that those offence types where clear-up rates are high are likely to include a high proportion cleared up directly, whilst those where clear-up rates are low are more likely to be cleared up indirectly. This would appear to be the case. When damage offences, of which only three were detected, are excluded, the correlation between the two ranked columns (for detection rate and percentage of detections which were indirect) is -0.78 using a Spearman correlation (P<0.05); i.e. those offences least likely to be cleared up are most likely to be detected indirectly.

Although this relationship is plausible, it is unlikely to be the only factor. For example, shopliftings tended to be almost always cleared up, and only 25.6% of shopliftings were cleared up indirectly. Yet it is probable that the proportion of shoplifters escaping arrest is relative-ly high compared with other offences. It may thus be that the police, in attempting to clear up offences on their books, are most likely to question offenders about certain types of offences and ignore others they consider less serious. Sex offences for example (which in this sample are mostly under age intercourse, would be unlikely to be cleared up indirectly, because the possibility that the offender had committed some would be of little interest to the police unless the offence in question was serious.

The relationship is perhaps best illustrated if we consider three elements - the detection rate, reporting agent and detection method. Here a twofold pattern emerges:

(i) A number of offence types have a high detection rate but low police involvement in the discovery and detection stages. That is, offences are frequently only reported to the police where an offender is known, e.g. shopliftings, meter thefts, fraud, violence and sex offences. In each case (except fraud) the percentage of indirect detections is low.

(ii) Alternatively some offences have low detection rates but high rates for police discovery, police detections and indirect detections, e.g. thefts of and from cars, breaking (other).

The implications from this pattern suggest that the distinctions be-tween the reporting and detection process may be less clear cut than has been assumed, although this is to some extent due to the exclusion of offence types which follow a rather different process. For example, housebreakings are infrequently discovered by the police, have a low detection rate, but have high rates for indirect detections and police detections.

The relationship is clarified somewhat if we consider, briefly, the relationship (for detected offences) between the reporting agent and the detection method, and figures 5.1 and 5.2 express this for the offence and offender samples separately, with regard to three reporting agents (police, victims and witnesses).

Figure 5.1
Relationship between reporting agents and detection methods
(excluding unknown detections)

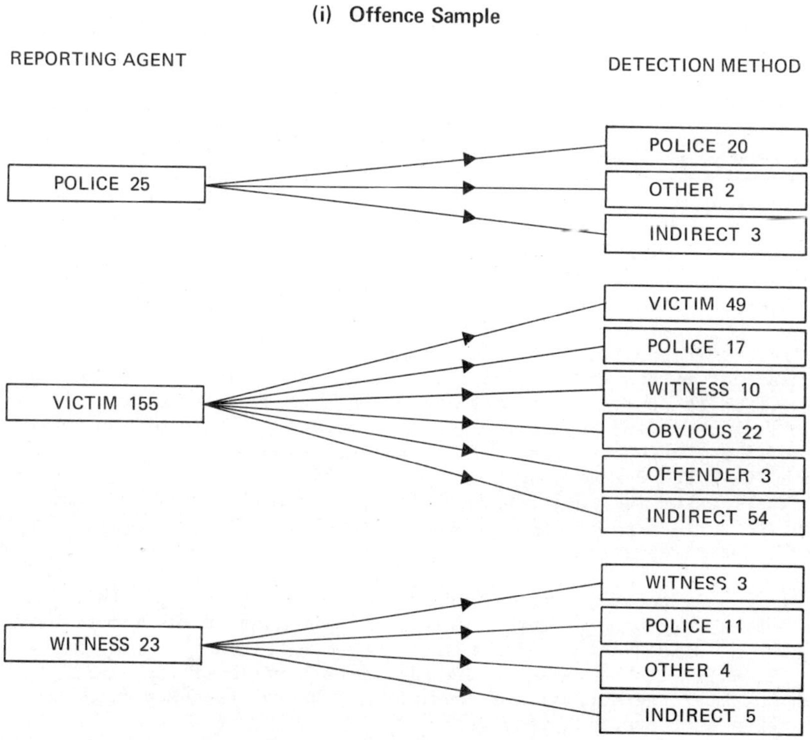

(i) Offence Sample

REPORTING AGENT   DETECTION METHOD

POLICE 25	→	POLICE 20
	→	OTHER 2
	→	INDIRECT 3

VICTIM 155	→	VICTIM 49
	→	POLICE 17
	→	WITNESS 10
	→	OBVIOUS 22
	→	OFFENDER 3
	→	INDIRECT 54

WITNESS 23	→	WITNESS 3
	→	POLICE 11
	→	OTHER 4
	→	INDIRECT 5

127

Figure 5.2
Relationship between reporting agents and detection methods
(excluding unknown detections)

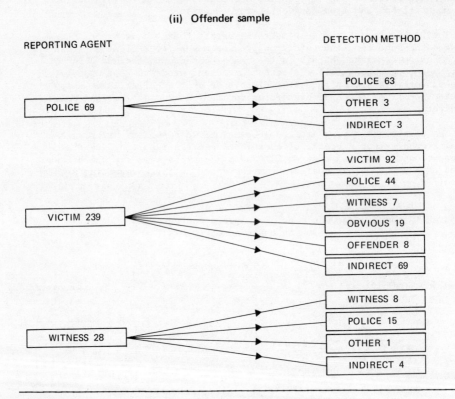

(ii) Offender sample

REPORTING AGENT · DETECTION METHOD

Because police records contained details of the time of arrest of each offender, rather than the time the offender was identified, it was not possible to demonstrate the time element conclusively. Nevertheless, it seemed that in the majority of directly detected cases, the offender was identified at approximately the same time that the offence was discovered. That is, although unfortunately no record was made of the detecting agent (i.e. whether a member of the detective or uniformed branch) it seemed that the detection process was rarely distinct from the reporting process (except for indirect detections). Thus in cases where the detection agent was a member of the public, in almost all cases this person was also the reporting agent.

This is, of course, typified in the example of the shoplifter. Where the police were brought into a case of shoplifting it was almost always a "cut and dried" situation - the police were "presented" with an offender. However, if the three numerically important reporting agents (other than the store detective) are considered, the relationship between reporting and detection is clear.

(i) <u>Police reporting</u>: Almost all police reportings which were directly cleared up were cleared up by the police and all but two were cleared up at the time of discovery of offence.

(ii) <u>Victim reporting</u>: A much lower proportion of victim reports were cleared up; however for both offender and offence sample the victim was the most common detecting agent for direct detections.

(iii) <u>Witness reporting</u>: Although some witness reportings were detected due to the witness catching, or naming, the offender, most detections were due to the police responding quickly to the call and thus catching the offender in the act.

In fact, of these three examples, the detection of offences reported by victims stand out as involving the majority of instances where the reporting and detection process were distinct. Here the police role in detecting "cold" cases (where these were cleared up) was not inconsiderable, whilst a high proportion of victim reportings which led to a detection were detected indirectly.

Consideration of the roles of various agencies in the discovery of crime, and the alternative means by which crimes were cleared up undermines much current academic thinking about policework. In the light of these findings it is therefore necessary to review the material collected on areal variations, specifically in terms of their effects on recorded crime <u>vis-à-vis</u> the nine areas.

SUMMARY: POLICEWORK AND RECORDED CRIME

In the previous sections, one of the basic assumptions of the research – the distinction between reporting and detection – was questioned. In summarising the major findings of this chapter and the last, it is perhaps pertinent to question the other major assumption, the distinction between offender and offence data.

A distinction has already been made for the offender sample according to whether reporting agents varied where the offence was committed locally. There it seemed that offences committed locally were less likely to be discovered directly by the police than were offences committed elsewhere. This parallels the finding that police proactivity was greater in the offender sample than the offence sample.

It is however possible to compare offence and offender data in another way, by considering whether offenders who committed their offences locally had them discovered, or detected, any differently from other offences committed in the nine areas. This is an important issue, given that many offences are cleared up due to victim or witness naming of the offender. On the other hand since definitions of a suspicious situation might vary according to whether the "suspect" is known or not, this may affect the distribution of reporting.

In tables 5.14 and 5.15 the offence data has been reconsidered according to whether or not it was attributed to a local offender. As can be seen, there appeared to be some differences in reporting and detection agents.

Table 5.14
The reporting of offences in the nine areas (excluding
indirect reporting) according to residence of offender

	Offender a resident	Offender a non-resident	Offender unknown
Victim	76	59.0	91.1
PLE	3.2	11.5	0.3
Witness	8.8	10.7	4.9
Offender	4.8	0	0
Alarm	0.8	4.1	1.0
Police	6.4	14.8	2.7
Total %	100.2	100.1	100.0
Total	125	122	370

Considering first the reporting of offences (table 5.14); it appears
that victims are more likely to be the reporting agents in the cases of
local offenders than nonlocal offenders, although this is largely compensated for by the opposite tendency in the case of reports by private law-
enforcers. On the other hand, there is a relatively large, and significant ($\chi^2 = 4.65$, $P<0.05$) difference in police discoveries, with the
police more likely to discover offences by non-residents than residents.
It would appear that, rather than the local police being more aware of
offences by residents (i.e. who may be known to them by reputation), if
anything, they are more likely to discover offences by non-residents.
This may be due to the types of offence committed by the different
categories, i.e. residents are more likely to commit "more private"
offences, but it may also relate to an aspect of policework discussed
earlier, namely the training of the police which is focussed on incon-
gruence. That is, the police may be more likely to discover offences by
non-residents because such offenders are rather conspicuously "on foreign
soil".

This suggestion is given some support by the findings from detection
data (table 5.15), where police detections are rather more common where
the offender is a non-resident. However, here the most notable difference
is for victim detections, with a higher proportion for "local offender"
offences.

Table 5.15
The detection of offences (excluding indirect detections)
in the nine areas, according to residence of offender

	Offender a resident	Offender a non-resident
Victim	33.7	22.1
PLE	4.2	15.1
Witness	6.3	10.5
Offender	6.3	1.2
Obvious	18.9	8.1
Police	26.3	33.7
Unknown	4.2	9.3
Total %	97.9	100.0
Total	95	86

This finding adds one further contradiction to the amplification theorists (Armstrong and Wilson, 1973). It has already been stressed that police saturation of problem areas will not necessarily "produce" higher offender rates for these areas, because crime there is commonly committed by non-residents. From this evidence it would appear, moreover, that the police are less likely to be instrumental in catching offenders in residential areas when the offender is a local resident. Instead, as one might suspect, the victim is more likely to be the detecting agent, since he is more likely to recognise a local offender.

The finding that witnesses and private law enforcers are less likely to detect local offenders is harder to explain. One might have expected witnesses to be more instrumental where the offender is local, just as is the victim. It is possible, on the other hand, that witnesses, with no personal involvement, may be more reluctant to supply information if the offender is a local, so as not to create animosity. Given the small numbers involved, this is, however, speculative.

The over involvement of store detectives in reporting offenders who are non-residents may be seen as a deliberate policy, with local, regular customers being informally cautioned. Alternatively, it is equally possible that shoplifting from supermarkets and stores is not a local activity, and that, just as many offenders go to the city centre to shoplift, so others go to out-of-town stores in an area some distance from where they live.

Overall, though, it is clear that police involvement in the discovery and detection of offences does not increase in the residential areas for offences committed by residents of those areas. Correspondingly, there is no evidence that police detection methods are such as to create or even magnify differences in offender rates between areas. To illustrate this point, in table 5.16 each offence committed by an offender living in the nine areas which was cleared up directly (excluding "unknowns") has been included and incorporated into the table, such that alternative "offender rates" may be compared, according to whether the detection is attributed to the police or another agency.

Table 5.16
"Offender rates" per 1000 population in the nine areas,
according to whether offences detected by police or other agents

	CHH	CHM	CHL	CFH	CFL	RHH	RHL	R'HL	OHL
Police	41.8	16.5	14.9	26.0	4.0	49.2	12.7	6.1	3.4
Rest	66.4	26.1	17.4	43.0	13.1	84.6	17.6	15.8	1.7

As is immediately obvious, the offender rates in the two columns are relatively similar (more so than for offence rate comparisons). Using a Spearman rank correlation, the relationship is highly significant ($r = 0.98$, $P < 0.001$).

This appears to confirm that there are differences in the offender and offence rates of the nine residential areas which cannot be explained as due to differential policing policies. The analysis of detection methods in this chapter has revealed differences according to offence type, victim type, and area of offence (comparing offences within the nine areas with elsewhere). On the other hand, when a number of individual offender variables were considered, most (including area of residence) appeared unrelated to detection method. The only exception here, notably, was for police detections to be most common for the 17-20 age group.

However, overall, the results of this and the last chapter have focused attention on offence and victim characteristics. It is therefore relevant at this stage to consider other types of crime data in more detail.

6 The Police Involvement with Marginal Crime

In the last two chapters, the relatively small part played by the police in the discovery of standard list offences, and the not insubstantial part played by other agents in the detection of known crimes, have been stressed. At the same time, two findings have immediate implications for this chapter - that police involvement varies according to the publicness of the crime and the status of the victim, and that a distinction frequently has to be drawn between the discovery and detection processes.

If we reconsider for one moment the types of marginal crime included in this research, the importance of these two points becomes clearer. Taking nonindictable offences, a distinction was made in chapter 2 between soliciting, other public order offences, vandalism, technical (drinking) and technical (other) offences. Although offence and offender data were collected vis-à-vis each area, police recording processes restrict offence data to those cases where the offence is cleared up. However, with the exception of vandalism, all the categories mentioned largely cover offences which are victimless in a strict sense of the word. Partly because of this the reporting or discovery of the offence directly implies the identification of an offender.

Turning to data which the police recorded as minor incidents of a noncriminal nature, it is evident in contrast that we are dealing with offences which by definition have been reported by a member of the public. However while at the one extreme disputes involve an identified "offender" and "victim" (even if it is unclear which is which) nuisance calls invariably result in the police reporting that the "offender" is no longer present.

In none of these cases, then, is it at all practicable to distinguish between discovery and detection. However, it might appear on the surface that whereas incident sheet data are dependent upon a victim or witness reporting the incident, nonindictable crime data are the pre-ogative of the police. This latter assumption will be questioned in the next section.

THE DISCOVERY AND REPORTING OF NONINDICTABLE CRIME

The number of vandalism incidents recorded was too small to analyse. However in table 6.1 the proportion of known incidents other than vandalism which were police discoveries has been considered for both offence and offender data.

What emerges from table 6.1 is a clear pattern, with soliciting and technical (drinking) offences always discovered by the police, and public order and technical (other) offences commonly discovered by both police and public.

Table 6.1
Nonindictable crime, 1971; percentage of known
cases which were direct police discoveries

	Offence Data		Offender Data	
	%	n	%	n
Public order offences	48.3	29	67.3	98
Soliciting	100	48	100	25
Technical (drinking)	100	32	100	83
Technical (other)	22.2	9	64.3	28

Data on arrests for soliciting (for the whole of Sheffield) will be
considered in more detail in chapter seven. Before that, however, it
is perhaps useful to refer briefly here to the role of the police in
the discovery of soliciting, and also technical (drinking) offences.

Soliciting is dealt with by each subdivision, as opposed to a central
department, and officers are seconded from normal duty, rather than
employed constantly in this work. However these "uniformed officers on
plain clothes duty" as they are called, seem to be regularly employed
in the work, patrolling in pairs under one or two sergeants. Technical
drinking offence patrols also tended to be handled on a district level,
but with less permanent organisation. Some offences, particularly
lunchtime after-hours drinking, were discovered by individual patrolling
officers. However most, including all under age drinking, was discovered by patrols (usually a sergeant and one or two constables) specifically assigned to the duty of checking public houses for possible
offences.

The role of this type of patrol, unlike drugs and soliciting, policing
has received no attention from criminologists, probably because the
offences discovered have been considered so petty that they were not
worth bothering about. However, in the present context it is relevant
to pose two questions, which, unfortunately, a statistical analysis of
arrest data cannot answer. First, do officers, or duty inspectors, use
their discretion over which public houses are "problems" to look for
offences there, and in so doing create differences between areas?
Second, how do officers looking for under age drinking decide which
drinkers to question? In relation to this second point, it is interesting to note that a high proportion of those charged with under age
drinking were girls. It could be that this is an offence commonly
committed by girls. On the other hand, two alternatives are that
(1) Girls who drink in pubs while under age tend to do so at a particular type of pub, or a particular occasion – at discotheques for
example, and these happen to be the ones the police are most likely to
check. Conversely, boys drinking in pubs while under age may frequent
their "local" which is relatively free from police patrols. (2) Police
on these patrols may consider themselves in the roles of "moral entre-
preneurs" and feel it more important that they concentrate on girls
rather than boys, on the grounds that under age drinking by girls is
likely to be a sympto of or lead to a wider deviant life style.

As can be seen if we refer back to the offence data in chapter two,
the position of CHH stands out, with police discoveries predominating in

that area. Turning to the offender data, clearly the extent to which police discretion may influence the resulting statistics is of direct relevance to the CHH offence rate.

With the exception of this one area, almost all the technical (drinking) offences were discovered by checks on city centre public houses. This in itself may "create" lower offence rates in some areas than in others, and, in so doing, also affect offender rates. Thus the offender rate for area CHH was high, while that for area CFH was fairly high, perhaps due to its proximity to the city centre. However, despite this, it seems that differences are not merely due to police patrolling policies - offenders from CHH were also frequently discovered in city centre pubs, whilst area CFL, although nearer to the city than CFH, had a lower offender rate.

Notable here is the low rate in area RHH. In part this may be due to the age structure of the population there. In addition, though, it is possible that much West Indian drinking in that area is at illegal drinking parties and clubs, and since police access here is difficult this may lead to an underestimation of technical (drinking) offences in the area and by residents.

Although differences in the deployment of police pub patrols is unlikely to affect substantially the proportions of offenders from the different areas, it is possible that choice of whom to arrest or whom to question may do. No evidence of this is available but, with the exception of area CHH it appears from the statistics that differences in offender rates are no more, perhaps less than for many offences. It therefore seems unlikely that any selectivity works towards creating differences.

Police proactivity seems to account for all arrests for soliciting and technical (drinking), put what of the role of the police vis-à-vis other nonindictable offences? Clearly a higher proportion of discoveries were police initiated than for standard list offences, but given the publicness and victimlessness of most of the incidents, the importance of proactivity might have been anticipated to be greater than appears in table 6.1.

However, there is a sense in which many of these crimes do involve a "victim" in the subjective sense. That is, particularly with sex offences - soliciting, exhibitionism - and other public order offences - urinating in the street, drunken and disorderly behaviour - it is possible that members of the public might be outraged or upset by the behaviour, and may consider themselves to have been victimised. This may in some cases have the effect that they call in the police.

This possibility is supported by a further feature of table 6.1. Comparing offence and offender data it seems that for both public order offences ($\chi^2 = 3.55$, $0.1 > P > 0.05$) and technical (other) offences ($\chi^2 = 3.41$, $0.1 > P > 0.05$) the police are somewhat less likely to discover offences from the offence sample. Moreover, combining the two categories, the difference is significant ($\chi^2 = 7.42$, $P < 0.01$), a notable fact considering the small numbers and the possibility of overlap.

To some extent this reflects the fact that the police presence is greater in the city centre than in residential areas, consequently leading them to discover more offences. As has already been noted, patrolling in residential areas is fairly constant; the number of foot beat patrols in the city centre is in excess of this, particularly at weekends. These officers were thus in an advantageous position regarding the arrest of, for example, drunks. In addition at weekends the city centre is policed by an extra agency, a police van with about a dozen officers, who ride around the night clubs and bars ready to deal with trouble at closing time. The numbers allow officers to be dispersed to different trouble spots where necessary, whilst the van used is large enough to "accommodate" about a dozen offenders. As a result, the police do not have to be selective in arresting troublesome drunks, but can handle almost any number.

In addition to this, though, it can be argued that the role of the public is likely to vary according to where the offence takes place. That is, citizens may be more willing to report offences committed in their area than those they witness in the city centre, both because they are more likely to see themselves as (to some extent) "victims" and because they are less able to take alternative (avoiding) action. Consequently some cases (like of a man masturbating in his car in the street, or urinating on the pavement outside a house) may elicit such a degree of moral outrage that citizens consider that they have been victimised and are motivated to report just as strongly as for standard list crimes.

Even if we accept this degree of public involvement, however, it is pertinent to consider, once more, whether the extent of police proactivity for public order and technical (other) offences varies according to residential areas. More specifically we can compare offences committed in the three high offender rate areas with the rest, or we can compare offenders who lived in the three high offender rate areas with those from the other areas.

In fact, taking offence data, only 38 cases were included in the two categories combined, and twenty-seven of these occurred in the three high rate areas. Nevertheless there were, if anything, a slightly higher proportion of incidents reported by the public in the high than in the low rate areas, the opposite to what an amplification model might suggest, but a finding which is consistent with that reported in earlier chapters.

Turning to the offender data, it seems unlikely that the police patrolling the city centre would be able to identify offenders directly in terms of their area of residence. Indeed it is more likely that the police working in the city centre will only coincidentally recognise any but the most regular drunks. Nevertheless it could be argued that if, as some studies have suggested, subjective factors - like demeanour, mode of dress, attitude - are important in determining an officer's response to a problematic situation, it could be that offenders living in different types of area react differently, when in the presence of the police, thereby "encouraging" (or discouraging) police attention. For example, where some areas have high offender rates, it could be argued that residents there have an antipathy to the police which results in confrontation in certain situations. This was tested by comparing the reporting methods used for public order offences and technical (other) offences, committed by offenders from high offender rate areas and other areas.

136

Taking public order offences only, it appears that police proactivity
is slightly higher for offenders from high offender rate areas – 69.9%
as against 60% – but this difference is insignificant (χ^2 = 0.81,
P 0.1). Even when public order and technical (other) offences are combined the difference is insignificant (χ^2 = 2.05, P 0.1). Moreover, in
this case the difference is distorted by one offender (from CFH) being
arrested proactively eleven times for street trading.

It must, therefore, be concluded that there is no evidence that the
police are more likely to arrest public order and technical (other)
offenders from high offender rate areas than from low rate areas. As
with other offender data the difference seems to be between areas where
offences are committed rather than areas where offenders live.

OTHER MARGINAL CRIME DATA

The incident sheet data were confined to cases reported to the police by
members of the public. Nevertheless, it was possible to distinguish between reporting agents in certain cases. Whereas neighbour disputes,
nuisances, and damage tended to be almost exclusively reported by the
person who considered himself to be the victim, it appeared that quite a
few domestic disputes (17%) were reported by a witness, generally a
neighbour who could hear the noise through an adjoining wall. Interestingly this corresponds with the high proportion of indictable violence
offences reported by witnesses. On the other hand, it does conflict
with evidence from other sources on wife battering, where the public are
castigated as ambivalent to the issue (Pizzey, 1974). It is therefore
useful to remind ourselves that these data only allow us to make
relative comparisons and moreover, the extent to which domestic violence
goes unreported, although heard or seen by neighbours, is unknown.

In considering the other recorded data, however, three points may be
stressed. First, the fact that using a source which is dependent upon
public reporting still reveals clear and consistent areal variations
adds to the evidence cited already to undermine a focus on the effect
of policing on areal rates. Similarly, the evidence of comparable area
differences when GPO data or television licence evasion and telephone
kiosk vandalism are considered supports the argument.

Secondly, although it was suggested in chapter one that the effect of
a "criminal subculture" could be that in certain areas public cooperation with the police might be less, leading to lower citizen reporting
rates, the evidence here does not support this. On the contrary, the
incident data seem to indicate that residents in the high offender rate
areas are only too eager to call the police, perhaps because, as one
American commentator has suggested, for such people the police are seen
as the automatic resource to exploit in times of need:

'(P)olice action is often used as a 'punishment' for the object of the
complaint. The complainant sees the police as an official adjudicatory
agency to relieve short term problems. Over the study period reported
here, it was observed that 'problem' families of this type generate
these situations cyclically – always returning to more stable arrange-
ments ... while low status persons may have little formal power in
economic and social spheres, they do exercise power over interpersonal
situations to the degree that they are willing to call the police.'
(Meyer, 1974, 77-81)

Finally, though, returning to the role of the police, two aspects of police discretion should be noted vis-à-vis the willingness of the police to record incidents as offences or no-crimes. On the one hand, the fact that incidents recorded on the noncriminal incident forms follow the same areal pattern as those recorded as offences rules out any suggestion that categories in which the police record incidents vary according to area. On the other hand, though, it is clear that some types of incident, most notably domestic disputes, are frequently included in the incident files whereas violence offences are comparatively rare amongst the standard list offence data (Mawby, 1978 (ii)). It therefore seems that, along with earlier studies, there is evidence that certain categories of incident are less likely than others to be recorded as crimes. This emphasis on the nature of the incident, related as it is to the status of the victim, indicates once again the importance of offence type in determining variations in police practice.

SUMMARY

The data referred to in this chapter are only infrequently considered in criminological studies, covering as they do the more marginal aspects of the law. Nevertheless, consideration of nonindictable crime sheets reveals that the role of the police is considerably more pronounced than was found in chapter four. On the other hand, the role of the public should not be discounted, and indeed citizens play a significant role in the reporting of incidents which occur in residential areas and which are subsequently categorised as nonindictable on incident sheet data.

However, although the distinction between standard list and nonindictable offences is frequently also a distinction between offences where a victim is involved and victimless crimes, this is not always the case. Indeed, in the next chapter three "victimless" offence categories have been considered in more detail, one of which is indictable (sexual intercourse with a girl under age), one hybrid (drugs) and one nonindictable (soliciting).

7 Policework and Victimless Crime: Policing Morality

INTRODUCTION

The role of criminal law and the operation of the police in the context
of victimless crimes have been the subject of heated debate, at least
since the professionalisation of the police in the nineteenth century.
Mills' (1966) essay on liberty is perhaps the text most often quoted in
this respect, but more directly, in the works of Victorian social
reformers, we can see a growing concern with increased police powers,
with the genesis of the policing of morality. The words of Josephine
Butler, in a speech in 1883, are equally familiar one hundred years
later:

'I am convinced that the province and the power of the law on the
question of virtue and morality as between men and women is exceedingly
limited ... On all hands we are very apt to fall back on Parliament and
on the law, and on its agents, the police, in order (I will not say
consciously) to rid ourselves of individual responsibility and work ...
Legislation on that subject cannot be carried into effect by men in
government livery, with sticks in their hands, whom we call policemen.
That cannot, must not be done ... The power of the State must be
exceedingly restricted when it comes to touch the morality of the
sexes.' (Butler, 1883)

The growth of police power in areas of morality, necessitating as it
did an intrusion into the lives of the wider population (Butler, 1879),
still causes concern. Academic social scientists, for example, have
been directly critical of police powers:

'Crimes of vice, for example, typically have no citizen complainants.
The man who uses heroin, or smokes marijuana, or bets on a football game,
or patronizes a prostitute, does not complain to the police that someone
has sold him narcotics, taken his bet, or has offered to go to bed with
him for a fee. In order to enforce these laws the police must develop
an information system.' (Skolnick and Woodworth, 1968; 459)

The operation of the police in compiling information, checking
sources, questioning known deviants, and ultimately in defining the
parameters of the crime problem, perhaps to their own advantage
(Dickson, 1968), has been the subject of a number of studies of victimless crime. One frequently cited example from Britain is the phenomenal
increase in recorded male importuning in Manchester, when a new Chief
Constable radically altered local policing practices (Whitaker, 1964).
Similarly in Wincanton, Gardiner and Olson (1969) show how crime rates
for vice and corruption offences follow a cyclical pattern in accordance
with the political climate.

It is indeed significant, as was suggested in Chapter One, that a high
proportion of studies which have focused on police discretion have been
concerned with victimless offences. Skolnick (1966) for example, deals
in detail with drug offences, prostitution and motoring offences while
vagrancy has been the subject of research by Bittner (1967) and

Chambliss (1964) among others. In each of these studies, quite clearly, the role of the police as a proactive agency, an initiator in the discovery process, is considerable.

In chapters 4 and 5, where police data on indictable crime was considered, attention centred on the role of the victim and the difficulties faced by the police. That is, where crimes involve a victim, the victim will in most cases be able to decide for himself whether or not to call the police, and only those cases not reported are potential police discoveries. Moreover the institution of privacy means that in many cases the police have no direct access to the situation of the offence, so that unless a citizen involves them their ability to discover the offence is minimal.

It is therefore not unexpected that the role of the police would be greater for victimless offences, and because of this the present chapter focuses on three. First, we shall consider consensual sex offences with a girl under 16 - i.e. unlawful sexual intercourse (USI) - where the law defines a victim but where the appropriateness of the definition is questionable. Second, we shall concentrate on soliciting by 'known prostitutes' where victimization is justified in terms of public embarrassment. Finally, policework in relation to drug offences will be described, where the victim is commonly either defined as the offender himself or more vaguely as the "straight" society whose values may be undermined.

Each of these cases involves, to a large extent, victimless crime. However, as will be argued, other differences may be important. For example, soliciting is an offence which takes place in a public and visible place which is of necessity well known to the police; consensual sex offences commonly take place in private, or at least in relatively hidden locations; drugs offences are usually committed in private.

Moreover, the formal structure of the police organisation varies in each case. Consensual sex offences are handled by the Uniformed Branch; after a case is discovered it is common for a female officer to handle it. Soliciting is, on the other hand, as noted in the last chapter, dealt with on a divisional level by the assignment of uniformed officers to plain clothes duty. Finally, in direct contrast, drugs offences, although sometimes discovered by the uniformed police, are the direct responsibility of an area Drugs Squad, with its own office in Sheffield.

Differences in the 'victim potential', publicness of the offence, and police organisation, and their effects on police operations, will become clear in the following sections. However, when these three offence types have been described in more detail, we shall reconsider them together in terms of the police role in the law enforcement of morality.

THE POLICE ROLE IN CASES OF USI (1)

USI, or unlawful sexual intercourse with a girl under the age of sixteen is an example of an indictable crime which, where appropriate, would have been included in the analysis in chapters 4 and 5. Here the data used are more extensive, covering a 50% sample of cases in the Sheffield and Rotherham crime files for 1971.

140

The singling out of this offence type for more detailed analysis may
be justified on a number of grounds. First, it is a good example of an
offence which is victimless to the extent that although the law defines
a victim, the victim "consented" to the offence and may not see herself
as a victim at all. Secondly, it is evident that the number of unreported crimes of USI is considerable, and that the dark figure of unrecorded
crime is proportionally greater in this case than in many others. For
example Schofield (1965) estimated that some 3% of girls under 16 had
had sexual intercourse, a figure well above that revealed for known cases
in official police statistics. Indeed, the number of maternities and
abortions to girls under 16 each year is slightly greater than the number of recorded offences!

Finally, USI is interesting because it is a type of offence which the
police themselves may consider marginal. The present study, which is
reported in more detail elsewhere (Mawby, 1979), for example, found that
in their reports the police appeared to draw a distinction between this
and other types of crime, almost implying that USI was not necessarily
a 'real crime'. Related to this, the cautioning rate is notably high.

For all these reasons, there has been considerable debate over the law
regarding USI, with recent recommendations that the age of consent should
be lowered.(2) In fact, concern over the law is certainly not new. When
the law was originally formulated as part of the Criminal Law Amendment
Act of 1885, Hopwood, a critical MP, prophesised that "if the Bill were
allowed to pass there would be a great danger of young men and even boys
being betrayed by designing creatures, whose object was to levy
'blackmail'". Further recognition of the problems involved with the
offender/victim distinction were recognised in the 1922 Act, which
incorporated a statutory defence against conviction, and this was re-
tained in the 1956 Sexual Offences Act which states that where the girl
is aged 13-15:

'A man is not guilty of an offence under this section because he has
unlawful sexual intercourse with a girl under the age of sixteen, if he
is under the age of twenty-four and has not previously been charged with
a like offence, and he believes her to be of the age of sixteen or over
and has reasonable cause for this belief.'

However, despite a widespread amount of contention over USI, the
number of research studies which have included any details of police
practices, either at the discovery/reporting stage or the cautioning
level is small.

If we focus on the discovery and reporting process, the most specific
study published is one carried out in two American cities by Skolnick
and Woodworth (1968). Describing one of the cities the authors report:

'It turned out that in Westville, the source reporting the complaint
to the police was neither the girl herself, nor her relatives. Rather,
the single most important source of information was the family support
division of the prosecutor's office. In general, the overwhelming
majority of cases were 'non-voluntary' in the sense that the facts were
brought to the Westville police as a result of information held by other
agencies. The adolescent girl applying for maternity assistance is
routinely sent to the police department where she is urged, and often
cajoled, into making a complaint.' (Skolnick and Woodward, 1968, 460)

141

This situation was in direct contrast to that in the other city studied by Skolnick and Woodward where the family support division pursued a different policy. The results of this difference were two-fold. First, the recorded rate of "statutory rapes" (i.e. USI) was higher in Westville. Secondly, the cases discovered tended to vary, such that in Westville a higher proportion involved victims who needed material help. If the father of the child (or the girl's parents) could afford to maintain the girl, no claim for assistance would be made and the offender would be relatively protected from the law.

The situation may, of course, be expected to differ somewhat in Britain. In fact only one study has included details of the discovery/reporting processes in USI cases, and this as part of a much wider survey of sex offences (Radzinowicz, 1957). This found that only a small percentage of offences were discovered directly by the police. Conversely most offences were reported to the police by the victim or her representative, often following a confirmation that the girl was pregnant.

In order to provide more recent details on USI all incidents of USI only[3] were abstracted from the files of the Sheffield and Rotherham police for a six month period in 1971. In total there were 36 cases involving 36 girls and 44 males, of whom 38 males were identified by the police. The characteristics of offenders and victims[4] may be briefly summarised:

(i) Age. Only 18% of offenders were aged 21 or more, with the modal age group being 16-17 which included 42% of the sample. Of the 36 girls involved, as many as 17 were aged 15 at the time of the offence, with a further 13 aged 14. Comparing the relative ages of the girls and their sexual partners, this meant that in a majority of cases the girl was no more than two years younger than her partner, and in only 19.0% of cases was there an age gap of 8 or more years.

(ii) Criminal Records. As many as 39.5% of males had a prior record, although only one of those included a sex offence. Moreover, comparing areas of residence of offenders and victims with the ED characteristics described by Baldwin and Bottoms (1976) it appeared that both groups, but males especially, were over represented in high offender rate areas.

(iii) Social Class. A similar comparison revealed that offenders were over represented in lower class areas.

(iv) Relationship between offender and victim. A classification was devised from police records, which allowed the girl/male relationship to be coded in 35 cases. These revealed 4 patterns:

(a) Casual meeting leading to intercourse (19).
(b) Brief acquaintanceship leading to intercourse (9).
(c) Girl and male knew each other well (e.g. at school together, family friend) (6).
(d) Relationship fairly permanent (11).

(v) Place of Offence. The very nature of the offence suggests that it might be expected to take place in private. However, taking all instances described in police reports, it appeared that some 41.7% occurred in public places, with a small majority (58.3%) in private (usually the home of either the girl or male). Of those instances which took place in public places, over half were in parks, woods, etc., and most of the rest occurred in derelict property or on wasteland.

The fact that so many incidents took place on public property, to which the police had legitimate access, suggests that the role of the police in the discovery process might be considerable. This is particularly so, given that if these results are compared with Schofield's interview survey into the sexual behaviour of teenagers it is evident that the proportion of acts of intercourse in public places is significantly higher for the Sheffield police sample.

Table 7.1
Method by which the victim of USI came
to the attention of the police

	n	%
Police Discovery	17	48.6
Caught in the act	3	8.6
Questioning – reported missing	6	17.1
– routine inquiries	5	14.3
– suspicious circumstances	3	8.6
Citizen Report	18	51.4
Victim	2	5.7
Victim's parents	13	37.1
Children's department	2	5.7
Offender	1	2.9
Unknown	1	–
Total	36	100.0

At first glance, the data in Table 7.1 apparently confirms this. Considering how each victim became officially identified, police discoveries accounted for no less than 48.6% of cases. However, in only three cases did the police actually catch the offender in the act. Rather, police discoveries typically followed from one of three other sets of circumstances:

(i) Reported missing. In 6 cases, the girl was reported missing from home by her parents and when she was subsequently located, police inquiries revealed a case of USI.

(ii) Routine inquiries. In 5 cases, the police had cause to question the girl on a matter not related to the offence, and in so doing uncovered a case of USI. Examples here include a case where the police questioned a girl who was witness to a crime, and one where they interviewed a girl who was hanging around a Remand Centre.

(iii) Suspicious circumstances. Three of the girls were questioned by the police because they were seen in notorious areas of the city. Here the police appeared to adopt a moral entrepreneurial stance and question young girls they found in disreputable cafes, or in the company of 'undesirables'.

Turning to those victims who were named by a member of the public it is notable that excluding the one report by the offender himself, only 2 of the remainder were reports by the victim herself. In 13 cases the parent was responsible for specifically reporting the sex offence to the police and in 2 cases the Children's Department, acting as guardian, did so.

It seems likely that where reports are made by the victim or her guardians, there may be some additional influence at play. As might be suspected, in no fewer than 9 of the 13 cases reported by parents and both cases reported by the Children's Department, the girl was pregnant, or suspected of so being.

In addition though, it seemed that while pregnancy might have been the factor which brought the affair to the notice of the parents or guardians, the motive to report was strengthened by other factors. On the one hand, in 3 cases it was clear that the parents brought the matter before the police because, acting on their daughter's description of the offence, they thought she had been forcibly raped. On the other hand, and most importantly, a reading of the official police files demonstrates that in a majority of cases reported by parents the revenge motive is foremost. Parents, unwilling to see their daughters as co-operative partners, define them as "seduced innocents", victims of men who deserve punishment. This revenge motive is particularly in evidence where the girl is pregnant, even where marriage to the offender is likely. Often this is because the offender and victim intend to marry but the girl's parents disapprove. In other cases, the discovery of the offence had led to a family feud between the parents of the girl and male, in which reporting the offence was one weapon used by the "injured parties".

It thus seems that despite the victimless nature of the offence, a high proportion of offences are reported by members of the public. This proportion increases if we include police discoveries following a girl being reported missing from home by her parents. The fact that sexual intercourse is likely to take place in private - whether in a legally private place or a relatively unobtrusive public place, clearly inhibits the role of the police. However, it seems that the police use their discretion to maximise their discovery powers. In one respect, they sometimes intervene to question girls who appear to be in suspicious circumstances - even though no offence is actually taking place. More commonly, once the police are given access to questionning under age girls on other matters - when they are reported missing or seen regarding some other crime or disturbance - the police are able to question them regarding their sexual behaviour.

We have already considered the types of girl likely to be included in police records of USI, and typical known offenders. It is however, pertinent to ask whether the different discovery methods lead to different types of offender and victim being uncovered. The numbers here are clearly too small for statistical analysis, and the results are consequently speculative. However one or two trends can be discerned.

For example:

(i) Considering cases uncovered due to police direct discovery or

144

using discretion to question girls found in suspicious circumstances: the girls involved were likely to be relatively young, as were the offenders; in almost all cases the relationship was a casual one, and most sexual intercourse (not only that discovered) appeared to have taken place in public places.

(ii) In contrast where the police discovered offences following routine inquiries, offences were in almost all cases likely to have taken place in private.

(iii) Where girls were reported missing, cases usually involved older girls and males, and offences tended to have taken place in public. Interestingly, although the numbers are small, only in these cases did the majority of offenders have previous convictions. This may, possibly, indicate therefore that reports on missing girls were made by parents whose daughters were going out with males of whom they did not approve.

(iv) Reports made to the police by citizens were likely to involve older girls, with a majority of incidents occurring in private.

In earlier chapters one of the principal focuses has been on the extent to which private places act as inhibitors on the proactive role of the police. Although the USI data are restricted to small numbers, it is nevertheless interesting to note that this pattern is maintained. The police role in discovery, even where there is no victim, is restricted by the fact that offences are not generally visible. In such circumstances the ability of the police to discover offences by following up routine inquiries, in particular, enables them to discover a number of offences which took place in private. The extent to which this is possible in other examples will be raised when we consider drug offences. Prior to that, however, it is relevant to turn to another victimless sex offence, soliciting.

"THE VICE SQUAD"

Although we are here concerned with data on soliciting in the whole of Sheffield, clearly this is of direct relevance to the area study since one of the nine areas (RHH) was notorious as the centre of the city's red light district and has a high offence and offender rate for soliciting (see chapter 2).

Police data on 'known prostitutes' arrested for soliciting in 1973 indeed revealed RHH as the centre of the market, although the area in which girls trawled for custom tended to be rather bigger than this, extending towards the edge of the city centre.

In addition, there appeared to be a second area for the trade, located in a privately rented sector to the north of the city, although rather fewer girls were arrested there. However, details on girls who were administered a formal caution, (although as noted in Chapter 2 incomplete) suggested that a rather greater proportion of inexperienced prostitutes operated in this second area, with the possible implication that they graduated to the main red light district at a later date.

Details from the records and from participant observation,(5) moreover, reveal that even where trade is apparently spatially restricted a number of complex patterns may be evident. Thus while many of the girls lived and worked in RHH, they would at times move outside the area to look for custom or avoid the police. Other girls worked in the area but lived elsewhere, perhaps renting 'business' flats locally. On the other hand, at the 'low prestige' end of the market some girls had no permanent flat and were often dependent on carrying out their transactions in their customers' cars or homes, a practice which brought with it considerable vulnerability.

This said, if we consider the official address given by arrested prostitutes who did not live in RHH, it is interesting that 22 out of 37 lived in low offender rate areas (according to Baldwin and Bottoms' analysis of the 1966 data), and only 4 in high offender rate areas. In addition, 12 lived in areas of predominantly owner-occupied housing, 11 in mixed areas, 5 in council areas and 9 in areas of privately rented accommodation.

Like much of the nonindictable crime data, police records for arrested prostitutes included only a minimum of information. Details of previous convictions were vague, although it seemed that only some 7 girls had no prior convictions (as opposed to cautions) for prostitution. This apart, age was the only variable commonly recorded, and was included on the files of 54 of the 56 girls. Of these the majority were in their twenties (22 aged 20–24 and 19 aged 25–29), with 7 younger than this and only 6 in their thirties.

Taking the 1973 arrests of 'known prostitutes' as a whole, the 56 girls were arrested on 110 occasions. Given that the police invest a considerable amount of time on vice patrols, an average of 2 arrests per week seems rather low in return. The operation of the police vis-à-vis prostitution is thus worth considering in more detail.

The police clearly recognised RHH as the centre of the prostitution trade, and focused their patrols on the area. To them, any suggestion that such policies 'created' area differences in respect to prostitution would be treated with some amusement. The chief soliciting areas are indeed likely to be easily located for obvious reasons. Prostitutes need clients, and in order to get them they must make public their addresses, or at least the areas where they can be located. If potential clients did not know that RHH was an area where prostitutes could be found, earnings would diminish. One, and only one, illustration of this dilemma was found in the 1973 records, with regard to an arrest of two prostitutes for soliciting on a main road out of the city and away from the normal areas of work. The arrest was made by uniformed officers on routine car patrol who seemed surprised to find the girls. So indeed, were other people, since it seems clear from the report that the girls were not having much custom!

On the other hand, it is feasible that prostitutes may work in other locations where they are able to operate within the law, and in this respect it makes sense to argue that police statistics give a misleading picture of where prostitutes can be found. For example, in Sheffield a high class call girl system is said to operate discreetly from the foyer of one of the largest hotels, but this, not surprisingly, is unrecognised in police records.

What then of the operation of the police in the main areas of soliciting? As already noted, the police invest a relatively large amount of manpower, but their results, in terms of arrest, are few. There would appear to be a number of reasons for this. First, the reactions of the girls themselves make the job of the police difficult. Police, even when in plain clothes, soon become known to locals (see also Skolnick, 1966) and certainly their private cars are readily identified. Therefore, given that the number of working girls is considerably greater than the number of patrolling police, it is relatively easy for a majority of the prostitutes to be working out of sight of the police, and in this they are aided by an informal but well developed warning network through which news of police presence is quickly transmitted through the neighbourhood.

Secondly, the police must attempt to arrest girls against whom they have a clear cut case.(6) This means that the police will choose to arrest prostitutes who solicit the most explicitly, and particularly where solicitation is successful (i.e. where a customer can be identified both before and after trading). In this respect the operation of the police is fascinating. They would appear to define their role as a crime prevention one (see below), within which they may concentrate to some extent on 'warning off' clients, for example by questioning males on the streets at night. However, when they arrest a girl, their attitude towards her customer is transformed, since he becomes a potential witness, and they will do all they can to get a written statement from him. To this end they may cajole, and even threaten him, but in some cases the opposite might be the case, and he might be invited to define himself as the innocent victim of seduction. The following case is extreme, but none the less revealing:

'Miss A had been arrested for soliciting when she and her customer emerged from her flat having gone in together some ten minutes previously. Her client, Mr. X, from Chesterfield, made a statement to the police in which he admitted being solicited. His 'story' was that he had come to Sheffield to attend a ballet class, but was unsure of the correct address, and for this reason had been circling the area slowly in his car. When he saw Miss A he stopped his car and went over to ask her if she knew where the ballet school was. At this point, quite unexpectedly, she suggested that he might like to go back with her to her room, and tempted on the spur of the moment he agreed.'

There is no doubt in this case that the police greeted this 'victim's' account with amusement, yet they accepted it because it meant that they had a clear cut case against the girl. In other examples, where the man refused to co-operate, or backed up the story of the girl, and where the girl was unsuccessful in attracting a customer, the police were on a less secure footing, and indeed there were 5 examples of cases which were dismissed or withdrawn. The police therefore were under pressure to make arrests only where they were sure of a conviction, and could be expected to use their discretion accordingly.

Finally, it is important to consider further the ways in which the police defined their role with regard to prostitution control. As already noted, to some degree they saw their role as preventative, in which case high visibility might be an effective deterrent to both girls and customers. On the other hand, there were also indications that they recognised a moralistic side to the job. That is, while they accepted that some prostitutes were professionals, who would not be deterred, they concentrated on newcomers to the area, in the hope that these could be deterred from 'the game'.

These twin concerns direct attention at two possible effects that police discretion may have on the arrest of prostitutes. On the one hand, a concern with prevention and order maintenance might lead to the police arresting some girls, i.e. troublemakers, more often than others. On the other hand, a distinction between professionals and novices might be expected to lead to girls being arrested an equal number of times each - that is, newcomers would always be arrested, girls working regularly in the area would be arrested in turn; a pattern which was apparently common prior to the Wolfenden Report.

Table 7.2
Number of times each prostitute
arrested for soliciting, 1973

	One	Two	Three	Four	Five	Six	Total
n	27	16	7	2	2	2	56
%	48.2	28.6	12.5	3.6	3.6	3.6	100.1

As is evident from Table 7.2, the data on the number of times each girl was arrested shows a bias towards the lower end, with almost half being arrested only once in the year, and, compared with a Poisson distribution, (7), relatively few girls arrested on four or more occasions. This is certainly, to some extent, due to the mobility of the girls, with many of them not working for the whole year, or at least not operating in the Sheffield area for the whole time period. In addition, some girls who were formally cautioned and arrested during the year would appear in the table only for actual arrests.

However, there was no indication that number of arrests was in any way related to experience. Taking age (as the only measurement of experience available) 51.3% of girls under 25 had been arrested more than once, only slightly less than the 56% of girls aged 25 or more.

If there did not appear to be any distinctive pattern in terms of which girls were arrested the most frequently the same cannot be said of the timing of arrests.

Considering first the time of day when arrests were made, an overwhelming majority, 79.1%, were in the 9 p.m. - 12 p.m. period, with the next highest period noon - 3 p.m. with 9.9%. This is what might have been anticipated but the lack of arrests after midnight (only two throughout the year) is perhaps surprising. The same bunching, to a lesser extent, was evident in terms of the day of the week for arrests. Only one arrest was made on a Sunday, compared with 25.5% on a Saturday and 19.6% on a Friday.

The relationship between arrest times, policing practices and soliciting are clearly tenuous. One could argue that the police patrol the area in the late evenings, especially at weekends, and the arrest pattern reflects this. On the other hand, it is tenable to suggest that the police in fact time their patrols such that they correspond to times of maximum activity, and it is not unreasonable to assume that these two factors interact to produce the temporal pattern.

However, when we consider the data on a monthly basis, it is less easy to discount the influence of differential policing. Taking the 12 month period, only 12.7% of arrests occurred in the fourth quarter, and only 2.0% in December. Since it seems likely that, with Christmas approaching the extent of soliciting might actually increase (as does other crime), the figures appear to indicate a reduction in police activity, perhaps due to the police accepting that prostitutes, like everyone else, needed a good Christmas!

It is evident from the above discussion that the police play a direct and monopolistic role in the arrest of prostitutes. All arrests were proactive, and all but one incident were due to the operation of a 'vice squad' of officers seconded for plain clothes duty. The lack of a victim and the visibility of the pickup, plus the spatial and temporal bunching of the trade, make soliciting the example par excellence of police proactivity.

DRUG OFFENCES (8)

In contrast to the policing of sex offences, drug offences are handled by a department specialising in drug related incidents, which was, in 1975, made up of some seven officers, headed by an inspector. As with sex offences, the enforcement of drug laws has been a subject of considerable controversy in recent years. In America, Dickson's (1968) work has been used to expose the relationship between the awakening recognition of a state of affairs (drug abuse) as problematic and the increasing status, power and prestige of the Agency devoted to its control. In Britain, law enforcement in the drugs field has been criticised on a number of counts. For example:

(i) Under Section 6 of the Dangerous Drugs Act 1967, the police were given the power to stop and search without warrant anyone 'reasonably suspected' of being in unlawful possession of drugs. This measure made the enforcement of law much easier and at the same time brought into question the logic of making law enforcement easier for the police in the case of drugs offences than for other offences.

(ii) It is clearly recognised that the 'dark figure' of unknown crime is particularly great for drugs offences, due to the invisibility of most offences. In this context a BBC Midweek survey in recent years estimated that there were some three million regular users of cannabis under 35, of whom only a fraction were known to the police.

(iii) In such a situation, recorded crime might be expected to reflect more the operational efficiency of the police than the extent and changing nature of drug use.

(iv) Similarly police data on known offenders and the drugs they have used will indicate more about law enforcement patterns than about typical drug users (Plant, 1975).

(v) Furthermore the difference between the numbers of drug takers and

arrested drug offenders means that the role of the police in determining
how to enforce the law may have considerable repercussions. Thus on the
one hand the police, in choosing who to arrest from allegedly 'a regular
source of fairly easily apprehendable villians' (Young, 1971; 172) may
discriminate between users and pushers, ignoring the former or using
them to aid in arresting the dealers (Plant, 1975; 246: Young, 1971;
188).

(vi) Finally, and crucial to the development of a contraculture,
police involvement may lead to an amplification process, involving the
isolation, stigmatisation and criminalisation of drug users and an
apparent increase in the use of drugs (Young, 1971; chapter 9).

In considering police records on drug use, we are clearly in an
unfavourable position compared with those who have been able to observe
directly the life styles of drug users (Young, 1971; Plant, 1975) or
the ongoing operational styles of the police (Skolnick, 1966). However,
it is possible, from the crime data, to consider policing methods and
the relationship between these methods and the types of offenders who
are identified.

In this context, Plant's research on drug takers in Cheltenham provides a useful backcloth. Plant (1975) dismisses research based on
medical and police (especially institutional) data and opts in his
research for techniques of participant observation and informal discussions with a sample of drug takers who were identified by using the
snowballing technique. As Plant himself recognised, the drug takers he
located are atypical of drug users in general, especially since the
research method ignores isolated users. However, in his methodological
critique of other research, and then more specifically in comparing
those in his sample who had police records with the rest, Plant draws
attention to the difficulties of using police records:

'One of the main disadvantages of criminal statistics is that they may
not give an accurate representation of the nature or extent of crime.
It is possible that those who are convicted differ from those who escape
attention and are unrecorded ... There was a significant association
between having been convicted of a drug offence and being classified as
physically dirty or very scruffy. As a group, those who had been convicted of a drug offence were more likely than other drug takers to be
neglected or conspicuous in their appearance' (Plant, 1975; 244, 246).

Plant compared drug users with criminal records for drug use with
unconvicted users, and found the former different in a number of other
respects - for example, they were more likely to be male, low status,
non-students, multi-users, delinquent and unemployed (Plant, 1975;
236-37, 245-46).

These differences may be related to the ways in which the police
operate vis-à-vis drug users. That is, drug taking in the privacy of the
home is unlikely to be discovered (Plant, 1975; 247) whilst those whose
external appearance is indicative of their allegiance to a bohemian life
style are particularly vulnerable to police arrest (Young, 1971; 174).
On the other hand, those who are designated by the police as users
rather than dealers may escape prosecution even when they are known to
the police.

150

However, although both Young and Plant accept that the police use informants in order to make arrests, both tend to underemphasise this detection method and concentrate more specifically on the proactive role of the police in stopping suspects in the street. Thus, almost certainly due to the different research techniques (as well as cultural differences) their references to the operations of the drug squad are in notable contrast with the account presented by Skolnick (1966) where the role of the informant attains almost monopolistic status. What is equally clear from all of these studies, however, is that an overview of the variety of discovery methods used by the police is lacking. The Sheffield data to a large extent fills this void. In addition, though, while we cannot in any sense demonstrate definitively any differences between the characteristics of users who are or are not known to the police, we can compare known offenders according to the ways in which their offences were discovered.

In considering cases recorded in the drug squad files for 1975, we distinguished the number of separate offences discovered directly and the number of offenders, counting offenders more than once where they were involved in different offences (9). In this way we distinguished 80 offences and 136 offenders for the year.

The records kept by the drug squad were, like those for standard list offences in general, extremely detailed. Moreover, because of the exclusive nature of the unit, officers were in many cases able to fill in details which were missing from the files. In consequence, the only piece of information kept which was commonly missing (in 20.7% of cases) was marital status.

If we refer briefly to the characteristics of drug offenders, a not unfamiliar pattern emerges. The majority were male (76.3%), single (71.0%) and under 30 (31.9% were under 21, 54.8% being 21-29). In addition a high proportion were unemployed (43.9%) and the non-British group (defined by birthplace) although by no means large, was over-represented (9.6%). Taking previous records, a minority (40.1%) were first offenders, but at the other extreme 34.7% had previous convictions for drug offences and rather more (45.0%) had convictions for non-drug offences. If we consider social class, where known, 24.4% were recorded as having professional, managerial or routine non-manual jobs and 31.0% as having semi- or un-skilled jobs. Finally it is noteable that although offenders' residences were distributed throughout the city, more lived in RHH than in any other enumeration district.

Turning to characteristics of offences and when they were discovered, data were collected on the drug involved and principal offence type, and the place and time of discovery. Not unexpectedly the most common drug identified was cannabis, which was recorded in 41.0% of cases. In 55% of offences, a drug only (possession or supply) was involved. However, in the remaining cases (a significant minority) a non-drug offence was also included - burglary in 15%, importation in 2.5% and offences involving forgery, handling and theft of prescriptions in 27.5% of cases (10). It is important to recognise the distinction between drug only cases and those involving non-drug offences, because the latter should be filed in the standard list offences files for 1975, and to this extent our data overlap that covered in chapters 4-5, although the year is different.

If we turn our attention from the offence to the place and time of discovery, some of the features behind the operation of the drug squad become clear. First, considering time, there were no notable differences in the number of cases filed per month throughout the year. However, on a daily basis there were some variations, with at one extreme 26.7% of cases discovered on a Saturday and at the other only 4.0% discovered on a Tuesday. A pattern was also evident in terms of the time of day of the discovery, with 21.2% in the 9 - 12 p.m. period and 18.2% in the 12 p.m. - 3 a.m. period. Moving from a consideration of the <u>time</u> of discovery to the <u>place</u> of discovery, the visibility factor becomes evident - only 17.5% of cases were discovered in an offender's home, compared with 32.5% in streets, car parks etc., 11.3% in clubs, cafes etc., and 23.8% in chemists' shops.

These then are the main characteristics of the population of drug offenders recorded in police files, their offences and the time and place of offence discovery. At this stage, they have been included to provide a general picture against which differences according to discovery methods may be considered. If we now focus on the ways in which offences were discovered, two words of explanation must be inserted. First, methods have been tabulated in three ways:

(i) The number of offences discovered in each way, where the total number of offences is 80.

(ii) The number of offenders directly identified by each method, where the total is 106.

(iii) The number of offenders overall who were identified due to an offence being discovered via a particular method, a total of 136. This includes an additional 30 offenders who were identified in one of two ways. Some were named by offenders who had already been caught by the police. Others were caught by what is perhaps best described as 'contamination' - that is, the police arrested one offender and in so doing discovered other offenders who would not have been suspected had they not been with the 'key' offender at the time of arrest.

Secondly, in Tables 7.3 and 7.4 these three sets of figures have been included according to eight different detection methods which we identified. These were:

(i) Proactive policing, where the police used their discretion to apprehend a suspect.

(ii) Information received, where the police made an arrest because of information they had been given by an informant.

(iii) Crime follow-up, where the police questioned the offender with regard to a non-drug crime and in so doing a drug offence came to light.

(iv) Chemists' reports, that is, where the police were called by a chemist (or in some cases doctor) who suspected that a prescription had been forged.

(v) Hospital calls, where the police investigated reported overdose cases.

(vi) External/customs inquiries, where the South Yorkshire police were informed of a suspect by another force or the customs' department.

(vii) Citizen information leading to an arrest.

(viii) Routine inspection, where a Home Office inspection of registered chemists and retailers revealed unauthorised drugs.

Table 7.3
Drug offences discovered directly
according to different methods

	n	%
Proactive policing	25	32.9
Information received	11	14.5
Crime follow-up	10	13.2
Chemists' reports	14	18.4
Hospital call	4	5.3
External/customs inquiry	6	7.9
Citizen information	5	6.6
Routine inspection	1	1.3
Unknown	4	-
Total	80	100.1

Table 7.4
Drug offenders identified
According to different methods

	Identified directly		Total	
	n	%	n	%
Proactive policing	36	35.3	43	32.6
Information received	17	16.7	19	14.4
Crime follow-up	11	10.8	23	17.4
Chemists' reports	19	18.6	19	14.4
Hospital call	4	3.9	5	3.8
External/customs inquiry	7	6.9	10	7.6
Citizen information	7	6.9	12	9.1
Routine inspection	1	1.0	1	0.8
Unknown	4	-	4	-
Total	106	100.1	136	100.1

In order to expand on these descriptions and consider the offence and offender characteristics common to each, the four major discovery types and others (combined) will be considered in more detail. Given the numbers involved, it is not surprising that overall statistical differences were not often evident, although employment/unemployment was significantly related to discovery method (χ^2_4 = 12.82, P<0.02). Therefore significant differences between individual discovery methods and the rest have been cited in the text, and other notable trends have been included. Having stressed this, it is time to consider the distinctive features of the different discovery methods.

(i) Proactive policing

Examples:

'Two men were stopped outside a Sheffield allnighter in the early morning by a Drug Squad Officer, because they allegedly showed signs of being under the influence of amphetamines.'

'A uniformed officer on patrol in the city centre at night saw two men walking towards him smoking hand rolled cigarettes. One of the men hid his cigarette behind his back when he saw the constable, who became suspicious and investigated.'

'A girl was observed in a drugged condition at a Sheffield allnighter by a female police officer in the early hours of the morning.'

Almost one third of all offences were discovered by the method of police direct proactivity towards people they suspected of drug use. Moreover, as is clear from the above examples, the Uniformed Branch were not infrequently involved in making these arrests. The drugs involved in such cases were as likely to be hard drugs as cannabis, and in the majority of cases (88.0%) no non-drug offences were involved.

Not surprisingly, eighteen of the twenty-five incidents occurred in the street, with seven in the late evening (9 - 12 p.m.) and seven in the early morning (12 p.m. - 3 a.m.). In addition sixteen of the incidents occurred in two city centre EDs, in particular around an all-nighter and a public house which were considered centres for drug users.

Turning to characteristics of offenders discovered by this method, a number of distinctions emerged. For example, six offenders lived in one area (RHH), and males were significantly more likely to be arrested by this method than were females ($P < 0.05$). However, two other features were evident which do not fit the model described by other researchers, like Young. Thus offenders discovered proactively were more likely than others to be first offenders ($P < 0.05$) and showed a tendency to include fewer unemployed offenders ($P < 0.10$).

(ii) Information received

The important part played by the informant net-work is clearly described by Skolnick, who starts by appreciating the dependence of the drug squad on the use of initiative:

'The work of the narcotics officer requires that he be an initiator of police activity, rather than a man who performs a service for an aggrieved citizen ...' (Skolnick, 1966; 117)

However, the form the initiative takes is not that of the vigilant officer 'combing the streets'. Rather:

'Much of the generative activity in enforcing narcotics crimes takes place within the police station. This is not because narcotics police are lazy but because the nature of narcotics crime requires that invoca-

tion of activity is based upon receipt of messages. Thus, all detectives,
but especially narcotics detectives, do a lot of work on the telephone.
Many of the informants (some of whom are transients) do not have teleph-
ones of their own, and others prefer not to be called at home by a
policeman. As a result, the narcotics policeman is continually being
called to the telephone.'

'Not all informing, however, takes place over the telephone. Petty
informants seem to enjoy wandering into the separate quarters of the
vice control squad, and narcotics officers must be available to greet
and chat with them. Indeed, due to the constant need for information,
narcotics officers encourage informants to 'drop in'.' (Skolnick, 1966;
140).

The informer network is, for Skolnick, the method par excellence of
the drug squad. In this respect, it is noticeably different from the
description of policing practices given by Plant and Young. Of course,
the latter two accept that the drug squad do act on information
received, but imply that this is largely a case of gaining information
on supplies from known offenders. In fact, in Sheffield police clearly
distinguish between information passed on by offenders they have directly discovered and details received from 'informants'. Whereas the
former individuals are explicitly identified in police reports, leading
to the distinction we made earlier between all discoveries and all
direct discoveries, the latter are characterised by deliberately vague
reports on the source of information (i.e. 'due to information received'):

For example:

'Drug Squad Officers went to address of offender with warrant under
Misuse of Drugs Act. Searched and found cannabis in offender's room and
some in another room which the offender also admitted was his.'

'Drug Squad Officers had a warrant under the Misuse of Drugs Act
(1971) to search offender's house. Offender admitted purchasing drugs
from bar in the City Centre.'

'The police stopped the suspect outside his own home getting into a
taxi. He had with him a polythene bag with 36 twists of cannabis in it.'

'Drug Squad Officers searched offender's house, (without warrant) in
early hours of morning and found quantities of opium etc. They were
acting on 'information received'.'

Discoveries based on 'information received' characteristically involved the Drug Squad, armed with a search warrant, contacting the suspect
either at his home or outside his home. In contrast to the impression
created by Skolnick, however, they accounted for only one sixth of all
offence discoveries. In addition, in contrast to police proactive
discoveries, the drug involved was more likely to be cannabis than a
hard drug and was never an amphetamine (P < 0.05), although once again
the offence was most likely to be a drug offence only.

If we consider the type of offender involved, other differences between
the two discovery methods emerge. Although offenders involved in
'information received' cases were also likely to be male (16 out of 19),
they were, interestingly, significantly more likely than other offenders

to have previous convictions ($P < 0.05$) (especially for non-drug offences) and to be unemployed. This group of possibly low status, 'drifter' offenders, which appear to fit in some ways Plant's description of known offenders, seem therefore, to be known to the police not because of police discrimination so much as the 'immorality' of their fellow users. (11)

(iii) Crime follow-up

In some 10% of cases, a drug offence was discovered because an offender was questioned for a non-drug offence (usually by a uniformed officer) and in the course of the inquiry a drug offence came to light. For example:

'The offender was stopped in London driving a car reported stolen from Rotherham and large quantities of various drugs were discovered inside.'

'The offender was arrested for an offence of criminal damage at a hotel in the city centre in the early hours of the morning. He was taken to the police station and searched, when a matchbox containing cannabis was found.'

'The offender was apprehended by a store detective for shoplifting in a city centre store. His flat was searched by the police and cannabis was found behind the ventilator grill.'

Considering the 10 cases involved in this category revealed no clear pattern according to drug type or characteristics of the offence and its discovery, although most offences were for drug offences only and no amphetamines were involved. The types of offender involved were, however, atypical in certain respects – they included a relatively high proportion of females ($P < 0.05$) and unemployed, and there was in addition a tendency for younger offenders (i.e. under 21) to be included in this category ($P < 0.10$).

The number of offenders discovered in this way is relatively small but is notable for at least two other reasons. First, it involves a detection process which until now appears to have been largely ignored. Secondly, in view of the controversy over the relationship between drug use and other types of criminal activity, it is worth speculating on how far the relationship between these variables is influenced by such a detection method, even where it involves only a minority of known drug offenders.

(iv) Chemists' reports

The relationship between drug and non-drug offences raises the question of how far drug users commit other types of offence in order to obtain drugs. Although quite clearly other property crimes may be a means of obtaining money to buy drugs, two more direct ways are represented in the files – first, where the offender breaks into a chemist's shop to steal drugs, secondly, where he attempts to forge a prescription. Cases of this latter sort characterise the group of discoveries based on chemists' reports. These stem from chemists calling the police because they are suspicious about prescriptions given them, either because a figure has been altered clumsily or because the doctor's signature is suspect. By definition, then, such offences include a related non-drug offence, which is either forgery/deception or theft/

156

handling of a stolen prescription. For example:

'Attended surgery, gave false name and address and obtained prescription for Mogadon. Went to pub, where he altered number of tablets from '20' to '80'. However, the alteration was clumsy and the chemist reported it.'

'Obtained prescription for 30 Duromine, ostensibly for the treatment of her mother-in-law (but without her knowledge). Altered quantity from 30 to 80, but chemist was suspicious.'

'Visited G.P. While she was out of room stole prescription pad and wrote himself a prescription for amphetamines. Chemist was suspicious and rang senior doctor who said it must have been prescribed by his locum. However he later realised it was not the locum and reported the matter to the police.'

'He went to a G.P. and stole a prescription form made out to a patient and left for her to collect. He added Tuinal and Ritalin to the prescription, which made chemist suspicious.'

This group of cases in fact was numerically the second largest, yet a review of the records makes it seem that similar examples may be numerous and that it is relatively easy to obtain drugs in such ways. As these examples indicate, it is when the offender becomes greedy and adds to the prescription, or alters the numbers clumsily that the chemist is suspicious, and it is likely that a host of undiscovered offences of this order exist.

If we consider the characteristics of offences and offenders discovered due to chemists' reports, it is at once clear that the pattern is distinct in many respects from that produced by other discovery methods. Not surprisingly, offences are likely to occur between 9 a.m. and 6 p.m. (usual opening times) and throughout the week. In addition narcotics (i.e. opiates and opiate-like drugs) ($P < 0.05$) and amphetamines ($P < 0.05$) were overrepresented. Moreover, this group of offenders were distinct — they were the only group with a majority of women ($P < 0.05$) and a majority of married people ($P < 0.05$), and did not include any offenders aged under 21 ($P < 0.05$).

The distinctiveness of this group of offenders is interesting because not only is the discovery method virtually ignored in other research, but it is also basically a reactive method. In general, however, a brief review of the preceding pages reveals a number of distinctions in the types of offenders discovered by different methods, and we may reconsider these shortly. Before doing so, however, it seems appropriate to mention briefly the other discovery methods evident in the 1975 files.

(v) Other discovery methods

Although we have discussed the four major discovery methods, these in fact accounted for only 79.0% of cases discovered and 78.8% of all offenders who were caught. Three other methods appeared more than once during the year. Six offences were discovered due to external inquiries, when customs officials, or the police from another force gave the Sheffield police information leading to an arrest. For example:

'Customs and Excise Officers intercepted a parcel addressed to the offender, alleged to contain a 'Glass Desk Set' but which was actually 32 grammes of cannabis.'

Another five cases were discovered because of a report made by a member of the public:

'A chemist's shop was burgled by two offenders. They then went to a Sheffield allnighter, hiding the drugs on a picnic site and later distributing them to four other offenders. However a local resident had seen the break-in and gave the police the offenders' car number, which led to the arrest of the car owner who implicated the other five.'

'A witness reported a break-in at a chemist's shop. A patrol car arrived and caught two of the offenders on the premises.'

Finally four offences were discovered due to the routine police practice of monitoring ambulance calls:

'The offender dialed an ambulance after taking an overdose. The police picked up the call and questioned him in hospital where they found cannabis in his clothes.'

(vi) Summary

The discovery of drug offences was, then, commonly an activity which involved, using Skolnick's terminology, the police as initiators. With most offences not involving a victim, it is notable that the two major reactive methods, citizen and chemist reports, covered in the main offences which involved something more than a drug offence and the presence of a victim – that is, they were either cases where a chemist's shop was broken into, or where deception was directed at either the doctor or the chemist himself. If we exclude external inquiries, we are then left with four discovery methods which stemmed from police initiative. Of these, the most direct, the stopping and searching of those defined as 'acting suspiciously' was the most common and was notable in being largely restricted to certain 'notorious' sites. Given, however, that drug offences are relatively invisible, the drug squad employed other, distinctive, methods, to gain information. Here the use of informants was the most common, but the interception of hospital calls provided another source which was exploited. In addition, 'crime follow-up' methods provide an interesting contrast with the USI data, where police involvement with the 'victim' rather than the offender was an equally useful means by which victimless offences were discovered.

Having focused on the role of the police, nevertheless, it is notable that there were differences in the types of offender discovered by the different methods. Indeed, if we reconsider the four most common discovery methods, differences are evident on six variables:

(a) Age. At one extreme all those involved in chemists' reports were aged over 21; at the other extreme 47.8% of those from the crime follow-up group were aged under 21.

(b) Sex. Over 80% of those discovered by police proactivity or information received were males, compared with 60.9% of follow-up and

158

47.4% of chemists' reports.

(c) Marital status. Here chemists' reports were atypical in contributing nine of the nineteen married offenders.

(d) Unemployment. The highest rate of unemployment was amongst the information received group (72.2%), the lowest the proactive group, with 32.5% unemployed.

(e) Criminal record. Similarly, the information received group included the highest proportion with a record (81.3%), the police proactivity group the lowest (45.9%).

(f) Drug. By definition, chemists' reports all involved hard drugs (in particular narcotics and amphetamines) but police proactivity cases also involved hard drugs in a majority of cases, unlike information received and follow-up cases, in neither of which were any amphetamines found.

If we consider these differences in total, a number of interesting points emerge. First, taking the position of female drug offenders, it seems that these form a relatively invisible group, and are not uncovered either by police proactivity or information received. Consequently it is in cases of chemists' reports, where (in order to get drugs but without subcultural channels) female offenders become visible, and in crime follow-ups (where the discovery is relatively coincidental) that the proportion of female offenders is greatest.

However, other differences are either less marked or in the opposite direction to expectations. For example, whilst we might have anticipated police proactive discoveries to include a relatively high proportion of younger, unemployed offenders, in the case of the latter the opposite was the case and the age of this group was not particularly distinctive. Just as there is no evidence of a bohemian subgroup of potsmokers being picked up on the streets by the police, as Young (1971) implies in Notting Hill, so the low status offender with prior convictions is more likely to be unearthed due to police informants than to proactive policing in the strict sense. On the other hand, if we focus on the drug itself, the relationship between discovery method and visibility is more comprehensible. Following the argument developed by Plant (1975) – that cannabis use is more likely to occur in private, but that hard drugs may be taken in public more commonly – as anticipated the methods whereby the invisibility barrier is broken down (crime follow-up and information received) are most commonly associated with the discovery of cannabis offences. On the other hand, the visibility of hard drug offences, either through use in public or at the stage of supply (through burglary or fraud) is reflected in the discovery of hard drugs via police proactivity and chemists' reports. In police reports on their reasons for stop and search proceedings, considerable emphasis is placed on the extent to which signs of drug use are visible. While we should treat these statements with scepticism, it should, however, be stressed that in terms of the variables considered here this approach is more consistent than one which focuses on more directly personal factors. In particular, there is no evidence of successful stop and search methods being deployed against those, for example of bohemian appearance, who might be associated with a drugs subculture.

This point may be surprising. It is therefore perhaps important to emphasise, finally, that whereas in earlier chapters it was stressed that for standard list offences different discovery and detection methods apparently produced similar area differences in crime rates, the same cannot be said here with regard to other variables. Quite clearly, an increase in the use of informants, police proactivity or whatever else could lead to a considerable shift in many characteristics of the known offender population. Similarly the amount of recorded drug use is directly resultant from the extent and types of police activity.

CONCLUSIONS

In this chapter, it has become quite clear that the role of the police in the discovery of crime is considerable when we consider various types of victimless crime. However there is also a degree of variation, with at one extreme the police responsible for the discovery of all recorded offences of soliciting, and at the other extreme the police discovering only some half of USI cases. The extent of police involvement is largely accounted for by two elements that have been considered in detail in this chapter, the feasibility of the victimless label and the visibility of the offence.

Taking first the assumption that USI, soliciting and drugs offences are examples of victimless offences, it is clear that the extent to which the label is contended, i.e. a victim is acknowledged by the public, determines the degree of citizen involvement. At one extreme, it is notable that despite the legal justifications, members of the public who are unsuccessfully solicited by prostitutes do not feel victimised to the point where any of them are motivated to call the police. (12) At the other extreme, in USI and drugs cases some citizens may define either themselves or others as victims. In the case of USI it was notable that parents were sometimes willing to consider their daughters as innocent victims. With regard to drugs offences there were numerous examples where the act of obtaining a drug (through burglary or deception) meant that there was in fact a victim with a motive to call the police.

The other aspect which is important here is the visibility of the offence. Soliciting by known prostitutes is highly visible, both because it takes place in public and because it occurs in specific places at specific times. The same is true of some drugs cases, where police patrolling of certain allnighters and public houses at night enables them to detain some drug users. However in other drugs cases, and most USI cases, the visibility of the offence is questionable.

This would appear to have two implications. On the one hand, the recognition of drug use as a serious crime combined with appreciation of the difficulties of discovery have led to the formation of a drug squad. In contrast, USI is not considered serious enough for special measures, while the temporal and spatial location of prostitution make the use of special plain clothes patrols sufficient.

On the other hand, lack of visibility combined with an unwillingness of the public to report offences mean that the police, in order to discover offences, are required to develop strategies which surmount the visibility barrier. One way of doing this is through police questioning of those to whom they already have legitimate access (i.e. crime follow-up cases for drug offences and routine inquiries and reported missing cases for USI). A second example is the use of other agencies' information - the interception of hospital calls for drug cases, which has no equivalent in USI records here, but is a clear parallel to the methods described by Skolnick and Woodward (1968) in America. A third example, of importance in the drugs field, is the development of an information network among drug users and their contacts. Finally, there are cases where the police may use their discretion to question people whose behaviour or status in public leads them to suspect either that an offence is taking place or that some offence has taken place in private. Perhaps surprisingly the information from the drugs department records provide little or no information to suggest that this is very common, or based on suspect characteristics (rather than directly pertinent behaviour) but three USI cases were noted where the police acted directly to question girls seen in 'suspicious circumstances'.

The twin problems of privacy and victimlessness result in a considerable gap between crimes committed and crimes recorded. In the case of prostitution and drugs offences, where police specialisation exists, the focus turns on the role of the police in the definition of appropriate crime levels. The argument that the police define their role as containment agents (in the cases of prostitution allied to order maintenance) gains credence from the effects on crime figures of one incident in 1975, namely the murder of a car park attendant in the city centre during the late summer. As a result of the murder, a large scale police inquiry was launched which lasted for the rest of the year and which led to the 'vice squad' and drugs squad operating at minimum strengths. The subjective reports we have of the effects of this on prostitution suggest that the degree of open solicitation in the red light district increased markedly, an illustration of the efficiency of the police in containing the problem at other times. On the other hand, despite feelings from the drug squad that their efficiency at that time was curtailed, our records show no evidence of a decrease in the number of offences discovered, and in particular no decrease in the extent of police proactivity and information received cases. It thus seems that even in this type of situation the drugs squad were able to maintain a fairly consistent level of offence discoveries.

Whereas much of this book has served to shift the focus for the level of recorded crime onto decisions made by members of the public, i.e. on whether or not to report offences to the police, the same cannot be said here. Most especially, it is clear that the role of the police is of primary importance in determining the recorded crime rates for some offences, for example soliciting, drugs offences and (referring back to Chapter 6) technical drinking offences.

8 Official Cautioning by the Police

INTRODUCTION

Earlier chapters have focused on the role of the police in the discovery and detection of crime, first using data on crimes associated with nine residential areas of the city, then concerning specific types of victimless crime. In this chapter we return to the area data to consider one final aspect of police decision making, the role of the police in cautioning of offenders. The importance of this aspect is well illustrated by La Fave, in his influential work Arrest:

'Perhaps the most significant feature of current criminal justice administration is the great amount of discretion which is exercised by police. Decisions not to arrest because of the nature of the offense, the circumstances of its commission, or some other factor are made routinely. The use of judgement in deciding whether one apparently guilty of criminal conduct should be subjected to the criminal process is an obviously important exercise of governmental power.' (La Fave, 1965; 61)

Of course, as has been stressed throughout, the data used here are dependent upon the decision to record. For example, police action which involves the discretionary 'turning a blind eye' either to suspicious behaviour or to an offender who has actually been spoken to, cannot by definition be quantified given the methods employed. Whilst the limited participant observations and discussions with the area constables implied that the unrecorded use of discretion is not frequent in cases of indictable offences, there is no guarantee that this is the case. On the other hand if as might be expected, such discretion is more common in the case of juveniles, there is other evidence that, at least since the Children and Young Persons Act (1969), discretion may have become more a part of the formal, recorded organisational process than being rooted in individual on-the-scene procedures. (Ditchfield, 1976)

In fact, a number of the American studies of discretion have also been based on officially recorded information (Terry, 1967 (i) (ii); Shannon, 1963). However, in this respect, there is considerable evidence available from British sources regarding the use of official cautioning by the police, and this is almost entirely due to the meticulous recording of such information by the Home Office.

The most detailed analysis of the data collected on official cautions is contained in a monograph by Steer, based largely on a sample of male offenders aged seventeen years or more, cautioned for indictable offences during the years 1965-67 in five English police forces:

'When an offence is reported, the chief constable or other senior officer may (except in the case of certain grave offences and offences by police officers which must be reported to the Director of Public Prosecutions) still decide to take no further action, or to issue the formal caution as an alternative to proceedings in court. If the formal caution is for an indictable offence, shoplifting for example, the

offender will most probably be asked to attend a police station where,
if the offence is admitted and the complainant does not insist on a
prosecution, he will be given a verbal caution by a senior police officer
in uniform. Otherwise the caution will be sent in the form of a letter
from the chief constable.' (Steer, 1970; 5)

As is indicated in the above quotation, one important element in the
decision to caution may be the reluctance, or otherwise, of the complainant to prosecute. In addition Steer noted that cautions may be given due
to the nature of the offence, especially where the 'victim' was a
participant (e.g. intercourse with a girl aged 13-15), where the police
had insufficient evidence or where the production of such evidence in
court might be difficult or costly. However, Steer also stressed that
in deciding whether or not to caution, the police took particular
account of the offender, his previous reputation, and the effect that
a court appearance might have on him. Thus cautioning was also related
to the age and criminal record of the offender.

In addition, Steer noted that there were considerable differences in
cautioning rates between different forces. Taking up this point,
Ditchfield, using police data for all ages in 1973 found that force
variations could only be partly explained by different patterns of
crime in different areas. (Ditchfield, 1976) However, there was a
relationship between cautioning rates and discharge rates. Thus where
forces tended not to use their cautioning powers, courts apparently
compensated by discharging more offenders.

Ditchfield was also concerned with differences in cautioning on an
individual level, relating it particularly to offence type and age of
offender.

In the latter case, he found considerable variation and moreover,
demonstrated the importance of the Children and Young Persons Act (1969)
in leading to increased cautioning rates for the younger age groups.
As table 8.1 demonstrates, since 1968 there has been a considerable
increase in cautioning for the 10-13, and 14-16 age groups which has not
been matched for the older age groups, leading to even more disparity
than was formerly the case.

Table 8.1
Those cautioned as a percentage of known offenders,
by age group, 1960-1974 (indictable and non-indictable
offences) (Ditchfield, 1976; 7)

Age Group	1960	1968	1969	1970	1971	1972	1973	1974
10-13	33.0	39.1	46.7	51.7	61.6	65.7	66.0	66.2
14-16	21.2	18.6	23.5	25.5	32.2	34.1	34.7	36.1
17-20	9.4	5.9	5.6	5.6	5.8	5.9	5.7	5.0
21+	8.9	5.4	4.7	4.8	5.6	5.5	5.4	5.2

As well as the monographs by Steer and Ditchfield which are specifically
devoted to cautioning material, the Home Office Criminal Statistics have,
in recent years, contained a great deal of evidence of variation in
cautioning rates, both in different forces and for different categories
of offender. For example, the Report for 1976 (Home Office, 1977; 30-39)

163

includes information relating to offence type, sex and age. As is
indicated in table 8.2, which is based on Home Office figures (Home
Office, 1977; 31-32, tables 3.2 - 3.3), cautioning rates are clearly
related to offence type, sex and age. Females are more likely to be
cautioned than males, juveniles than adults, and those committing
apparently 'less serious' offences (like sex, theft/handling) are more
likely to be cautioned than those committing 'more serious' offences
(like robbery and violence offences).

Table 8.2
Persons cautioned as a percentage of those cautioned or
found guilty, England and Wales, 1976

	Males				
	Under 14	14-16	17-20	21+	Total
Indictable					
Violence	57.9	22.6	2.3	4.5	8.2
Sex	78.2	67.9	54.5	12.9	34.7
Burglary	46.8	17.7	0.8	0.6	14.6
Robbery	30.3	7.0	0.2	0.3	2.8
Theft/handling	72.6	39.8	2.8	3.5	21.1
Fraud/forgery	60.7	32.9	2.3	1.7	4.6
Crim. Dam.	56.6	28.3	2.7	2.1	19.3
Other	57.5	22.6	2.7	1.6	2.8
Total	63.5	31.9	3.5	3.2	17.2
Non-indictable					
Excl. motoring	60.8	35.1	4.8	4.8	7.2
	Females				
Indictable					
Violence	61.0	36.6	8.7	14.2	23.1
Sex	84.2	90.9	81.3	47.6	63.3
Burglary	55.9	26.4	3.4	5.2	25.0
Robbery	23.1	8.2	0	0	0.6
Theft/handling	84.7	60.0	5.1	10.7	30.4
Fraud/forgery	70.7	46.0	5.2	5.5	10.4
Crim. Dam.	64.8	40.0	5.2	5.4	18.7
Other	82.1	55.6	5.2	3.9	6.4
Total	81.4	54.8	5.3	10.0	27.7
Non-indictable					
Excl. motoring	58.9	32.0	27.4	11.1	14.6

There are, however, some interesting variations to the pattern. Thus,
whilst the 17-20 age group in general tend to be treated rather more like
the 21+ group than the 14-15 group, this is not the case for sex offences.
In addition, whilst females are more likely to be cautioned than males,
this does not hold for robbery offences or, in the case of those under
17, non-indictable (excluding motoring). Moreover, as has been noted
elsewhere (Mawby, 1977; (iii)), the pattern is complicated by the lack

of any control for previous convictions. Where, as was shown in the first stage of this research (Baldwin and Bottoms, 1976; 70) male offenders are more likely to be recidivists than are females, this factor could well account for the differential cautioning rates.

Although the American research has considered the relationship between cautioning and factors such as social class and area of residence, the British material has been less comprehensive. The result is that although only some three pages of The Urban Criminal (Baldwin and Bottoms, 1976; 134-36) were devoted to cautioning patterns, these are important in providing some information on the relationship between social class, area of residence and cautioning at least as far as the under 20 age group was concerned.

In fact, the findings proved to be interesting. On the one hand, there was a significant difference between owner occupied areas, with some 24% of juveniles cautioned, and other tenure type areas, with 13% of juveniles in council areas and 20% in privately rented areas cautioned. However, dividing areas within each tenure type according to social class of area produced no significant differences within tenure types; and comparing 'low status' owner occupied areas with 'high status' council and privately rented areas (all these being roughly equivalent in social class composition), still revealed considerable differences between tenure types. This led Baldwin and Bottoms to conclude:

"the data thus appear to indicate tentatively that in Sheffield some difference exists in police decisions according to tenure types. Possibly the most likely explanation of this is that owner occupied houses are typically better kept than council or rented houses, and that the standards of upkeep of home seems (on impressionistic evidence from police records) to be an important consideration in the decision to caution juveniles.' (Baldwin and Bottoms, 1976; 136)

The second stage of the research makes it possible to consider these points further, although, given the small numbers involved in a comparison of only nine areas, the findings are nowhere near conclusive. (In addition of course, differences between owner occupied and other areas cannot be considered fully due to the small numbers.) However, it is possible to consider cautioning rates according to the offender rates of each area. Thus one can ask whether the proportion of cautions given, or the reasons given for cautions, vary between areas. In chapter three a considerable amount of information was included which suggested that area constables had rather vague ideas of the offender rates of 'their' areas, and this implies that cautioning rates would not vary by this criterion. Nevertheless, in the following two sections, various aspects of the cautioning process will be considered to see whether differences do in fact exist according to areal or any other factors.

THE CAUTIONING OF OFFENDERS FROM THE NINE AREAS

Data collected at this stage of the project may be handled in two ways. First, it is possible to consider cautions given to offenders living in the nine areas in detail. Secondly it is possible to analyse the justifications given in the official reports for employing a caution (for a parallel use of these two sets of data see Stanfield and Maher, 1968).

Table 8.3
Cautioning in the nine areas (2)

Males	CHH	CHM	CHL	CFH	CFL	RHH	RHL	R'HL	OHL	Total
Cautioned	11	9	1	3	5	6	2	4	0	41
Found guilty	65	19	16	35	11	76	20	8	5	255
Total	76	28	17	38	16	82	22	12	5	296
% cautioned	14.5	32.1	5.9	7.9	31.3	7.3	9.1	33.3	0	13.9

Females	CHH	CHM	CHL	CFH	CFL	RHH	RHL	R'HL	OHL	Total
Cautioned	2	10	4	8	1	5	0	3	1	34
Found guilty	8	3	5	16	2	11	3	3	0	51
Total	10	13	9	24	3	16	3	6	1	85
% cautioned	20.0	76.9	44.4	33.3	33.3	31.3	0	50.0	(100)	40.0

Table 8.4
Percentage cautioned by sex and offender
rate of area

	High rate	CHM	Low rate	Total
Males	10.2	32.1	15.7	13.9
Females	30.0	76.9	40.4	40.0

In tables 8.3 and 8.4 each decision (i.e. by the police or the court) has been treated separately. That is, an offender who was cautioned once and found guilty in court once during 1971 would be included twice, as would an offender cautioned twice, whilst an offender cautioned once for two incidents would be counted once. As can be seen, in general the low rate areas tended to have a higher proportion of offenders cautioned than did the high rate areas, and within the low rate areas males from CFL and RHL stand out as being apparently favourably treated. However, quite unexpectedly, CHM is clearly distinct from the other areas in having a high cautioning rate, with 32.1% of males and 76.9% of females cautioned and it is this, rather than the high/low offender rate distinction, which makes areal variations significantly different (for males comparing high/ CHM χ^2 = 9.32, P < 0.01 for females comparing high/CHM/low, χ_2^2 = 9.46, P < 0.05).

But at this stage, no allowance has been made for differences in the types of offenders living in the different areas. Since there are differences in the ages, offences committed and criminal records of offenders from different areas, and since these three factors have all been shown elsewhere to be related to cautioning, it is at least possible that areal differences are more a reflection of variations between offenders than of police policy being explicitly directed at specific areas.

As table 8.5 illustrates, cautioning is, in these areas, strongly related to age, with cautioning common for the under 17 age group and rare for males in the 17-19 age group. For males, it appears that, irrespective of area those 17-19 are unlikely to be cautioned, and given the small number of females in this age group, it is only really practicable to consider those under 17 and 20 or over.

Table 8.5
Cautioning by age of offender

Males	Cautioned	Found guilty	% cautioned
Under 17	26	73	26.3
17-19	1	53	1.9
20+	14	129	9.8
Females			
Under 17	21	9	70.0
17-19	2	3	-
20+	11	41	21.2

Table 8.6
Cautioning by offender rate of areas

	Under 17			20+		
	High	CHM	Low	High	CHM	Low
Males						
Cautioned	16	8	3	5	1	8
Found guilty	51	9	13	92	6	31
% cautioned	23.9	47.1	18.8	5.2	(14.3)	20.5
Females						
Cautioned	10	6	5	5	2	4
Found guilty	6	0	3	26	3	12
% cautioned	62.5	(100)	(62.5)	16.1	(40)	25.0

The numbers involved particularly in CHM, and for females in general, are small and should be treated with circumspection. However, considering males there is no evidence that those under 17 from the low rate areas are more likely to be cautioned than are those from the high rate areas, but it would seem that for the older age group there is an areal difference (χ^2 = 6.00, P < 0.05). For females, despite the small numbers, the areal difference is similar being apparently confined to the older age group.

Ideally, it should be possible to compare areas including a control for criminal records. If this is done, numbers in each box become increasingly smaller and must be treated with ever more care. Nevertheless, confining our attention to the under 17 and 20+ age groups, it can be seen (from table 8.7) that:

(i) A higher proportion of females than males are cautioned although the difference is negligible for first offenders over 20 (the only significant difference is for first offenders under 17, χ^2 = 4.13, P < 0.05).

167

(ii) A considerably higher proportion of first offenders than recidivists are cautioned, the difference being especially prevalent for males.

(iii) The under 17 age groups are more likely to receive a caution than are the 20+ age groups, especially in the case of first offenders.

Table 8.7
Cautioning according to age, police record
and area of residence

	No previous police record				Previous police record			
	High	CHM	Low	Total	High	CHM	Low	Total
Males 20+								
Cautioned	3	1	6	10	2	0	2	4
Guilty	20	1	13	34	72	3	18	93
% cautioned	13.0	–	31.6	22.7	2.7	–	10.0	4.1
Males under 17								
Cautioned	14	5	3	22	1	3	0	4
Guilty	14	3	7	24	37	6	6	49
% cautioned	50.0	(62.5)	30.0	47.8	2.6	(33.3)	(0)	7.5
Females 20+								
Cautioned	5	0	4	9	0	2	0	2
Guilty	17	3	9	29	9	0	3	10
% cautioned	22.7	–	30.8	23.7	–	–	–	14.3
Females under 17								
Cautioned	9	5	5	19	1	1	0	2
Guilty	4	0	1	5	2	0	2	4
% cautioned	69.2	(100)	(83.3)	79.2	–	–	–	–

These differences are all fairly clear. On the other hand, controlling for these three factors seems to minimise many of the areal differences. Thus, comparing offenders from high rate areas with offenders from low rate areas, it appears that:

(i) For males 20+ those from low rate areas are most likely to be cautioned, for both first offender and recidivists groups.

(ii) For males under 17 there is no such trend, and if anything it seems that first offenders from high rate areas were more commonly cautioned than those from low rate areas.

(iii) The female categories are very small, but for females with no previous convictions it appears that those from low rate areas were relatively more frequently cautioned, for both the under 17 and 20+ groups but the differences are far from statistically significant.

These differences are not, however, pronounced, and are certainly not

great enough to be statistically significant, which, given the numbers
involved, is perhaps not surprising. However, it must be stressed that,
while on the one hand the inclusion of other variables, like offence type,
or a sharper age distinction for the older age group, might narrow the
differences further, clearly age, record and even sex are considerably
more significant factors than is area of residence. Since for the 17-19
age group it also appeared that males from all areas were highly unlikely
to be cautioned, the main conclusion of this section must be that for
males, where numbers are at least large enough to show some pattern,
there are no clear areal differences for the under 17 and 17-19 age
groups but there may be differences for the older age groups. Even here,
however, differences are minimal in comparison with differences on other
variables, like age and record, a finding which is broadly similar to
that of other research. (Shannon, 1963)

In terms of the wider implications of this data, it appears that the
effects of differential cautioning policies on differences in area
'offender' rates would be minimal. However, before returning to this
point, it is pertinent to consider the justification given for cautions
in the areas.

JUSTIFICATIONS FOR RECOMMENDING AN OFFICIAL CAUTION

The policy in South Yorkshire in 1971 was for the officer in charge of
a case to state, in his report, the reasons why he was recommending a
particular caution. In fact, whilst there were only two cases recorded
where the officer recommended a caution but none was given, there were a
number of instances where the senior officer decided to issue a caution
without a written recommendation. It is possible, of course, that in
some cases a caution would have been recommended verbally. Nevertheless,
it can be seen from table 8.8 that cases where cautions were given but
not recommended in writing were restricted to the high and medium
offender rate areas.

Table 8.8
Cautions recommended in writing by officer in
charge, by offender rate of area

	High	CHM	Low	Total
Caution recommended and given	18	11	21	50
Caution given but not recommended	17	8	0	25
Total	35	19	21	75
% cautions recommended	51.4	57.9	100	66.7

Whereas in general two thirds of cautions followed a written recommendation, all cautions in low rate areas were backed up by a recommendation
but only about half those in high rate areas ($\chi^2 = 14.80$, $P < 0.001$).
What then, was the substance of written recommendations?

In the last section it was suggested that factors like age and record
were considerably more important discriminators in determining cautioning
rates than was area of residence. Similarly, an analysis of the reasons
given for a caution showed that the home circumstances of the offender
were mentioned comparatively less than other factors, and there were no

cases in which the wider area was discussed. In all, there were seven
different types of justifications given for a caution:

(i) The officer might stress that the offender had no previous
convictions.

(ii) Alternatively, or in addition, he might include details of the
offender's attitude - for example that he was sorry, or had co-operated
fully with the police. That is, in such cases, the offender might be
portrayed as accepting the police definition of the situation.

(iii) On the other hand, in some cases the officer in charge included
details of the more general circumstances of the offender - his background, work record, etc.

(iv) Similarly, particularly in the case of juveniles, the offender's
home and family might be described.

(v) Alternatively, extenuating circumstances might be mentioned to
'explain' the offence - particularly the fact that the offender was very
young or old, or had been ill.

(vi) On the other hand, in many cases the officer focused on the
offence itself, recommending a caution on the grounds that it was not
serious - not much had been stolen, or everything had been recovered.

(vii) Finally, specific mention was made in a number of cases that the
victim had expressed a wish that a caution should be given - or at least
had not objected to the police suggestion that a caution might be
appropriate. Conversely, only once was a caution given when the victim
was recorded as expressing a desire for prosecution.

In table 8.9 the reasons given have been tabulated in two ways. First,
each reason given for each offender has been counted separately (A).
Secondly, only one reason within each of the classifications has been
used for each offender (B) (although as can be seen, multiple reasons
across different categories are still included).

Table 8.9
Justifications cited for cautioning

	A	B
No criminal record	34	34
Offender was sorry or co-operative	12	12
Offender's social background	16	16
Situation in the home, family	18	13
Extenuating circumstances	20	19
Offence not serious	46	38
Victim's wish for caution	40	40
Total justifications	186	172
Total cases	50	50
Justifications per case	3.7	3.4

As can be seen from table 8.9, as might be expected, in thirty-four of
the fifty cases the lack of a criminal record was stressed. However, the

170

nature of the offence and the victim's wish appeared to be the most common justifications cited. On the other hand, a number of other factors related to the offender, his background, family and attitude, and any extenuating circumstances were each cited in a not insignificant minority of cases and in fact in total accounted for 35.4% of all justifications.

Whilst the victim's wishes and the lack of a criminal record could clearly be stated only once for each case, it is notable that for other justifications it sometimes happened that a similar point was made in a number of ways (as reflected in A > B) - this was particularly so in cases where the minor nature of the offence, and the home circumstances of the offender were stressed.

Of course it cannot be too often emphasised that these are the reasons given by the officer-in-charge, and may reflect his perception of the circumstances, his idea of the frame of reference used by his superior officer, or his judgement over the most likely tactics to 'pay off' in a particular case. Nevertheless, having accepted that the data cited here is in no sense an objective portrayal of the actual circumstances pertaining to each case, it is still pertinent to consider what differences there were in terms of the justifications given for different types of offender and different areas.

Here numbers make it impossible to classify according to more than one variable at once. However, considering three characteristics of offenders - age (comparing those under 17 with 17+), sex and area of residence it is possible to estimate the relative importance of each of these.

Even taking each factor separately, the small numbers involved make statistical analysis difficult, but one can at least note trends. Thus, as is illustrated in table 8.10, comparing those under 17 with those 17+, the minor nature of the offence was significantly more likely to be mentioned in the case of the younger age group (χ^2 = 14.46, P < 0.001) and the wishes of the victim were apparently also more commonly cited for this group. On the other hand, whilst as might be expected the home circumstances of the offender were much more commonly mentioned for those under 17 (χ^2 = 9.34, P < 0.01) this was compensated for by an emphasis on more general social background factors in the case of those 17+ (χ^2 = 5.98, P < 0.02).

Whilst these differences are pronounced, there are rather less clear differences between the sexes. The only significant (indeed the only clear) difference between the sexes is in references to extenuating circumstances, this being more common for females (χ^2 = 6.33, P < 0.02).

Turning to the types of justification made according to area of residence of the offender, the most significant finding is that areal differences, at least between high and low offender rate areas, are minimal. There is no evidence that home circumstances, social background, attitude or extenuating circumstances are more commonly cited in the low rate areas compared with the high rate areas. The attitude of the offender and home circumstances were cited most frequently in CHM, but the numbers involved are small and should be treated with care. On the other hand, whilst in the last section it appeared that factors such as age and previous convictions were more closely related to cautioning rates than area of residence, in this section, similarly, area of residence seems to be of less importance than age and sex.

Table 8.10
Justifications cited for cautions (B)
according to age, sex and area of residence

	Age		Sex		Residence		
	17	17+	M	F	H	CHM	L
No criminal record	18	16	17	17	11	8	15
Offender was sorry or cooperative	7	5	8	4	3	5	4
Offender's social background	5	11	9	7	6	2	8
Situation in home, family	12	1	8	5	3	7	3
Extenuating circumstances	12	7	6	13	7	5	7
Offence not serious	27	11	21	17	14	10	14
Victim's wish for caution	25	15	21	19	13	9	18
Total justifications	106	65	90	82	57	46	69
Total cases	28	22	27	23	18	11	21
Justifications per case	3.8	3.0	3.3	3.6	3.2	4.2	3.3

The evidence produced in this chapter has thus tended to confirm the finding of previous studies, in that factors such as sex, age, and previous convictions appear to be more strongly related to cautioning patterns than do more general factors (in this case area of residence). Similarly there is no evidence of any marked variation between high and low offender rate areas in terms of the number of justifications given for a caution, or the factors stressed in the officers' reports.

These points must however be qualified. The numbers dealt with here are very small, and in addition the interrelationship between the different variables is difficult to assess. The results are therefore suggestive rather than conclusive.

Moreover, there does appear to be a difference between areas in the readiness of the officer-in-charge of a case to recommend a caution, at least as far as the written records indicate. Cautioning rates in high and low offender rate areas were not markedly different; but in the low rate areas all cautions given were recommended in writing by the officer-in-charge, whilst in the high rate areas there was evidence of recommendations in only some half the cases, a difference which may indicate a policy, explicit or otherwise, of superior officers compensating for the discriminatory practices of the officers-in-charge.

However, the precise nature of these 'negotiations' cannot be assessed from the records available retrospectively, and indeed may well have changed with the further implementation of the Children and Young Persons Act since 1971.

On the other hand, in the present context it is pertinent to consider the extent to which decisions, such as who to caution and which cases to drop for lack of evidence, plus decisions made in the courts over sentencing, affect alternative measurements of the offender rates in the different areas.

This study was not designed as an examination of variations in sentencing practice between offenders from different areas, and the numbers involved are clearly too small to allow such comparisons to be made. Nevertheless, it is clearly relevant to consider what effect cautioning policy has on area rates where for example, only those found guilty in court are considered. Similarly, this research has used a police-based definition of guilt and it could be argued that this might affect areal differences, while on the other hand, the different measurement of offender rate between this and the first stage of the research may be significant.

Taking these factors into consideration, it is possible to construct four alternative measurements of offender rate other than the one used throughout this study.

This study has used an offender rate based on all those considered by the police to be guilty (as indicated by their being named on the incident form), including those who were not brought to court because of a lack of evidence, or because it was otherwise inexpedient to prosecute (including those under age of criminal responsibility), and those who were found not guilty. However, each individual was counted only once. An offender who was at one time in 1971 found not guilty but at another time found guilty would be counted only once, as would an offender found guilty on two separate occasions.

Clearly the area offender rates constructed by this means might be modified if all those who were either found not guilty or not formally charged for lack of evidence or other reasons, were excluded. In fact this involved only seven individuals. Five of these were either found not guilty or not charged, the remaining two were serving sentences for offences committed in 1970 and were not charged with offences they admitted from the 1971 files. Despite the small numbers involved, an offender rate (B) has been constructed for each area, in which these cases are excluded from the total.

Alternatively, one can start from a different base, as did Baldwin and Bottoms in the first stage of the research, by including offenders more than once, according to the number of times a decision was made on how to deal with each. This allows two rates to be used, corresponding to the two originally described, namely, including (C) and excluding (D) cases where the suspect was either found not guilty or where no proceedings were initiated. In addition, one can exclude all cases which were not taken to court (i.e. cautions and other inexpedient to prosecute cases) and construct a rate based only on guilty findings in court (E).

At this stage we have four measures of offender rate, which could be used as alternatives to the one chosen for the present survey. However, it is also possible to consider other measurements of offender rates, which are less easily justified but which have been utilised by past researchers. One obvious example here is a rate based on probation (or supervision) cases (P) similar to that used by Morris in his Croydon study (Morris, 1957). Alternatively, a number of studies have used an even more selective group, those sentenced to a custodial sentence (I). Here the definition of a custodial sentence has been widened so as to include as many cases as possible, for example attendance centres, suspended sentences and care orders (although many of these may not be institutionalised).

In table 8.11 these six alternative measurements are presented alongside the offender rate (A) used in the rest of this book. Taking the
first five measurements, it is clear from tables 8.11 and 8.12 that
whichever measurement is used the rank ordering of areas is largely the
same, the only difference being a shift round of two low rate areas,
CFL and R'HL. At the same time, there is, within this overall picture
of similarity, some change of emphasis. Using only guilty findings,
the gap between RHH and CHH is lessened and RHL becomes more clearly
distinguished from CFL and R'HL. Similarly the atypical pattern of
cautioning in CHM is reflected in a relative fall in its rate on the E
measurement.

Table 8.11
Alternative offender rates for the nine areas

	CHH	CHM	CHL	CFH	CFL	RHH	RHL	R'HL	OHL
A	96.7	46.6	32.4	76.7	22.2	141.5	25.5	21.9	5.2
B	95.3	46.6	31.2	75.4	21.2	136.9	25.5	21.9	5.2
C	131.3	57.6	36.1	83.3	24.2	166.2	25.5	23.1	5.2
D	129.9	57.6	32.4	82.0	22.2	156.9	25.5	21.9	5.2
E	105.3	30.2	26.2	66.4	13.1	133.8	22.5	13.4	4.3
P	27.4	9.6	7.5	9.1	2.0	23.1	7.8	2.4	0
I	17.3	8.2	3.7	13.0	4.0	46.2	5.9	1.2	0.9

Table 8.12
Rank order of areas for alternative offender
rates (1 = highest rate; 9 = lowest)

	CHH	CHM	CHL	CFH	CFL	RHH	RHL	R'HL	OHL
A	2	4	5	3	7	1	6	8	9
B	2	4	5	3	8	1	6	7	9
C	2	4	5	3	7	1	6	8	9
D	2	4	5	3	7	1	6	8	9
E	2	4	5	3	8	1	6	7	9
P	1	3	6	4	8	2	5	7	9
I	2	4	7	3	6	1	5	8	9

On the other hand, the picture is somewhat more different when rates
are worked out on the basis of probation or custodial sentences only.
Taking the probation rate (P), the change is illustrated by this being
the only rate on which RHH is displaced as the highest rate area, and
additionally CHM has a higher rate than the third high rate area CFH.
Considering the actual rates, rather than their ranking, re-emphasises
this. Thus, were one working only from a rate based on the probation
data, the nine areas could most easily be distinguished as three groups,
two with high rates (CHH, RHH), four with medium rates (CHM, CFH, RHL
and CHL) and three with low rates (R'HL, CFL and OHL).

The case of the probation rate is particularly interesting because it
is rather less similar to the other rates than is the custodial offender
rate (I). It has been suggested at various stages in chapter two, that

174

offenders from the high rate areas might commit more serious offences
than those from the low rate areas, and, more significantly, they appear
to be more frequently recidivist. One might therefore expect areal
differences to be clearer, rather than otherwise, taking this type of
measurement. Certainly, as can be seen from table 8.12, the rank order
is similar to that using rates A-E. However, rather than showing a
polarisation of high and low rate areas, the custodial offender rate
distinguishes RHH from the other areas. Whereas on measures A-E, RHH
has a rate some 21% to 46% higher than CHH, on rate I it has a rate no
less than 167% higher.

Seemingly then, decisions on whether or not to charge an offender
have relatively minor effects on areal variation in offender rates.
However rates based on actual court decisions regarding a particular
sentence are considerably more questionable. It is not of course,
possible from the present data to discover why this is so: it may be
partly due to different sentencing practices; it is certainly likely to
be affected by the different types of offender living in the different
areas, in terms of such factors as age, record and sex. That is, to
state the case baldly, offenders from CHH seem to be considered relatively good probation potential, offenders from RHH rather more as requiring
an institutional sentence. Whatever the reason, clearly the findings
here cast some doubts on studies, such as that by Morris (1957), which
use data related to specific sentences, at least as far as this is a
sentence of probation or some form of custody.

This is, moreover, to ignore the fact that similarity between overall
rates may mask considerable differences between the types of offenders
included within those rates. On the level of cautioning, for example,
it was demonstrated that younger first offenders were highly likely to
be cautioned. Exclusion of cautioning data from analysis could therefore mean that areas with high proportions of young offenders, or first
offenders (or both) would not be represented adequately. Similarly, if
two areas have comparable rates on, say, both scale A and scale P used
here, this could be because in one area adult recidivists and in the
other area adult first offenders tend to be placed on probation. Thus,
whilst the ratio of offender rates may well be similar, the types of
offenders compared across areas may not be adequately reflected.

CONCLUSIONS

This study utilised the widest possible definition of 'offender', for
two reasons. First, in so doing the maximum number of cases was included where police discretion might be considered. Secondly, it enabled
a number of alternative measurements to be constructed, such that the
direct influence of that discretion - at the levels of deciding who was
the offender (according to police rather than judicial definitions)
and who should be cautioned - on the offender rates could be measured.

In fact, in each of these cases it appears that the findings, like
those of previous chapters, tend to show that the discriminatory role
of the police, at least as far as areal differences are concerned, may
have been overemphasised in previous literature. At the level of
cautioning, areal differences were slight (being only marked in the
case of CHM) although this may have been due to a complementary policy
employed by commanding officers. However, an analysis of the justifica-

tions given for recommending a caution also revealed no clear area differences.

On the other hand, whilst differences between areas were relatively consistent whether one defined 'offender' at the one extreme according to police definitions and at the other only whether there was a court finding of guilt, using specific sentences as measurements appeared to be of questionable validity.

Nevertheless, the findings of this chapter are similar to those reported earlier. That is, it appears that, in so far as one can approximate 'real' differences in offender rates between different areas, a number of alternative measures used here would appear consistently to reveal such differences.

Put another way, there is no evidence here or elsewhere in the research that differential areal offender rates were 'created' by the law enforcement process, up to and including a finding of guilt. In the final chapter the evidence for this assertion will be reconsidered within the general framework of policework.

9 Conclusions

This research started from the assumption that the police played a
pivotal discretionary role in the law enforcement process, with the
result that data on crime rates which were based on police returns would
be highly suspect. It will be clear from the general tone of the findings reported in chapters four and five that with regard to indictable
crime at least, the power of the police is extremely limited. The
results are surprising, to the author no less than to the reader. The
aim of this chapter is, consequently, to summarise the main findings
and suggest reasons why the situation is so. In this section, the
focus will be on the role of the police in general. Then, in the next
section, I will concentrate on the areal dimensions and the extent to
which official statistics provide a reliable and valid measurement
instrument.

Quite clearly, the findings of this research clash with other
perspectives on the role of the police in modern society. Those working
from a conflict theory model have often considered the police as outsiders intervening in the lives of those whose social order is different,
not inferior or less moral, from that of the law makers and law
enforcers. The importance placed herein on the role of the public as
complainants, not only in terms of indictable crimes but also minor
incidents, shows very clearly that residents of 'disreputable'
neighbourhoods are only too eager to involve the police in their lives
on numerous occasions. Here the work of Meyer (1974) on noncriminal
incidents has already been cited as support. In addition, though, there
are other indications of the willingness of lower-class citizens to seek
help from the police. For example, as one American study in 'Midcity'
revealed, there may be a distinction between residents' public attitudes
towards the police and their actual behaviour:

'The 'official' line of urban slum residents, particularly the more
criminally inclined, resonates the bitter, venomous 'lousy copper'
ethic so frequently represented by writers - particularly authors of
gangster and prison movies - as constituting the true feelings of lower
class people. In Midcity, relations between the police and local
residents were in actuality, quite amiable and of clear benefit to the
populace. The local police station was the first resource they turned
to in the event of a wider variety of problems typically facing slum
residents - illness and accidents, drunken husbands, fights in bar
rooms, runaway children and more. Residents of Midcity - particularly
mothers in husbandless households - even turned to the police for
assistance in problems only remotely involving police functions, as,
for example, trouble with the hotwater heater. With some exceptions,
the police accepted these responsibilities with good grace and performed
the requested services with considerable efficiency.' (Miller et al,
1968; 93)

Here two additional points of relevance may be noted from the Sheffield
research. First it was clear, using the juvenile self-report data, that

schoolboys in the high rate council housing estate (CHH) expressed
significantly more hostile attitudes to the police than did boys from
the low rate estate (CHL) (Mawby, 1978 (i); 291-92). On the other hand,
comparing the same estates it was equally clear that residents of CHH
were some three times as likely as residents of CHL to ask the police to
make surveillance checks on their homes while they were away on holiday,
and a similar pattern emerged for the privately rented sector for which
details were also available (Mawby, 1978 (i); 290). The difference
here seems to reflect a correct appreciation by residents of high crime
rate areas of their need for additional protection. Put another way,
such an awareness is quite clearly more important to residents than any
feelings they may have about the police, in determining whether or not
they involve the police. It seems then, that both in response to
crimes and minor deviant incidents and as a precaution against crime,
there is no evidence of those in 'disreputable' areas being less willing
to involve the police than those in other areas. (1)

What then of the role of police discretion at the discovery and detection stages of the criminal process? A number of studies have placed
central importance on the operational discretion of the police, whereby
they are enabled to select from the routine normality of their work task
those situations which are problematic and need to be investigated
further. In reply, it should first be stressed that the results of
this study in no way contradict these assumptions. Quite clearly the
police through experience and training, do learn to make normative
distinctions between different types of citizen encounter. However the
two crucial points that need to be made here are first with regard to
the extent to which discretion is used (especially as regards an outcome
as a recorded criminal statistic), and secondly the types of criteria on
which discretion is based. Thus, taking Matza's model with its emphasis
on the 'method of suspicion' (Matza, 1969), I have argued that there is
no evidence, from police arrest data, that the method is significant as
a detection method. This is not to say that the police do not operate
a method of suspicion, only that the extent to which it is operational-
ised successfully (i.e. it results in an arrest) is quite clearly
minimal. Moreover, where there are cases in the records of the use of
police discretion, it is notable that area of residence of the offender
does not appear as a distinguishing factor, either for the indictable or
nonindictable data. Furthermore, when in chapter five an additional
analysis was carried out on other individual variables, it was evident
that police detections were no more common for offences involving more
than one offender, nor for offenders with criminal records. Indeed the
only variable which was distinct was age. It seemed that offenders in
the 17-20 age group were most commonly picked up due to police initiative.
This may have been related to the types of crimes they committed. On the
other hand, it was also notable that this group were also the least likely
to receive an official caution. The possibility thus exists that males
in the 17-20 age group are distinguished by the police (perhaps being
seen as more of a threat and more dangerous than other offenders) leading
to their being observed more carefully and cautioned infrequently.

However, with this one exception the role of the police in distinguishing between suspects in terms of personal characteristics appears to be
minimal. What then are the reasons for this? Central to the argument
in this work has been an appreciation that the police role is subject to
a number of constraints. It is through an understanding of these constraints that we can better understand many of the surprising, perhaps to

178

some unpalatable, findings of the study. Therefore it is appropriate at
this juncture to refer to them once again. At least four constraints
have been noted in previous chapters, related to the victim, the visibility factor, the knowledge base and manpower:

(i)   The victim

Other studies have assumed that the presence or absence of a victim
exerts considerable influence on the importance of police discoveries,
and the present research confirms this. Where an offence has been
committed which involves a victim, a very high proportion of recorded
offences are reported to the police by the victim; at the other
extreme, as revealed in chapters six and seven, for 'victimless' crime
the role of the police is more crucial. However, even in these cases,
it is possible that citizens may consider themselves to be 'victims'
and report incidents to the police - for example a relatively high
proportion of public order offences (excluding soliciting) in the nine
areas were citizen reports, and the material on USI cases revealed a
number of instances where the girl's parents defined her as a victim
and reported the incident. At the other extreme, the analysis of
indictable records (chapters four and five) demonstrated that the nature
of the victim was important. That is, where the victim was an individual,
rather than a corporate body (like a shop) offences were particularly
likely to be victim reported and unlikely to be police direct discoveries. Irrespective of the ability of the police to discover crime, then,
in many cases the victim has first (perhaps the only) 'option' on whether
to involve the police. Moreover in many cases the victim may also have
information which allows the police to make an automatic arrest, with
the result that the role of the victim at the detection stage is not
insignificant.

(ii) Visibility

However, despite the high proportion of victim reports, victim studies
confirm that the majority of crimes are not reported to the police.
Consequently, after the victim has made a decision not to call the
police, there are an enormous number of crimes which the police may
possibly discover. The fact that they do not, and that, as a result,
most offences are either reported by the victim or remain undiscovered -
even where police manning levels are increased (Bright, 1970) - is
principally due to the visibility factor. This is well illustrated if
we consider the types of crime discovered by the police. Housebreaking
and thefts (other than metal thefts) were rarely police discovered;
on the other hand, offences which were more public, like vandalism and
thefts of and from cars were more commonly police discovered.

The importance of the offence visibility raises a number of problems
with regard to victimless offences in private or secluded places. In
this respect, much of the data in chapter seven provides insight. Drug
offences and USI, despite having no apparent victim involvement, are
discovered by the police only in a minority of cases, since both types
of offence, by their nature, are unlikely to take place in the open.
Consequently the police utilise various strategies to surmount the
visibility barrier. For example, in the case of USI they may question
girls who they have cause to speak to on other matters; with regard to
drugs they follow up hospital calls, gather information from users etc.
However, quite clearly where information of this type is not readily

179

available, the proactive ability of the police is muted. In this light, the recent debate in London between the present police commissioner and his predecessor over the ability of the police to deal with house burglaries is somewhat superfluous – as we have seen, police involvement in the discovery of residential burglary is negligible, the detection rate is low, and there is a heavy dependence upon indirect detection.

(iii) The knowledge base

The nature of detection methods raises the whole question of the knowledge base from which the police work. I have argued, in chapters three to six, that academics have been guilty of an overromanticised view of police management practices. Let us take one example of this as it affected the present researcher.

When I was first introduced to the South Yorkshire police and voiced an interest in offence and offender data from different areas of the city, I had expected some rationally structural response from the police, in terms of their records of crime in Sheffield. Specifically I had anticipated a tour round the police 'operations rooms', the walls of which would be lined with maps, coloured flags marking the spot where each crime was committed. Instead I was given a very hazy impression of the spatial aspects of crime, and little evidence of any developed conceptions of offence/offender distinctions. In terms of where offenders lived, each police official I spoke to had some ideas of particularly notorious areas, but these were not necessarily those which rated highly according to our quantitative information. (2) Considering offence data, the picture was even more vague, and although the police clearly distinguished between the city centre and commercial and industrial areas and the rest of Sheffield, they made little or no distinction within the residential sector.

The implications of this are pertinent at both the discovery and detection stages. In terms of the discovery of crime, the evidence from chapters three and four makes it unequivocally clear that the police have only vague ideas of intra-residential area distinctions and that the extent of police presence between residential areas varies only slightly. This is reflected in a lack of any clear differences between the proportion of offences discovered directly by the police in different residential areas, although in contrast there is a difference between the nine residential areas and other parts of the city, which reflects police policy vis-a-vis city centre, industrial and commercial areas.

These conclusions are perhaps surprising. However, if we consider the implications for this on detection patterns, an even more provocative picture emerges. The overwhelming conclusion of chapter five is that detection is commonly instantaneous. When the offence is discovered or reported, a suspect may be identified at that stage, commonly due either to the victim naming him or to the police catching him in the act. Conversely, it is quite clear that if an offender is not identified at that stage, the ability of the police to clear up the offence, other than by indirect detection, is negligible. From this perspective, the suggestion that the police commonly and successfully apply a strategy such as 'the method of suspicion' is at best naive, at worst farcical. It is to ascribe to the police a level of knowledge which they do not ·have, and which is perhaps in the last analysis unobtainable. Unless the police assume that the offence is 'down to' a local resident, or

unless it is so distinct (3) as to make a <u>modus operandi</u> identification
feasible, quite clearly the ability of the police to link an offence to
even a reasonably small number of suspects is muted. Both at the discovery stage and in the detection process, the direct role of the police
is constrained by their lack of precise knowledge either about spatial
patterns of where offences are committed or as to who might have committed a known offence.

In this respect, quite clearly, it is easier for the police to operate
according to easily identifiable personal characteristics than according
to details which require a comprehensive knowledge base. The nature of
the area where a suspect resided, and his previous record, may well be
useful indicators to the police, but are not necessarily available. On
the other hand, age and sex are. At the stage where decisions are made
on whether an offender should be prosecuted or formally cautioned,
criminal record details are available to the police and these are an
important element in the decision making process. However in terms of
<u>who</u> is formally cautioned there is less evidence of area differences,
and in terms of what data are included in police submissions there is
no indication that area of residence is in any way a salient issue at
this stage of the process.

(iv) <u>Manpower</u>

This is not, however, to suggest that the police would ignore information on the nature of the area where the offender lives, were it
available. Quite clearly, if we consider the ways in which the police
would like to operate, as opposed to the base from which they actually
do operate, the extent to which a broader spectrum of relevant data might
be used is considerable. However the role of the collator is a small
part of police organisation, and the police are unable to patrol many
areas as much as they would wish. Consequently, decision making may be
based on details which are readily available, rather than on wider information which requires unearthing. In particular here, the police may
make a distinction between residential and non-residential areas and
assign manpower accordingly, but they neither have the resources to
consider variations between residential areas nor the manpower to police
some residential areas more than others. The theoretical arguments with
regard to amplification may thus be sound as well as persuasive. That
does not however mean that they are practicable in a particular situation.

In arguing that constraints imposed by the presence of a victim, the
visibility factor, the knowledge base with which the police operate, and
the manpower situation are of fundamental importance in limiting the
ability of the police to play a pivotal role in the law enforcement process,
I am aware that my emphasis contrasts vividly with earlier writings. On
the other hand, recent research lends some support to the present findings. As was noted in chapter one for example, Chatterton's (1976) material reveals a lack of police discretion at the arrest stage. In addition,
one recent study of juvenile crime mentions a lack of evidence of the
method of suspicion for this group:

'Arrest on suspicion does not seem therefore to involve the police
'picking on' known faces for routine 'turnovers' or 'liftings' during
which, by the law of averages, some offence behaviour comes to light.
Labelling theorists insist that this is one way in which 'deviant
identity' is formed. There is little support for this notion in these

181

data, and none in what we know about the children who were first brought to notice as a direct result of police activity. Hardly any of these, so far as the records show, were the result of stop and search activities, but the detection by policemen of children 'in flagrante delicto'' (Priestley et al, 1977; 52).

CRIME STATISTICS AND AREA DIFFERENCES

The finding that the discretionary role of the police as regards the discovery and detection of offences is considerably muted, allied to the apparent willingness of residents of high crime rate areas to call the police, seems to question widespread assumptions that police policies create area differences in crime rates. If we consider the area analysis conducted in chapters four - six and chapter eight, it is evident that the recorded information shows no indication of area differences being radically altered due to the different actions of the police (or indeed the public) in different areas. Taking the four stages of the law enforcement processes distinguished in chapter one, this is well illustrated:

(i) The discovery and reporting of crime

There was no evidence of differences between residential areas in the ways in which crimes came to be known to the police. There were indications that the police role in the discovery process is more important in non-residential areas, resulting in a possible inflating of the recorded offence rates in non-residential areas. However in no way could differences in offence or offender rates between the nine residential areas in this study be attributed to differences in police discovery or citizen reporting patterns.

(ii) Detection

Similarly, comparing offenders from high and low offender rate areas there was no evidence either that the police role in the detection process was proportionally greater in high offender rate areas, or that the police used more discretionary detection methods with regard to offenders from high rate areas.

(iii) Dealing with offenders

In contrast, there were some slight indications of area differences in cautioning rates, at least as far as some males were concerned. It seemed that for males aged twenty or more, those offenders living in high offender rate areas were less likely to receive a caution than those living in low rate areas. Nevertheless, not only was this difference not reflected for the younger age groups, but it was also clear that age and record differences were more important factors in determining cautioning rates. Consideration of the justifications given for cautions similarly revealed little evidence of area distinctions. Moreover, overall it was clear that most area differences in offender rates were maintained whether or not cautioning data were included, although rather more differences emerged where area offender rates were based on data restricted to those receiving probation or custodial sentences.

182

(iv) Police responses to reports made by the public

It is necessary to stress once again that since these data are based on police records, they may be suspect where police decisions on whether or not to record incidents are concerned. The use of other sources was one way of safeguarding against this (see below). However, due to the introduction of the incident sheet procedure in South Yorkshire, it seemed likely that non-recording practices in this authority at least, might be minimal. In addition the incident form material allows us to check whether area differences were present in the ways 'in which incidents were recorded. Given that the area pattern for these 'noncriminal' incidents is similar to that for other police records, it seems highly unlikely that differences of this order exist on an areal level, although as the domestic dispute details indicate (Mawby, 1978 (ii)) certain types of incident may be almost always defined as 'noncriminal'.

The police records thus show no evidence of area crime differences being created due to particular aspects of the law enforcement process. In addition though, our confidence in there being 'real' crime rate differences between these areas is increased by the results of other research approaches used on the project. Information collected by the GPO on television licence evasion and telephone kiosk vandalism largely produced similar area variations. These findings are important because they show that data from non-police law enforcement agencies of a non-professional kind (in the case of the licence evasion department) and agencies where discretion is irrelevant (in the case of kiosk vandalism) confirm the pattern of the police data.

More telling, however, is the fact that the use of sources which directly tap residents of the areas (i.e. the household victim survey and the juvenile self-report study) produced a generally similar picture of contrasting areas. In no way can one argue that any one of these gives a 'correct' image of area crime rates. Nevertheless, the fact that similar patterns are produced when we use a variety of sources with quite different strengths and weaknesses, suggests forcibly that the area differences with which we began the study cannot be dismissed as artefacts of police procedures.

This conclusion in itself allows us to go on to consider other factors which may be involved in producing different crime rates in different areas, and alsewhere the project has focused on some other explanations (Bottoms et al, forthcoming). More generally, the finding that area differences in one study cannot be 'explained away' suggests that differences elsewhere should be considered on a multi-dimensional level rather than being sceptically written off as due to policing practices.

Nevertheless, it is arguable that Sheffield presents a special case, or that the research here is so specific as to prevent the results being generalised to other parts of Britain, much less to other countries.

It seems to me that three distinctions could be drawn here, of which two may have some substance. First, one could argue that the social-geographical structure of Sheffield is such that perceptions of area differences (as for example by the police) might be anticipated as less distinct than in other cities. This is possible, but from what we know of Sheffield highly unlikely. As noted in chapter two and in the first stage of the research (Baldwin and Bottoms, 1976), Sheffield is commonly

considered an amalgamation of 'villages', with strong links to the local
community and a clear distinction between different areas. If anything,
therefore, we might expect area differences to be more clearly distinguished in Sheffield than elsewhere.

Secondly, however, it is more convincing to suggest that the area
definitions used here are such as to preclude the emergence of different
patterns. In fact, the policy here has been to consider areas which are
small enough to be meaningful entities to the residents, and which are
similar in other respects - for example in terms of social class. Most
other studies of policing which have incorporated an areal dimension have
considered much larger areas than this. The result is that differences
which are attributed to the crime situation may in fact reflect differences in police policy vis-à-vis large areas of the city with considerable
social class differences. Only one area of owner-occupied housing was
included in this study, and consequently we cannot consider differences
of this order - however it is certainly possible that in Sheffield a
comparison of the middle class South Westerly sector of the city
(Baldwin and Bottoms, 1976) with the northern working class areas would
reveal area differences in policing patterns. Where the areas compared
are defined in terms of police divisions, or where large areas of slum-
developments or ghettos are concerned, the picture may be even more
distinct. These are, however, only qualifying statements, and we would
argue that where we are considering the factors behind area crime
differences, our concentration on areas of this size (and where other
variables are controlled for) is preferable.

Finally, we may consider how far the procedures used by the South
Yorkshire police may be distinct and consequently influential in producing a particular pattern. Obviously without similar studies in
other areas of the country it is impossible to pursue the question to
any extent. However in one respect there are notable differences
between Sheffield and possibly two other areas which have been examined,
that is, in terms of the use of vague charges by the police. In both
the Easterhouse area of Glasgow where police amplification is alleged
(Armstrong and Wilson, 1973) and the Luke Street area of Liverpool,
where it is to some extent demonstrated (Gill, 1977), there is a
considerable focus on the police use of 'holding' charges (specifying
vague offences like loitering on suspicion, creating an affray,
assaulting a police officer, being drunk and disorderly) as ways in
which they control the 'suspicious' behaviour of residents (especially
teenage residents) of problem areas. Gill in particular shows that the
criminal records of younger Luke Street residents were littered with
charges of this nature. In contrast, as the evidence from chapter six
in particular reveals, there is no evidence in Sheffield either that
these charges are commonly employed, or that there are area differences
in their use. It is therefore quite possible that where the use of
public order charges is recognised as a normal and regular feature of
policework, a well used weapon in the armoury of control, differential
policing policies may emerge. To this extent at least it is possible
that the policies of the Sheffield police may be distinct, although it
is no less possible that the situation in Luke Street and Easterhouse
is distinct, especially since the focus in these studies has been on
one specific area in each city.

184

SUMMARY

In the first two sections of this final chapter, the emphasis has been on two focal concerns of the research - namely the role of the police and the extent to which area crime rate differences are influenced by different processes at the law enforcement stage. The title of the book, however, Policing the City, has been specifically chosen to reflect the much wider findings of the study. In essence, policing the city relates not merely to the role of the police but to the part played by all those agents involved in the criminal process. The importance of the public in the policing process has been stressed by Reiss (1971) in particular. However, here the role of the public has been considered in rather more detail.

In chapter four, the role of different agents in the reporting of crime was assessed. In line with other studies, the results showed that police proactivity was comparatively rare, and that most recorded crimes were reported by member of the public. Moreover, even where there was no 'victim' in a strict sense, reports by members of the public were not uncommon (chapter six). However, given that the role of the public is crucial at the reporting stage, much of the data in chapter four breaks new ground where an attempt has been made to distinguish between different types of citizen report. Here, although a variety of reporting agents were distinguished, the role of the witness in the reporting process has been considered as one which has been ignored in almost all criminological research and yet is of considerable practical importance.

In chapter five, the emphasis moved to the detection process, where, not surprisingly, the role of the police was considerably greater. Even here though, the importance of identification by victims or private law enforcement agencies needs to be stressed. Moreover, police detections were commonly associated with two types of situations - where the police caught the offender in the act following a call from a member of the public, and where the police simultaneously discovered offence and offender. Within this latter category, the use of discretion by the police was relatively common, especially with regard to certain types of offence. However where no early arrest was made, it was unlikely that an offence would be cleared up other than by indirect detection.

Consideration of nonindictable crime and specific types of victimless crime revealed a more crucial role for the police, although two additional points of interest should be noted. First, it is clear that even in these situations members of the public may decide to involve the police, perhaps because they consider themselves or others to have been victimised. Secondly, in many situations the role of the police is constrained by the privacy of the incident, and here the strategies used by the police to surmount the visibility barrier have been described in some detail, especially with regard to USI and drugs offences.

Throughout the research though, the role of the public in the policing process has been assigned a considerable degree of importance. Clearly the public are willing to involve the police in their lives on numerous occasions, not only where a crime has been committed and unambiguously recognised as such, but also where citizens think the police should intervene in marginal situations which are eventually categorised as nonindictable crimes or 'non-criminal' incidents. Victim studies have unequivocally revealed the extent of non reporting by the public.

Despite this, if we consider the role of the public from the perspective of input to the police organisation, it is evident that the police are highly dependent upon the requests and help they receive from private citizens. Policing the City is consequently largely a study of the general public.

FUTURE POSSIBILITIES

It is perhaps inevitable that academics phrase their conclusions mainly in terms of generalities bounded by a submission that more research is needed. As is evident, the present study was seen primarily as a test as to whether area crime rate differences warranted further study, and to this extent we are able to reconsider these area patterns with some confidence that they are not the result of policing policies. However, at varying stages of the research, points have been raised which were not covered by the study. Some of these are perhaps best described as 'sins of omission', others are points which have been clarified by the research findings themselves. It is perhaps appropriate to end by citing the need for research in some of these areas:

(i)   The role of the police

The focus of this work has been the data kept by the police as this relates to the reporting and detection of crime. In one respect at least the role of the police has been inadequately covered, with few details of the operation of the detective branch and a detailed exam- ination of this aspect of policework would be useful. Additionally, the data on reporting and detection processes reveal clear differences according to offence types and suggests that other variations may exist - for example for the small group of offences which are profession- ally planned. Research on the role of the police in relation to specialist aspects, like the detection of burglary offences or car thefts, may well provide a totally different picture of police procedures.

(ii)   The area dimension

Here the discussion has centred on differences between nine areas, eight of which could clearly be described as working class, and where in all nine there was a relationship between offence and offender rates. In hindsight, it seems possible that policing patterns on an area basis may be entirely different if one considered middle class, or upper middle class areas, particularly those where offences such as burglary are common but where offender rates are low. No such area was included here, with the result that we have no information about the role of the police in these areas.

(iii)   The role of the witness

At various stages in this report, the role of the witness has been described. While reports to the police by witnesses are relatively common, in terms of the proportion of reports made by different agents, there has been considerable concern in recent years over the 'unresponsive bystander' (Latane and Darley, 1970). Very few witnesses to crime may be sufficiently motivated to call the police and the police are themselves often critical of the level of public co-operation. Yet where witnesses do call the police, a relatively high detection rate was found, and witnesses were partly responsible for clearing up many crimes either due to their direct involvement or through their speed in reporting situations. It is therefore regretable that when we consider questions on why bystanders become involved and how their intervention varies, we are dependent upon experimental psychological literature for most of the few answers which have been attempted.

In these three areas then, the present study raised points which could be further explained in future research. The present study has been concerned with the role of the police and other agents in the discovery, detection and handling of crime, and the influence of these processes on the resulting crime statistics. In this respect, like some other studies (West and Farrington, 1973) (4), the results suggest that if sufficient caution is used criminal statistics may indeed tell us some things about crime rather than merely reflect the police process. In addition though, much of the detail is of interest in its own right as providing information on the part played by the police and various other agents in the reporting and clearing up of crimes.

Notes

INTRODUCTION

(1) Because this study is concerned with the exercise of discretion by the police I have attempted to maximise the area covered by taking a police definition of 'offender'. That is, I have included as offenders all those recorded by the police as guilty, whether or not they were subsequently charged with or cautioned for the offence, and irrespective of a finding of guilt. In fact, as I will show later (chapter eight) the number of additional suspects included through this method is negligible.

CHAPTER 2

(1) The three-letter code has been used throughout the second stage of the project. The first letter refers to the tenure type of the area (council, rented privately or owner occupied); the second letter refers to the design type predominating in the area (houses, flats); the third letter refers to the offender rate in the area, using the 1971 standard list file data (high, medium, low).

(2) A second important factor which influenced the decision to include the second high rise area was the publication of Newman's study of crime rate differences according to design principles (Newman, 1973). In considering area crime rate differences, standard list data for the one area (CFH) refer to seven months of the year, and the annual rate has been adjusted accordingly. However, in discussing total figures the unadjusted data have been used. Strictly speaking, a reweighting should have been carried out. However since the overall total is in no way representative of Sheffield as a whole, being dependent on the types of areas chosen and their relative size, the figures have been left unadjusted.

(3) The household survey was financed by a grant from the SSRC and later from the Home Office.

(4) The definitions for social groups or social grades D/E are slightly wider than those for social classes IV and V, and include all those whose standard of living is low. Grade D refers to semi and unskilled manual workers and E to casual labourers, part-time workers and those who through age, sickness or unemployment depend on pensions or supplementary benefits.

(5) The categorization of offences is similar to that employed in the first stage of the research. However three perhaps controversial classification decisions should be noted:

  (i) Fraud etc. - included here are fraud, forgery and handling offences.

  (ii) Meter thefts - are only included in this category where the offender is a resident. Offences where the police suspect an outsider are included in the theft (other) or B and E (houses) categories.

(iii) Thefts from pubs, clubs etc. are included with shop thefts.

CHAPTER 3

(1) 'Blackacre' is the estate described by Baldwin (1974 (ii)), which had a high offender rate.

(2) A large traffic island in the city centre.

CHAPTER 4

(1) The most significant contribution to theoretical analysis of witness motivation has in fact been made by psychologists - see Latane and Darley, 1970.

CHAPTER 7

(1) The data on USI are described in more detail in an extended paper (Mawby, 1979) which includes a consideration of the cautioning process.

(2) See for example:

   NCCL (1976) 'Sexual Offences: Evidence to the Criminal Law
      Revision Committee', NCCL Report No. 13.

   Butt, R. (1976) 'Who really wants a change in the age of consent?',
      Times, 24 January, 14.

   Grey, A. (1975) 'Sexual Law Reform Society Working Party Report',
      CLR 323-335.

   Hansard (1976) volume 904, 271, 397;
                  volume 907, 615-616, 283;
                  volume 910, 293-294;
                  volume 914, 191.

(3) i.e., excluding offences which also involved incest.

(4) For purposes of convenience I have here distinguished between the male 'offender' and female 'victim'.

(5) Area RHH was the subject of a special study within the Sheffield project, based on participant observations. I am indebted to Dave Wall for some of the details contained here.

(6) It is however noticeable that the police did not encounter difficulties to the same extent as those described by Skolnick (1966), and solicitation arrests included cases where no customers were identified, including attempts to solicit the drivers of passing cars. The apparent ease of proving soliciting in Sheffield also means that the various complex police strategies described by Skolnick were unnecessary.

(7)   Comparison with a Poisson distribution is however, an approximation, given that the data lack a 'no arrests' category.

(8)   The data quoted in this section were originally collected by A. E. Bottoms and I am grateful for his permission to analyse and describe some of the details. A more complete description of the material, particularly covering characteristics of known drug offenders in more detail, will be included in a forthcoming paper.

(9)   Two offences were discovered indirectly and have been excluded from subsequent analysis. The lack of any number of indirect detections is an indication of the police being uninterested in recording past drug offences, and results in the number of offenders exceeding the number of offences. It should also be noted here that, as in the wider study, the term offender has been used to describe police definitions and includes those who were formally cautioned and those against whom no further action was taken. We shall discuss the point more fully elsewhere, but in the present context it is important to recognise that the proportion of 'no further action' cases is considerably larger for drugs offenders than for other offenders.

(10)   It should be noted here that in other cases <u>unrelated</u> non-drug offences were also recorded, and the distinction in this section between drug only and drug and non-drug offences relates to the drug offence situation <u>only</u>.

(11)   The extent to which police/drug interaction takes place at an informal and casual level is well illustrated in a recent account by Willis (1978). As an example Willis notes occasions where drug users use 'informing the police' as a means of controlling the market and ridding themselves of unwanted drug pushers.

(12)   It should however be noted that citizens <u>may</u> complain in general terms about the level of solicitation in the areas and that comments of this type made to the police patrols may be used to justify maintaining a high level of 'vice squad' activity.

CHAPTER 9

(1)   There is however one exception here, namely the owner occupied area (OHL). As noted in chapter 2, rates for some minor incident data were slightly higher than might have been anticipated. Similarly rates of requests for police surveillance were considerably higher than in the other low offence rate areas (but still lower than in the high rate areas) suggesting that there may be a distinction between owner occupied and other areas in terms of residents' willingness to involve the police <u>in</u> some situations. For the matched areas, however, this was not the case.

(2)   In this respect an experience during the first stage of the research is revealing. Following the writing of his PhD, John Baldwin was involved with the police in discussions over the confidentiality of his presentation of the data. One example used by the police was his discription of 'Blackacre' which according to one senior official could be easily identified. Ironically the identification which was made was incorrect!

(3) An offence may be considered distinct either because there is some
idiosyncratic feature present, or because it is serious enough and
professional enough to limit the number of possible suspects. Needless
to say, most crimes fit neither of these pictures.

(4) It should however be noted that the present study does not share
the positivistic and individualistic assumptions of the West and
Farrington research.

Bibliography

Armstrong, G. and Wilson, M. (1973). 'City Politics and Deviancy Amplification'. 61-89 in Taylor, I. and Taylor, L. - Politics and Deviance, Penguin, Harmondsworth.

Baldwin, J. (1972). 'Social Aspects of Crime in Sheffield' - PhD. Thesis, University of Sheffield.

(1974) (i). 'Problem Housing Estates - Perceptions of Tenants, City Officials and Criminologists'. Social and Economic Administration, 8, 16-35.

(1974) (ii). 'Social Area Analysis and Studies of Delinquency' - Social Science Research, 3, 151-168.

Baldwin, J. and Bottoms, A. (1976). The Urban Criminal - Tavistock, London.

Banton, M. (1964). The Policeman in the Community - Tavistock, London.

Becker, H. (1963). Outsiders - Free Press, New York.

Belson, W. (1975). The Public and the Police - Harper and Row, London.

Bideman, A. et al. (1967). 'Report of a Pilot Study in the District of Columbia on Victimization and Attitudes towards Law-Enforcement' in President's Commission on Law Enforcement and Administration of Justice. Field Surveys I.

Bittner, E. (1967). 'The Police on Skid Row' - ASR, 32.

Boland, B. (1976). 'Patterns of Urban Crime' - 27-41 in Skogan, W. (1976), Op cit.

Bottomley, A. (1973). Decisions in the Penal Process - Robertson, London.

Bottomley, A. and Coleman, C. (1976). 'Criminal Statistics: The Police Role in the Discovery and Detection of Crime' in International Journal of Criminology and Penology, 4.

Bottoms, A. (1974). Book review of Defensible Space, British Journal of Criminology, 14, 203-06.

Bottoms, A. et al. (Forthcoming). Urban Crime and the Housing Market.

Brantingham, P. and Brantingham, P. (1975). 'The Spatial Patterning of Burglary' - Howard Journal, XIV.

Bright, J. (1970). Beat Patrol Experiment - H.O. Police Research and Development Branch, London.

Butler, J. (1879). Government by Police - Dyer Bros., London.

(1883). <u>Dangers of Legislation in Matters of Social Purity</u> - Pamphlet based on a speech to Friends' Association.

Cain, M. (1973). <u>Society and the Policeman's Role</u> - Routledge, London.

Cameron, M. (1964). <u>The Booster and the Snitch</u> - Free Press, Glencoe.

Chambliss, W. (1969). <u>Crime and the Legal Process</u> - McGraw-Hill, New York.

Chappell, D. (1965). 'The Development and Administration of the English Law Relating to Breaking, and Entering' - Unpublished PhD. Thesis, University of Cambridge.

Chatterton, M. (1976). 'Police in Social Control' - 104-22 in King, J. (1976), <u>Control without Custody</u>, Cambridge University.

Chesney, K. (1970). '<u>The Victorian Underworld</u>' - Temple Smith, London.

Cicourel, A. (1976). <u>The Social Organisation of Juvenile Justice</u> - Heinemann, London.

Cohen, L. and Stark, R. (1974). 'Discriminatory Labelling and the Five-Finger Discount' - <u>Journal of Research in Crime and Delinquency, 11</u>, 25-39.

Conlin, J. (1967). <u>Local and Central Government - Police Administration</u> Cassell, London.

Cressey, D. (1964). <u>Delinquency, Crime and Differential Association</u> - Mortinus Nijhoff, The Hague.

Cumming, E. et al. (1965). 'Policeman as Philosopher, Guide and Friend' - <u>Social Problems</u>, 12, 276.

Damer, S. (1976). 'Wine Alley: the Sociology of a Dreadful Enclosure' - 175-206 in Wiles, P. (1976). <u>The Sociology of Crime and Delinquency in Britain, Vol. 2.</u> Martin Robertson, London.

Dickens, C. (1858). 'On Duty with Inspector Field' - 513-23 in <u>Reprinted Pieces</u>.

Dickson, D. T. (1968). 'Bureaucracy and Morality: An Organisational Perspective on a Moral Crusade' - <u>Social Problems</u>, 16, 143-56.

Ditchfield, J. (1976). <u>Police Cautioning: England and Wales</u> - HORU, HMSO.

Douglas, J. (1967). <u>The Social Meaning of Suicide</u> - Princetown, University Press.

Duster, T. (1970). <u>The Legislation of Morality</u> - Free Press, New York.

Ennis, P. (1967). 'Criminal Victimization in the United States' - in President's Commission on Law Enforcement and Administration of Justice, <u>Field Surveys II</u>.

Foote, C. (1969). 'Vagrancy-type Law and its Administration' - 295-330 in Chambliss, Op cit.

Gardiner, J. and Olson, D. (1969), 'Wincanton: the Politics of Corruption' - 103-135 in Chambliss, Op cit.

Garfinkel, H. (1967). Studies in Ethnomethodology - Penguin, Harmondsworth.

Gill, O. (1977). Luke Street - Macmillan, London.

Goldman, N. (1963). The Differential Selection of Juvenile Offenders for Court Appearance - NCCD, New York.

Hansard (1856). Police (Counties and Buroughs) Bill.

Herbert, D. (1976). 'The Study of Delinquency Areas' - Transactions of the Institute of British Geographers, 1, 472-492.

Hindelang, M. (1974). 'Decisions of Shoplifting Victims to Invoke the Criminal Justice Process' - Social Problems, 21, 580-93.

(1976). Criminal Victimisation in Eight American Cities - Ballinger, Cambridge, Massachusetts.

Hindess, B. (1973). The Use of Official Statistics in Sociology - Macmillan, London.

Holdaway, S. (1977). 'Changes in Urban Policing' - BJS, 28, 119-137.

Home Office (1938). Report on the Departmental Committee on Detective Work - Procedure, Vol. 1 - HMSO.

(1966). Report of the Working Party on Operational Efficiency and Management - HMSO.

(1977). Criminal Statistics, 1976 - HMSO.

Hood, R. and Sparks R. (1970). Key Issues in Criminology - Weidenfeld and Nicolson, London.

House of Commons (1975). Report from the Select Committee on Violence in Marriage - HMSO.

Jephcott, P. and Carter, M. (1954). 'The Social Background of Delinquency' - Unpublished Manuscript, University of Nottingham.

Jones, H. (1958). 'Approaches to an Ecological Study' - BJD 8, 277-293.

King, R. and Elliott, K. (1978). Albany - Routledge, London.

Kitsuse, J. and Cicourel, A. (1963). 'A note on the uses of official statistics' - Social Problems, 11.

La Fave, W. (1965). Arrest - Little, Brown and Co.

Lambert, J. (1970). Crime, Police and Race Relations - Oxford University Press, London.

Latane, B. and Darley, J. (1970). 'The Unresponsive Bystander: Why doesn't he help?' - Appleton-Century-Crofts, New York.

McCabe, S. and Sutcliffe, F. (1978). Defining Crime - Blackwell, Oxford.

McClintock, F. (1963). Crimes of Violence - Macmillan, London.

McClintock, F. and Avison, N. (1968). Crime in England and Wales - Heineman, London.

McDonald, N. (1976). The Sociology of Law and Order - Faber and Faber, London.

Maccoby, E. et al. (1958). 'Community Integration and the Social Control of Juvenile Delinquency' - Journal of Social Issues, 38, 38-51.

Mannheim, H. (1948). Juvenile Delinquency in an English Middletown - Kegan Paul, London.

Martin, D. (1962). Offenders as Employees - Macmillan, London.

Matza, D. (1969). Becoming Deviant - Prentice-Hall, New Jersey.

Mawby, R. I. (1977) (i). 'Kiosk Vandalism' - British Journal of Criminology, 17, 30-46.

   (1977) (ii). 'Defensible Space: a Theoretical and Empirical Appraisal' - Urban Studies, 14, 169-179.

   (1977) (iii). 'Sexual Discrimination and the Law' - Probation Journal, 24.2, 38-43.

   (1978) (i). "Crime and Law-Enforcement in Residential Areas of the city? of Sheffield' - PhD Thesis, University of Sheffield.

   (1978) (ii). 'A Note on Domestic Disputes Reported to the Police' - Howard Journal, 17.3, 160-168.

   (1979) (i). 'Television License Evasion: A case study of crime and law-enforcement' - Forthcoming, British Journal of Criminology.

   (1979) (ii). 'The Victimization of Juveniles' - Journal of Research in Crime and Delinquency, 16.1.

   (1979) (iii). 'Policing the Age of Consent' - Journal of Adolescence, 2.1.

Meyer, J. (1974). 'Patterns of Reporting Non-criminal Incidents to the Police' - Criminology, 12.

Mill, J. S. (1966). 'On Liberty', 126-250 in Utilitarianism - Fontana, London.

Miller, W. et al. (1968). 'Delinquency Prevention and Organisational Relations' - in Wheeler, S., Controlling Delinquents, Wiley, New York.

Morris, T. (1957). The Criminal Area - Routledge, London.

Morrish, R. (1940). The Police and Crime Detection Today - Oxford University Press, London.

Newman, O. (1973). Defensible Space - Architectural Press, London.

Parker, H. (1974). View from the Boys - David and Charles, London.

Parnas, R. (1967). 'Police Responses to the Domestic Disturbance' - Winconsin Law Review, 914-960.

Piliavin, I. and Briar, S. (1969). 'Police Encounters with Juveniles' - 165-174 in Chambliss, Op cit.

Pizzey, E. (1974). Scream Quietly or the Neighbours will Hear - Penguin, Harmondsworth.

Plant, M. (1975). Drugtaking in an English Town - Tavistock, London.

Priestley, P. et al. (1977). Justice for Juveniles - Routledge, London.

Punch, N. and Naylor, T. (1973). 'The Police as a Social Service' - New Society, 17 June.

Radzinowicz, L. (1957). English Studies in Criminal Science, IX: Sex Offences - Macmillan, London.

Reiss, A. (1967) (i). 'Measurement of the Nature and Amount of Crime' - in Presidents' Commission Field Surveys III.

(1967) (ii). 'Public Perceptions and Recollections about Crime, Law Enforcement and Criminal Justice' in Field Surveys III, Op cit.

(1971). Police and Public - Yale University Press.

Rex, J. (1968). 'The Sociology of a Zone of Transition' - in Pahl, R., Readings in Urban Sociology - Pergamon, Oxford.

Robin, G. (1970). 'The Corporate and Judicial Disposition of Employee Thieves' - in Smigel, E. and Ross, H., Crimes Against Bureaucracy - Reinhold, New York.

Rock, P. (1973). Deviant Behaviour - Hutchinson.

Sacks, H. (1972). 'Notes on Police Assessment of Moral Character' - in Sudnow, D., Studies in Social Interaction - Free Press, New York.

Schofield, M. (1965). The Sexual Behaviour of Young People - Longmans.

Sellin, T. and Wolfgang, M. (1964). The Measurement of Delinquency - Wiley, New York.

Shannon, L. (1963). 'Types and Patterns of Delinquency Referral in a Middle-Sized City' - British Journal of Criminology, 4, 24-36.

Shaw, C. and McKay, H. (1969). Juvenile Delinquency and Urban Areas - University of Chicago Press, Chicago.

Skogan, W. (1976). <u>Sample Surveys of the Victims of Crime</u> - Ballinger, Massachusetts.

Skolnick, J. (1966). <u>Justice without Trial</u> - Wiley, New York.

Skolnick, J. and Woodworth, J. (1968). 'Bureaucracy, Information and Social Control: a Study of a Morals Detail' - 458-63 in Schwartz, R. and Skolnick, J., <u>Society and Legal Order</u> - Basic Books, New York.

Sparks, R. et al. (1977). <u>Surveying Victims</u> - Wiley, New York.

Stanfield, R. and Maher, B. (1968). 'Clinical and Actuarial Predictions of Juvenile Delinquency ' - in Wheeler, S., <u>Controlling Delinquents</u> - Wiley, New York.

Steer, D. (1970). <u>Police Cautions</u> - Oxford University Press, London.

Steffensmeier, D. and Steffensmeier, R. (1977). 'Who Reports Shoplifters?' - <u>International Journal of Criminology and Penology, 5,</u> 79-95.

Stinchcombe, A. (1963). 'Institutions of Privacy in the Determination of Police Administrative Practice' - <u>AJS, 69,</u> 150-160.

Sutherland, E. and Cressey, D. (1960). <u>Principles of Criminology</u> - 6th edition, Lippincott, Chicago.

Taylor, I. et al. (1973). <u>The New Criminology</u> - Routledge, London.

Terry, R. (1967) (i). 'The Screening of Juvenile Offenders' - <u>Journal of Criminal Law, Criminology and Police Science,</u> 58, 173-81.

(1967) (ii). 'Discrimination in the Handling of Juvenile Offenders by Social Control Agencies' - <u>Journal Research in Crime and Delinquency,</u> 4, 218-30.

Turk, A. (1969). <u>Criminality and Legal Order</u> - Rand McNally.

Turner, S. (1969). 'Delinquency and Distance' - in Sellin, T. and Wolfgang, M., (1969), <u>Delinquency: Selected Studies</u> - Wiley, New York.

Werthman, C. and Piliavin, I. (1967). 'Gang Members and the Police' - in Bordua, D. (1967), <u>The Police: Six Sociological Essays</u> - Wiley, New York.

West, D. and Farrington, D. (1973). <u>Who Becomes Delinquent</u> - Heineman, London.

Whitaker, B. (1964). <u>The Police</u> - Penguin, Harmondsworth.

Wilcox, A. (1974). 'Police 1964-1973' - <u>Criminal Law Review,</u> 144-57.

Wiles, P. (1975). 'Criminal Statistics and Sociological Explanations of Crime' - 198-219 in Carson, W. and Wiles, P., <u>The Sociology of Crime and Delinquency in Britain, Vol. 1</u> - Robertson, London.

Willis, P. (1978). <u>Profane Culture</u> - Routledge, London.

Wilson, J. (1968) (i). 'The Police and the Delinquent in Two Cities' - in Wheeler, S., Op cit.

(1968) (ii). Varieties of Police Behaviour - Harvard University Press.

Young, J. (1972). The Drugtakers - Paladin, London.

Index